Understanding Urban Policy

Understanding Urban Policy

A Critical Approach

Allan Cochrane

 **Blackwell** Publishing

BLACKWELL PUBLISHING
350 Main Street, Malden, MA 02148-5020, USA
9600 Garsington Road, Oxford OX4 2DQ, UK
550 Swanston Street, Carlton, Victoria 3053, Australia

First published 2007 by Blackwell Publishing Ltd

2   2007

Library of Congress Cataloging-in-Publication Data
Cochrane, Allan.
  Understanding urban policy : a critical approach / Allan Cochrane.
    p. cm.
  Includes bibliographical references and index.
  ISBN: 978-0-631-21120-4 (hardback : alk. paper)
  ISBN: 978-0-631-21121-1 (pbk. : alk. paper)
  1. Urban policy. 2. Community development, Urban. 3. Sociology, Urban. I. Title.
  HT151.C5995 2007
  307.76–dc22

                                                    2006018674

A catalogue record for this title is available from the British Library.

Set in 10/12.5 pt Dante
by Newgen Imaging Systems (P) Ltd., Chennai, India

The publisher's policy is to use permanent paper from mills that operate a sustainable forestry policy, and which has been manufactured from pulp processed using acid-free and elementary chlorine-free practices. Furthermore, the publisher ensures that the text paper and cover board used have met acceptable environmental accreditation standards.

For further information on
Blackwell Publishing, visit our website:
www.blackwellpublishing.com

For Amanda

Contents

Chapter 1

What is Urban Policy?

The question posed in the chapter title is an obvious one to start with. Before we explore the nature of urban policy we need to be reasonably clear what it is (and – perhaps just as important – what it isn't).

But maybe the answer to the question is already equally obvious. Perhaps we all know what urban policy is and can go on from there without too much difficulty to consider the details of particular policy initiatives. That certainly seems to be the way most discussion of urban policy is approached. Most ambitiously the object of urban policy is sometimes simply taken to be what happens in urban areas because of the way in which different aspects of policy come together to shape opportunities and welfare outcomes, since, as the foreword to the British urban white paper *Our Towns and Cities* (DETR 2000) puts it, "How we live our lives is shaped by where we live our lives." Surely urban policy is nothing more nor less than the cluster of initiatives aimed at dealing with the problems of cities or the inner cities, or – more positively – initiatives intended to take advantage of the innovation, "buzz" and excitement associated with cities. However, this starting point does not help much in actually understanding why policy has changed or why first one initiative and then another has been replaced and superseded by the next.

There is surprisingly little shared understanding about what constitute urban problems – or urban possibilities. And (perhaps equally surprisingly) there is little consensus about what constitute the cities or the "urban" to which it is expected urban policies will be applied. Assessing quite why one particular form of policy intervention attracts the soubriquet "urban," while another does not, simply adds to the difficulties. It would be hard to argue that the development of urban policy has followed a continuing process of learning based on a clear and continuing set of aims and ambitions (see Cochrane 2000, pp. 184–8). On the contrary, as Atkinson and Moon note tersely in their review of British urban policy, it is "at least in Western society, a chaotic conception" (Atkinson and Moon 1994, p. 20) because there has been no shared understanding of the problem around which policy might be defined. At no time, they conclude, can one realistically talk of "a coherent urban policy" (Atkinson and Moon 1994, p. 271).

So, the point here is not to argue about the effectiveness (or lack of effectiveness) of different antipoverty strategies or different forms of urban policy. Instead, the approach adopted seeks to understand why particular clusters become identified as specifically *urban* problems suitable for intervention through urban policies and spatial targeting at one time while they might be understood quite differently at other times and in different places. They might, for example, be seen as problems that affect older people or lone parents; people in particular social classes; women or men; or members of particular racialized groups, most of whom also just happen to live in urban areas. The problems of unemployment, which tend to be concentrated in inner urban areas, might be defined in terms which emphasize that they are *urban* problems (and require specifically urban solutions such as investment in economic infrastructure); in ways which suggest that national economic growth will create demand for labor; or in ways which suggest that people need to be moved from "welfare to work" with the help of individualized packages of training and compulsion (see, e.g. Peck 1996, 2001). In other words, sometimes they will be interpreted as "urban" problems, requiring urban policy solutions, while at other times the same problems may be interpreted quite differently.

Certainly we could all probably list a series of urban "problems" that urban policy might be expected to tackle (from crime to family breakdown; poverty to dereliction; joblessness to low educational attainment; pollution and environmental sustainability to poor health; over-crowding to vacant property). But being clear at what point any of these becomes an object of policy is much more difficult, as it moves from what C. Wright Mills called a "personal trouble" to become a "public issue," that is from something that can be handled within households, families or even communities, to something that is subject to forms of public policy inter-vention or regulation (Mills 1959, pp. 7–9). More broadly any consideration of urban policy makes it necessary to actively explore what Foucault calls the process of "problematization," that is "how and why certain things (behavior, phenomena, processes) became a *problem*. Why, for example, certain forms of behavior were characterized as "madness" while other similar forms were completely neglected at a given historical moment" (Foucault 2000, p. 171). The same question might be posed with equal force about urban problems.

It reinforces the need to explore the process by which urban policy develops and defines itself in practice, rather than assuming that there is some universal definition waiting to be rolled out wherever the term is used to describe particular clusters of policy. The protean form of urban policy reflects changing understandings of cities and their role in economic and social development, as well as the way in which definitions of social policy have changed in the context of global neo-liberalism and its local variants.

The focus of this book is on the emergence of what Edwards (1995, 1997) describes as "urban social policy" and it might similarly be asked quite what it is that makes policy intervention on urban issues urban policy, as something distinct from (if related to and often overlapping with) urban planning or housing policy. Some basic principles might be involved – urban social policy can be assumed to have a direct concern with issues of social welfare, to mobilize a wide range of policy tools to engage with them and to make claims to having holistic ambitions that go beyond those of particular professional areas. It might be summarized in the (admittedly somewhat rather bland while at the same time utopian) notion that no one should be disadvantaged because of where he or she lives (a principle that in Britain has been articulated by the politicians of New Labour). But the precise form and significance of urban policy cannot be defined and delimited in advance.

In their powerful, and highly prescient, critique of the British Urban Programme of the 1970s, Edwards and Batley (1978, pp. 220–1) stress the importance of the social construction of "urban deprivation," the ways in which it was defined as a social problem suitable for or requiring policy intervention. They outline the ways in which the problem was constructed through government circulars from a range of different departments and argue that "the Urban Programme ... never developed a coherent policy or a clear definition of what is meant by 'social deprivation', 'areas of deprivation', or 'acute social need' " (Edwards and Batley 1978, p. 221). They criticize the "muddled thinking" of the policy makers and complain that "a host of ... causally-unrelated social issues ... have at one time or another been defined as social problems ... all of which have on occasion been incorporated ... under the umbrella of 'urban deprivation' " (Edwards and Batley 1978, p. 243). Delinquency, vandalism, poor parenting, and illegitimacy were included alongside problems of housing, poverty, unemployment, and education, only linked by the urban label which was given to them and which they were intended to define. What had changed, suggest Higgins et al., "was not so much the nature of the problem as our social construction of it" (Higgins et al. 1983, p. 9).

Perhaps, however, the main distinctive and shared feature of the various programs labeled urban policy has been that they have had a territorial or area focus (although seldom the same one), rather than a focus on a particular client group, the provision of a particular service, or the distribution of benefits (whether universal or means tested). Other social policies are concerned with the delivery of services or the provision of support to "clients," "users," "consumers" or even "customers." Urban social policy, by contrast, focuses on places and spatially delimited areas or the groups of people associated with them. Its problem definition starts from area rather than individual or even social group, although, of course, a concern with an area is often used as a coded way of referring to a concern about the particular groups which are believed to be concentrated in it.

The value to policy makers of the discovery of urban policy and the identification of an urban problem was that they could be used to isolate and symbolize particular clusters of problems and forms of intervention. By redefining social problems in ways that identified them with particular areas, rather than as a consequence of structural inequalities, it became possible to develop area-based policies to deal with them. So, for example, instead of attempting to provide a more or less "universal" welfare safety net, urban deprivation (indeed multiple deprivation) was identified as an exceptional problem outside the normal, so that policy could be targeted by area (if not yet by means testing).

Instead of solving the difficulty of definition, however, this merely compounds it. It remains necessary to define the area – in practice different "urban" policies define their areas or territories differently. Although an area focus provides a useful starting point for analysis it also masks a very wide range of policy initiatives, concerned with dramatically different definitions of the problems faced either "by" urban areas or by those living in them. Cox points out that the use of the word "urban" is simply another example of spatial category that is used to "carve up the world" and warns us that like other similar categories ("region, the rural, the national, the international, the local, the global, the 'country' ") we need to treat such terms "with great caution" (Cox 2001, p. 761).

The definition of the "urban" being "regenerated" and, indeed, the understanding of "regeneration" have varied according to the initiative being pursued, even if this has rarely been acknowledged by those making or implementing the policies. So, for example in some approaches, it is local communities or neighborhoods that are being regenerated or renewed (learning to become self-reliant). In others, it is urban economies that are being revitalized or restructured with a view to achieving the economic well-being of residents and in order to make cities competitive. In yet others it is the physical and commercial infrastructure that is being regenerated, in order to make urban land economically productive once again. And there has also been a drive towards place marketing (and even "branding"), in which it is the image (both self-image and external perception) of cities that has to be transformed.

Another – rather unfortunate – shared feature of urban policies is that the widespread academic and professional consensus seems to be that in terms of their stated or implicit aims, they have all been rather unsuccessful. In Britain, for example, it has been concluded that they have neither significantly improved the social and economic position of those living in the inner cities and peripheral estates nor have they succeeded in delivering the hoped for economic revival (see, e.g. Atkinson 1995; Gripaios 2002). Meanwhile, as Jones and Ward (2002) point out, "Old policies are recycled and 'new' ones are borrowed from elsewhere through speeded-up policy transfer" (Jones and Ward 2002, p. 481). Some commentators are more harshly critical than others, but at least they all do seem to agree that little progress has been made; some blame the shortsightedness of policy makers, others the intractability of the problems; some blame the incoherence of the aims, others the lack of coordination; some simply think the levels of expenditure are inadequate for the tasks in hand (see, e.g. among many others, Edwards and Batley 1978; Audit Commission 1991; Atkinson and Moon 1994; Robson et al. 1994; Edwards 1995, 1997; Lawless 1996; Burton 1997; Parkinson et al. 2005).

Instead of being discouraged by this apparent chaos, policy analysts seem to have been encouraged further to call for the development of a more coherent approach. Burton (1997, p. 433), for example, has acknowledged that there is an urban policy mess and that limited (or even the wrong) lessons have been learned, but goes on to endorse the search "for a more sensible and coherent urban policy." Similar criticisms of urban and inner city policy have emerged throughout its life. The need for coordination is a perennial complaint of the analysts of urban policy both in the United Kingdom (see, e.g. Robson et al. 1994) and in the United States (where at an early stage Marris and Rein 1972 made similar criticisms of the US "War on Poverty").

Another reaction seems to have been a strong emphasis on looking for "what works," so that grand claims are eschewed in favor of pragmatic claims about the potential of particular initiatives, and even particular localized projects. Much writing in the field has focused on the identification and discussion of particular projects and the sharing of "best practice" – often reflected in a series of stories or case studies. So, for example, in the United Kingdom (although examples of similar approaches could be drawn from many other contexts, see, e.g. Walker 2002; European Commission 2003) reports prepared by the Social Exclusion Unit (1998) and the Urban Task Force (Rogers 1999) both include a series of carefully boxed case studies of best practice, from which it is expected that agencies and professionals in the field will learn. Like many management text books, the messages about change are embedded in the success stories reported in these boxes. However, looking for "what works" is ultimately unlikely to be very helpful in understanding what actually happens, in interpreting the policies that are developed or assessing the initiatives that are launched. It leaves us with a fragmented set of understandings to match the fragmented policy process.

When was Urban Policy?

In this context a related question must also be asked – namely, when was urban policy? Of course, there have always been policies that affect the ways in which people lived their lives in cities and the ways in which cities themselves developed, but when did some of them come together under a specifically "urban" label – to be understood as parts of a distinctive urban policy? Some aspects of the prehistory of urban policy are important in their own right, and have certainly gone on to influence its development. But they have their own autonomous status.

So, for example, town and country planning from its earliest years carried within it an implicit and sometimes explicit critique of contemporary cities and life within them. The vision embedded in Ebenezer Howard's writings (Howard 1902/1965) and the policies that flowed from them were a direct response to the problems of the cities as he understood them at the start of the twentieth century, even if the solution he proposed was to leave the city and construct new settlements combining town and country (see, e.g. Mellor 1977 for a discussion of the – contested – rise of anti-urban ideologies in underpinning dominant British understandings of the city). The new town legislation that followed in the second half of the twentieth century was similarly focused on moving population out of the "overcrowded" cities into a modern future of family housing and green spaces (see, e.g. Schaffer 1970; Osborn and Whittick 1978).

Other policies from the late nineteenth and early twentieth centuries with an urban bias, such as those focused on slum clearance, the provision of subsidized housing and on the alleviation of poverty were central to the rise of the welfare state, rather than specifically being understood as "urban" (Driver 1993). The work of Booth (1902) and Rowntree (1902), who systematically charted the distribution of urban poverty in Britain's cities, played a major part in influencing the way in which modern cities are understood. They also helped to underpin the development of policy (initially undertaken by voluntary organizations and local government), but the policies being developed were understood as policies for managing the poor rather than "urban" policies, that is policies for the cities as such. Even local initiative, expressed for example in the radical policies developed by some local Poor Law Boards and other local authorities in the 1920s and 1930s, were understood in these terms (see, e.g. Branson 1979; Macintyre 1980). Rowntree himself went on to undertake research on agricultural poverty, and also contributed to the development of policy on old age pensions and national insurance. Similarly, the emphasis on slum clearance and the provision of council or social housing which characterized public housing policy in the first half of the twentieth century helped to shape our cities in fundamental ways, but it was only when the emphasis shifted towards urban renewal and regeneration expressed in attempts to retain the housing of the nineteenth century and – in principle at any rate – the communities that lived in them (inspired by Jacobs 1961) that housing policy was explicitly understood as urban policy.

In the United States of the 1950s the focus of policy attention relating to cities was on the impact of suburbanization, what one popular collection labeled "the exploding metropolis" (Editors of Fortune 1958). The questions were whether this process could or should be resisted, whether it was the product of architectural and planning fashion (i.e. the attempt to plan out disorder through rational urban design), and whether it was possible to find ways of retaining the civilizing features of urbanism – the creative coming together of different groups, land uses, residential forms and architectural styles in an urban environment. In some respects this collection is remarkably consistent with today's policy debates about the city (almost a manifesto for gentrification, with its pictures of streetscapes and Jane Jacobs' slogan that "downtown is for people") (Editors of Fortune 1958, pp. 18ff and 138ff; Jacobs 1958). But its definition of the problem and of the issues to be tackled through urban policy were very different from the ones that came to define urban policy in the next decade.

It might, of course, be possible (and interesting) to draw out a complex lineage – or genealogy – for urban policy, tracing the various strands back into a series of prehistories. But the term urban policy is not one that was commonly used until the late 1960s when it began to be applied to a range of initiatives then being introduced in the United States (from the War on Poverty onwards). Indeed it has even been suggested that urban policy (as an explicit social policy field) was not given official status until President Nixon set up a Council for Urban Affairs 1969 with the specified task of assisting the President in the "development of a national urban policy" (Moynihan 1970, p. 6), although paradoxically this could also be seen as the moment when the gradual retreat from active federal engagement with urban welfare issues began.

Theorizing Urban Policy

It is necessary to step back and think rather more carefully about how to understand and interpret the rise and (frequent) reconfiguration of urban policy since its emergence as a policy area in the 1960s. One way of doing this might be to consider rather more closely some of the theoretical approaches that have so far been mobilized to explain the nature of urban policy at particular times and in particular places.

A great deal of ink has been spilled at various times by people seeking to define what is meant by the "urban" to which one might expect urban policy to apply. An equal amount has probably been spilled on looking for definitions of "policy." There have been several quite distinctive attempts to find some means of identifying some fundamental understanding of urban policy, which is nevertheless capable of capturing and reflecting its full complexity. Some of the earliest analysts of urban policy saw its rise as a response to political pressure (whether expressed through the threat or reality of riots or the need to incorporate a rising black middle class) (see, e.g. Piven and Cloward 1972). This is an issue explored more fully in Chapter 2 and the importance of political pressure in helping to generate urban policy in its early years should not be dismissed (particularly in the United States, where such pressures were significantly greater than in the United Kingdom). No doubt, from time to time – when particular urban social movements gain support or dramatic events (such as urban riots) highlight the fragility of existing social or political arrangements – urban policy responses will follow. Gough (2002), for example, argues that it was precisely the threats from a series of struggles around "class, gender, sexuality, and race" that led to the adoption of neo-liberalism as a strategy to be imposed from above when, a "majority feeling emerged among the elite that something radical had to be done to defuse this threat" (Gough 2002, p. 410). But the way in which urban policy made its transatlantic migration (and has since gone on to become a global phenomenon) suggests that it is not enough to focus on its role as a response to popular pressures.

Another early explanation for the rise of urban policy saw it as an expression of the rise of a new political class, new professionals in government and academia seeking to stake their own position as an alternative policy elite, based around the rise of the social sciences and what has come to be called evidence-based policy making, rather than the traditional culture of the civil service or public bureaucracy (see, e.g. Marris and Rein 1972). In the 1960s Moynihan was sharply critical of this group, describing them as "reformers first, professionals second" (Moynihan 1969, p. 94). They were often blamed for the difficulties that later emerged, for example allegedly being dismissed by President Johnson as "kooks and sociologists" (Marris and Rein 1972, p. 244; the debate is summarized and interrogated by Piven and Cloward 1972, Ch. 9). Moynihan is explicit in blaming "those liberal, policy-oriented intellectuals who gathered in Washington and in a significant sense came to power, in the early 1960s" (quoted in Piven and Cloward 1972, p. 248). Although, Marris and Rein (1972) also highlight the influence of the "reformers" and chart a series of linkages within policy communities that led to the emergence of a new policy framework, their critique is a basically sympathetic one. They suggest that the new initiatives reflected a concern about a sense of breakdown in the institutions that should be distributing the benefits of an affluent society more effectively – in other words what was identified was a technical problem, to which there should be a technical solution.

This interpretation has its attractions, since it fits well with the shift away from the traditional bureau-professionalism of the Keynesian (or Fordist) welfare state that has been widely recognized as a central feature of state restructuring since the 1970s, and that is considered more fully in Chapter 3 (see, e.g. Clarke and Newman 1997; Clarke et al. 2000). However, the extent to which urban policy can be closely identified with the rise of a new professional class remains questionable, not least because it seems to have been proved difficult to sustain any professional continuity across the decades. In other words the putative new class or even professional group has turned out to be rather elusive. They may have provided a convenient target for critics, but they do not seem to have built a sustainable professional culture.

The emergence of urban policy in practice was accompanied by an explosion of critical theory which set out to place the new agenda in a wider context. At the core of this explosion were approaches that focused on issues of social reproduction, whether described as "collective consumption" (Castells 1977, 1978) by neo-Marxists or "social consumption" (Saunders 1984, 1986) by neo-Weberians. The important point about these approaches, in the context of the arguments developed in this book, was that they offered the prospect of identifying an object of study that was not simply reducible to what was (confusingly and inconsistently) labeled "urban" in everyday speech or even in the language used by those emerging as new professionals in the field. They also (implicitly at least) highlighted the central role of urban policy in the reshaping of the postwar welfare settlement – the "urban" was placed at the heart of political life and policy debate.

Castells was explicit in arguing that, "The essential problems regarding the urban are in fact bound up with the processes of 'collective consumption' or what Marxists call the organization of the collective means of reproduction of labor power" (Castells 1977, p. 440). What matters here is the emphasis on the "collective," since clearly there are many aspects of the reproduction of labor power (the means by which a labor force is created, prepared for work and sustained mentally and physically) that take place in the home or in the individual pursuit of leisure activity. The addition of the word "collective" indicates that it was concerned with the education system, the health service and even the transport infrastructure and more – that is, almost everything provided by the state or other social organizations to support the lives of citizens. Since in this formulation the "urban" is itself defined by policy – the delivery of services and goods provided by or through the state to support the reproduction of labor power – in a sense "urban policy" becomes a redundant term, or alternatively, core aspects of social policy must be redefined as urban policy.

Although the theoretical starting point is rather different, similar conclusions could be drawn from the arguments of those who developed what was called the "dual state" thesis (Saunders 1984, 1986). According to this approach the central (the national level) state was largely concerned with issues of economy and production and its politics was corporatist, while the local state was responsible for consumption issues and its politics were best characterized as pluralist. Whatever the precise theoretical differences, the overall message was clear enough, identifying a distinctive and "relatively" autonomous sphere (in this case the "local") within which the politics of social consumption was pursued. Although the emphasis in this literature was on notions of "locality" rather than strictly the "urban," the framework was one in which "locality" was effectively used as a synonym for the "urban" (to the extent that almost all "locality" research focused on urban areas – see, e.g. Cooke 1989).

Duncan and Goodwin (1988) highlighted what they saw as the inevitable conflict between locally based (and implicitly urban) pluralist politics and the corporatist center. They argued that the local state was more accessible to popular democratic and community-based pressures, whereas the central state was captured by the corporate interests of big business and (to a lesser extent) the trade union leaders. In this model, local politics works to challenge the economic logic represented by the corporatist center, because of the way in which it generates increasing demands for welfare spending to support the process of social reproduction – that is, those activities which help to define the ways in which people live their daily lives. For Duncan and Goodwin (1988) the central–local division was underpinned by processes of uneven development which implied relentless conflict between central and local government, as (corporatist) central government attempted to gain financial control over (pluralist) local government.

In their different ways, both of these approaches sought to identify the potential for a popular urban politics (focused on the conflicts and opportunities offered by the development of urban policy, or social policy reinterpreted as urban policy). And at the same time in the United States, Piven and Cloward (1977) were similarly engaged in identifying the basis of political movements outside the mainstream, even if for them the focus was on the potential of "poor people's movements," rather than any specifically "urban" movements. Castells identified collective consumption as a fundamental basis for urban social movements, which would help generate cross-class radical alliances of resistance and for more positive change. He argued that it was with respect to struggle over issues of "collective consumption" that sections of the middle and working classes could be brought together in campaigns that challenged capital – "it is," he said, "in urban protest that they [the salaried classes] most easily discover a similarity of interest with the working class" (Castells, 1978, p. 172). Although there was some uncertainty and disagreement about how urban social movements might relate to working class politics Cockburn (1977) powerfully argued that it was possible to identify a gender-based politics organized around issues of social reproduction – or "community" – at local level (see also Castells 1978, 1983; Touraine 1983; Lowe 1986).

The state was understood not as a monolithic institution (against which it was necessary to take a similarly unified stance) but as the condensation of sets of social relations, which meant that it was also possible, in a slogan of the time, to work "in and against the state."

It was argued that "because the state is a form of relations, its workers and clients, if they do not struggle against it, help to perpetuate it . . . Our struggle against it must be a continual one, creating shape as the struggle itself, and the state's response to it, create new opportunities" (London-Edinburgh Weekend Return Group 1979, pp. 48–49). In other words, this form of analysis helped to provide a basis on which radical state professionals (whether in community work, town planning, teaching or social work) could define roles for themselves in seeking to mobilize communities and generate social change (for just one example of this, in the form of Britain's Community Development Projects, see, Loney 1983). In Britain's cities, at least, it was suggested that the traditional municipal politics of the left were being challenged by a "new urban left" (see, e.g. Boddy and Fudge 1984; Cochrane 1986b). This was urban policy from the bottom up, driven by the needs of communities and the campaigns of the left.

However, these approaches were not only used to help explain or justify particular (urban) political campaigns, movements or activities. They also provided a framework within which broader political tensions were located. Castells' work explained the nature of the "urban crisis," along lines that were consistent with the arguments about the "fiscal crisis of the state" developed by O'Connor (1973) (see also Offe 1984). In other words, it was argued that the smooth running of the capitalist system increasingly required the intervention of the state to act as "collective capitalist" in supplying those services which underpinned processes of social reproduction. Castells saw the relationships associated with these activities as defining the "urban" (just as for "dual state" theorists they tended to define local politics).

This also meant that they could not easily or directly be controlled by capital, through traditional corporatist politics or the operation of the market, and – instead – expenditure on these activities became subject to pressure from popular movements. For capital, there was an inherent contradiction between the need to support the process of social reproduction, while seeking to generate profits (the more expended on social reproduction, the lower the profits), and this was said to be exacerbated by the workings of urban politics, whether through the impact of urban social movements or the operation of (a pluralist) local politics. For political optimists, this meant that urban politics offered the prospect of generating movements capable of developing powerful reformist (or even revolutionary) change; for the pessimists, it presaged the new right's attacks on welfare expenditure which characterized the late 1970s and 1980s in the United States and the United Kingdom and across the countries of the West.

One of the strengths of the approaches that focused on collective or social reproduction also turned out to be a weakness, since, by identifying a separate sphere for the urban or a more or less autonomous space for local politics, they effectively excluded from consideration some of the policy initiatives that increasingly came to define the politics of and shape the experience of life in urban areas. As we have seen Castells defined the "urban" through public policy – for him the "urban" was where collective consumption took place, and collective consumption was effectively understood to be the consumption services provided through the welfare state (Castells 1977). Unfortunately such a circular definition – however elegant – is not very helpful for our purposes, since many of the policies that are not "urban" in this sense help to define the experience of urban life (including policing and economic development, as well as transfer payments through the social security and benefits systems). Equally important, spending on some programs (such as education and health) might qualify as collective consumption, but they are generally only seen as "urban" when specific area-based initiatives are launched.

The problem with interpreting urban politics as a separate sphere concerned with social reproduction was that it seemed to make it impossible to engage with issues of production, employment and unemployment. It made it difficult to get any hold on urban space as having anything to do with economic production (as well as social reproduction). It displaced such concerns to the national (and even global) level. From this perspective, it might be possible to imagine an urban policy (driven by the demands of production and economic restructuring) since that would be the province of national or regional institutions. Although it was always recognized that many of the issues that faced us in our daily lives were fundamentally influenced by economic change, the emphasis on collective consumption seemed to imply that urban residents were simply victims of wider forces. At best cities became the spaces or sites across which various economic logics played themselves out. At worst a more or less sharp division was made between economic context – something which was given by the operations of global capitalism – and the separate sphere of urban politics which simply had to take the context as given.

The discovery of any actually existing "urban social movements" (at least with the potential identified by Castells) also turned out to be more of a challenge than the identification of their theoretical possibility (and, indeed, necessity), so it may seem strange to revive these debates. But they provide a salutary reminder of the centrality of urban policy to the ways in which social policy has been reshaped over recent decades. And they remind us that political conflicts over issues of collective consumption remain significant (see, e.g. the discussion of urban social movements in Fainstein and Hirst 1995). They highlighted some of the key tensions within the postwar welfare settlements in the countries of the West and North and sought to interrogate them. They also sought to identify the potential of new forms of political engagement, and may have been less successful in doing that. But at their core is perceptive reflection on the principles and the conflicts around which restructuring was to take place. For all their strengths and the insights they provided, however, these approaches ultimately failed to capture the dynamic of urban policy and its development, even if they remain particularly helpful in considering the continued power of the "community" metaphor explored more fully in Chapter 3. And, indeed, until recently they seem to have been almost completely (and conveniently) forgotten in most contemporary discussion of urban policy (but see, e.g. Cochrane 1999; Ward and Jonas 2004).

Perhaps, instead of taking an approach that starts from the identification of a specific set of activities (or an identifiable social sub system) which then goes on to define the "urban" it might be more helpful to turn the approach on its head, starting with urban areas (forgetting for a moment the challenge of defining what these are) and identifying as urban policy the policies that affect such areas. This is effectively what has been done by Blackman (1995), who operates on the principle that urban policy is best understood as all aspects of public policy that affect people living in cities. While this way of thinking is tempting, there is a real danger that it might make the notion virtually meaningless and unworkable as a means of distinguishing what is urban policy and what is not. Since the vast majority of people in North America and Europe live in cities or urban areas – and almost all of the rest are dependent on cities for employment, income, and cultural activities – then almost every piece of social (and economic) policy could be reinterpreted as urban policy.

Nevertheless, from a rather different (political economy) perspective, Fainstein and Fainstein show the value of taking a broader view along similar lines. They argue that urban policy is "state activity which affects urbanism" or, more fully that it is, "state activity affecting the use of space and the built environment relative to the process of accumulation and the social occupation of space relative to the distribution of consumption opportunities" (Fainstein and Fainstein 1982, p. 16). They identify a key tension (which is revisited in each particular historical expression of urban policy in practice) between the "function of urban areas as residential areas for the mass of the population" and the "use of urban space as a vehicle for accumulation" (Fainstein and Fainstein 1982, p. 9). This more sophisticated interpretation provides a helpful way into debates about the ways in which a range of state policies (whatever their stated purpose) shape urban development and the experience of those living in cities. But it remains less successful as a means of delimiting and defining a specific policy field that might be identified as urban policy. So, for example, it might allow us to explore the urban consequences of a general program of privatization, without making it any easier to determine which policy initiatives should be seen as aspects of an explicitly developed urban policy and which should not.

If the debates of the 1970s focused on the role of the urban in processes of social reproduction, by the mid 1980s the emphasis had shifted dramatically. Now it was placed increasingly clearly on the role of cities in processes of production, or on the realization of profits from real estate development. So, for example, in a powerful phrase Logan and Molotch (1987) identified the city as a "growth machine" (see also Molotch 1976). They argue that: *"local conflicts* over growth are central to the organization of cities . . . not only the economic imperative of the larger system but also the striving of *parochial actors* to make money"* (Logan and Molotch 1987, p. viii). From a related but distinct perspective, others suggested that it was more appropriate to understand urban politics in terms of growth coalitions, based around the priorities of locally dependent capital rooted in localized conditions of profitability – a "particular local or urban product/service/labor/housing market or local government jurisdiction: some patterned set of local interaction in other words" (Cox 1998, p. 20. See also Cox and Mair 1989). Stone's work has also been used to reinforce arguments that see growth and its positive outcomes for business (as well as the promise of positive outcomes for citizens) as the basis on which localized urban policy may be developed to build urban regimes and partnerships drawing public, private and community sectors together under a broad agenda of business success (Stone 1989, 1993; Stoker 1995).

In some important respects the insights of these theorists are helpful, particularly because they seem to fit with key aspects of today's actually existing urban policy. They are consistent with some of the policy shifts that have led to the identification of the "entrepreneurial" or the "competitive" city, that is the policy approach that sees economic success as the necessary precondition for the well-being (or welfare) of citizens rather than the existence of an extensive (social-democratic) welfare state (see, e.g. from rather different perspectives, Harvey 1989b and Begg 2002). For some, this understanding has come to form the basis of a critique; for others it provided the basis of normative policy making (see, e.g. Buck et al. 2005 for a review of what they call the "new conventional wisdom"). The broader issues associated with the notion of the entrepreneurial or competitive city are discussed further in Chapters 6 and 7.

But the underlying theoretical approaches of the urban growth theorists (whether they use the term machine, coalition, or regime) also have their own weaknesses. If Castells and others overemphasized the significance of cities as places of collective consumption then this approach understates them.

In a sense they represent an inversion of the approach that sees the urban as defined by collective consumption, since they define urban politics through the drive to realize exchange value and generate profits from growth (through rising property values) or from the necessary relations associated with locally dependent business. The existence of welfare infrastructure is simply ignored or taken for granted. And aspects of urban policy that might be focused on other forms of social consumption (e.g. community) are automatically ruled out as irrelevant, or redefined as instrumental infrastructure. Although the tension identified by Fainstein and Fainstein (1982) is initially acknowledged, in practice it is soon marginalized since the emphasis is squarely placed on the side of production (that is the production or realization of exchange value). So, for example, therefore the significance of urban policy as an attempt to control the disorderly and manage disordered spaces (discussed more fully in Chapter 5) (see, e.g. Davis 2002, p. 244) fits uneasily with a structural emphasis on growth as driver of urban policy. Similarly, while it might be possible to claim community-based initiatives (and communitarian thinking) in terms that relate them to issues of production and the competitiveness of cities, the tension between a community-based agenda and a more narrowly defined competitiveness-oriented agenda is hard to ignore (these issues are explored more fully in Chapter 6). In other words, the role of cities in providing social infrastructure tends to be understated.

More recently, attempts have been made to position urban policy rather more explicitly within broader shifts in economy, public policy and state restructuring. One aspect of this is reflected in the major critique launched by those who see in its contemporary development and definition the working out of a global neo-liberal agenda (see, e.g. Brenner and Theodore 2002a). The extent to which it is helpful to understand urban policy as an expression of neo-liberalism is explored further in Chapter 8, but what matters here is that this approach invites us to understand urban policy as part of a wider process of change, while also positioning the city as an active agent in shaping that change (see also Harding 2005 for a discussion of ways of bringing the different conceptual understandings together).

A related but distinct approach sees urban policy as having had, and continuing to have, a key role in the reshaping of postwar welfare states (sometimes called the Keynesian welfare state) and the settlements associated with them, without necessarily finding it helpful to make use of the all-encompassing label of neo-liberalism to describe the process (but see also Jessop 2002b). The rise of urban policy effectively coincides with the moment of Fordist restructuring. Its continued development helped to constitute (as well as reflect) the policy upheavals and state restructuring that characterized the fraying of the Keynesian welfare state and the unsettling of the political, economic and welfare settlement implied by it. In its contemporary form(s) it begins to suggest the possibility of a new political and welfare settlement, even if it is one that remains highly provisional and contested.

In this context the (empirically evident) rise of the "competitive city" may be interpreted as important evidence of the direction of change, which finds its expression on a wider global stage, and not one restricted to the countries of the West. The rise of mega projects, the reimagination of cities as cultural centers and "global cities" is marked in the Pacific-Asian Region as much as in the United States and Western Europe. Within the emergent set of arrangements, the nature of the urban "problem" may also be interpreted differently – instead of a catalog of decline, which urban policy needs to reverse, in some expressions of a new urban policy cities become potential (and actual) sources of growth and development as long as the right policies are adopted (see, e.g. World Bank Infrastructure Group Urban Development 2000; Buck et al. 2005). Not only has there been a broad shift from the state as regulator of the market (which could be seen as the social democratic or Keynesian model) to the state as agent of the market – the explicit focus of policy is on capitalist production (and specifically the generation of profit) rather than social reproduction (see Smith 2002). From this perspective the new urban policy may be seen as a core aspect (or at least a harbinger) of a new welfare (or postwelfare) settlement (or unstable set of settlements).

Many Meanings, Not Just One

There is no final answer which makes it possible to pin down the meaning of "urban policy" for all time, so we should not be disappointed that one cannot be found. It is not that there is no "real" problem, or cluster of problems, but the questions that are of interest are both:

1   why a particular urban problem is identified as one requiring social policy intervention at any particular time, and;
2   why it is defined or understood as it is, in ways that often bear little or no relationship to what those who are apparently the targets (or supposed beneficiaries) see as the problem.

Urban policy is both an expression of contemporary understandings of the urban, of what makes cities what they are, and itself helps to shape those understandings (as well as the cities themselves).

This approach helps to provide the basis on which the book is constructed – not a linear history, but instead a review of urban policy as the product of a complex interweaving of meanings, producing a changing pattern but with recognizable continuities. So each chapter focuses on one theme that has been associated with urban policy. None of these themes can be understood in isolation from the others, but at different times and in different places, the lead emphasis of urban policy has varied, which makes it important to understand the cross-cutting and overlapping patterns of meaning that emerge. There is also an understanding that, although social policy tends to be discussed either in national boxes or in explicitly comparative terms, it is only through an analysis that consciously links developments across national boundaries that the development of urban policy can be understood. The book seeks to explore the complex interaction between urban policy definition, its development and meaning since the late 1960s.

In doing so, it largely draws on arguments and evidence from the United Kingdom but frequently with explicit cross reference to developments in the United States, not least because of the ways in which the development of urban policy in the two countries has (from time to time) been so intertwined. The development of social policy, particularly in the years of what Jessop (2002a) calls the Keynesian welfare national state and the first phase of its restructuring, played itself out on a series of more or less loosely connected national stages, so the analysis of any particular aspect of social policy requires a focus on those national experiences. Urban policy, like other areas of social policy, has been actively produced through a series of particular engagements that vary between national contexts, which makes it important to understand the nature of those engagements, since the form taken by any actually existing urban policy will be "path dependent" (Brenner and Theodore 2002b).

To understand the nature and meaning of urban policy, it is necessary to explore the ways in which it has been constructed in practice. In any exploration of social policy it is important to recognize the route that is being taken into wider debates and in this case it begins from the experience of a small island off the coast of Europe, which is connected into global policy networks in particular ways, for example, both as the home of a "world city" and as an ex-colonial power; and both in its subaltern role to the United States within those global networks and in its position within the European Union.

In this book, in other words, the empirical focus, particularly at first, is largely on the UK experience. But from the start it is also understood that no national experience can be understood as completely autonomous and, in this case, the complex relationship with the United States both as source of policy lessons and as vision of (positive and negative, utopian and dystopian) urban futures is recognized as being of particular significance. Britain, of course, also represents a rather peculiar "national" formation, constituted as it is from its own component nations (and quasi nations), while its cities are fundamentally shaped by sets of colonial and postcolonial linkages which have themselves helped to define urban policy in quite fundamental ways.

The core aim of this book is not to present and develop a more or less convincing "history" or story of urban policy in Britain (although, of course, it is important that the story presented is, at least, plausible). There may also be a danger that the "origin" story presented in the next chapter is stated too confidently as some sort of "universal" origin. Instead the aim is to suggest a way of approaching – of analyzing – urban policy in a wide range of contexts. In that sense the United Kingdom is simply one case and its experience is used to provide an example of how such an approach might be developed in practice. Not all of the themes or policy approaches discussed in the following chapters will be relevant to all the national or local histories of urban policy, and others that are absent may be mobilized in other contexts and at other times. But it is the coming together that matters – the recognition that urban policy is constantly in the process of being redefined and reimagined, drawing on a particular menu but combining its elements in different ways at different times and in different places.

Despite the extent to which supporting evidence is drawn from a particular case, the argument of the book is underpinned by an understanding that the case itself has to be located within wider processes of change and can only be understood in connection with the experience of other cases and the linkages between them. This means that examples from other cities and other policy contexts are also mobilized through the book. More important, perhaps, the rise of the entrepreneurial city which is discussed in Chapter 6 suggests a wider post-Keynesian take on urban policy, which may be undermining the possibility of (autonomous) nationally based policy development, while Chapter 7 considers the ways in which this has found an expression in a new emphasis on forms of cultural policy. Chapter 8 turns to a consideration of the emergence of globalized forms of urban policy since the mid 1990s.

The concluding chapter turns to bigger questions that focus on the hopes and possibilities that might be contained within urban policy. Deep in the rhetoric of urban policy, there continues to be a belief in cities as drivers of social progress, as places of civilization where conflicts may be translated into democratic engagement and "emancipation," as sites across which battles over social justice and equity are played out (see, e.g. Lees 2004). The ambiguities and tensions, the conflicts between managing the disorderly urban and creating spaces of popular empowerment, or even just for the maintenance of popular well-being, remain at the political heart of urban policy.

Chapter 2

Exploring the Roots: "Race," Disorder, and Poverty

It is always dangerous to identify any particular moment as the defining point at which any sort of change is initiated, and the uncertain nature of urban policy should perhaps make one still more cautious about doing so. Nevertheless, it is hard to avoid the conclusion that the explosion of urban social policy as an identifiable phenomenon had its roots in the United States of the 1960s, even if at first it was not explicitly described as urban policy.

It grew out of President Johnson's promise of "The Great Society" and the inauguration of what was called "The War on Poverty," declared in Johnson's State of the Union Message to Congress in 1964 with the stated objective of "total victory" (quoted in Lynn 1977, p. 63), which in turn built on a series of earlier initiatives, including the Ford Foundation's Grey Areas Program and the President's Committee on Juvenile Delinquency. At first the explicit emphasis was on developing an antipoverty strategy, with no particular expectation that this necessarily implied an urban focus – the valleys of Appalachia and the rural South had been equally strongly identified as places of poverty in Harrington's now almost mythical "The Other America" (1962) which is often identified as having played a key role in raising the profile of the issue and even persuading first Kennedy and then Johnson that action was required. Many of the recurrent themes of urban policy were brought together for the first time in this context and it is for that reason that this chapter begins with a review of the emergence of urban policy in the United States of the 1960s, before turning to a consideration of the ways in which it "drifted" across the Atlantic.

From the Rediscovery of Poverty to the Invention of Urban Policy

Even at this early stage, some of the central principles that were to underpin a more directly urban policy were already becoming clear. Poverty, it was said, was no longer something seen (let alone experienced) by the middle class majority – the poor were no longer a majority but a minority separated by segregation from the mainstream of suburban America. Above all poverty was being identified not in absolute terms, but in terms of marginalization (even if the notion of social exclusion was not yet commonplace), and also in the existence of what came to be called a "culture of poverty," that is a self-reinforcing culture which ensures that the poor remain poor (Lewis 1967).

Harrington himself forcefully summed up this understanding: "Today's poor ... are the first minority poor in history, the first poor not to be seen, the first poor whom the politicians could leave alone ... the new poverty is constructed so as to destroy aspiration; it is a system designed to be impervious to hope" (Harrington 1962, pp. 16–17). "Poverty in the United States," he continued, "is a culture, an institution, a way of life ... . To be impoverished is to be an internal alien, to grow up in a culture that is radically different from the one that dominates the society" (Harrington 1962, pp. 22–4). Since the culture of poverty was an interconnected system, said Harrington, it was not enough to tackle one symptom, but it was necessary to launch a comprehensive and coordinated attack in which the Federal Government needed to take the lead:

> Washington is essential in a double sense: as a source of the considerable funds needed to mount a campaign against the other America, and as a place for co-ordination, for planning, and the establishment of national standards. The actual implementation of a program to abolish poverty can be carried out through myriad institutions, and the closer they are to the specific local area, the better the results. (Harrington 1962, p. 167).

The extent to which Harrington's book directly shaped the emergent policy area is questionable, but it certainly had a symbolic role in marking its emergence. Despite not having an urban focus (except in a powerful chapter which focused on the experience of black people in the cities, entitled, "If You're Black, Stay Back") it also – perhaps unintentionally – pointed towards some of the ways in which first antipoverty policy and later urban policy would develop. So, for example, it effectively presaged a move away from the promotion of universal welfare services towards interventions targeted on particular areas and groups, to help reverse the culture of poverty, and it raised the recurrent theme of coordination and the interdependence of a wide range of policies. By arguing for a strong role for Federal government it also reinforced the view that that the old service bureaucracies and their associated professions could not meet the challenges being set for them by the "new" poverty.

The core programs of the War on Poverty were rolled out through Congress between 1964 and 1966, in legislation such as the Economic Opportunity Act (1964), and the Model Cities Act (1966). It is easy to get lost in the detail of the various initiatives clustered together in this policy explosion. So for our purposes it is perhaps enough to identify a number of key principles that run across them, as well as some of the tensions and inconsistencies that characterized them (another feature that seems to echo down the years of urban policy in practice). Above all, they include:

- A belief in the value of multiple initiatives, each relevant to the broader ambition of tackling poverty – so, for example, programs included those targeted on education (pre-school in the case of Head Start, but also at older ages, including high school and college in the case of Upward Bound); on employment and job training (in the case of Job Corps); on crime and disorder (in the case of the Neighbourhood Youth Corps); and on legal services (which had its own program).

- Following from this, a commitment to coordination – since poverty was understood to be multi-causal and systemic, only a coordinated attack could work effectively. It was said to be necessary to move beyond the boundaries created by professional disciplines, bureaucratic structures and government divisions. As the compilation prepared for the Congressional select sub-committee on poverty in 1964 made clear: "Since the causes of poverty are complex ... The most successful community action ... usually includes the political business, labour and religious leaders, the schoolboard, the employment service, the public welfare department, private social welfare agencies, and neighbourhood houses in a co-ordinated attack on local poverty" (quoted in Marris and Rein 1972, p. 113). At national level this was the task of the Office of Economic Opportunity, and at local level it was to be the task of the Community Action Agencies. The Community Action Program (CAP) promised a direct link between the federal government and the urban poor, since the federally funded community action agencies were expected both to deliver services and to coordinate their local delivery (Barnekov et al. 1989, p. 50).

- In principle, a move away from the old system of welfare based on "transfer payments" (such as social security or the payment of means tested benefits) towards one that enabled the poor to reenter the labor market and other aspects of "normal society." In its Second Annual Report published in 1967, the Office of Economic opportunity summarized this approach in the statement: "Give a poor man only a hand-out and he stays poor, but give the same man a skill and he rises from poverty" (quoted in Friedman 1977, p. 37). As Johnson himself put it: "We are not content to accept the endless growth of relief roles or welfare roles. We want to offer the forgotten fifth of our people opportunity, not doles" (quoted in Marwick 1998, p. 269).

- As so often in the history of social policy, of course, this belief in the need to offer poor people the "opportunity" to save themselves was accompanied by the view that this meant they had to change, too. Friedman (1977, p. 36) argues that "The war on poverty adopted, as its basic strategy, the tactic of changing the poor rather than enriching them, adapting *them* to the existing system." He goes on to quote Lampman (1971, p. 10) to the effect that the aims of the War on Poverty were to change "the attitudes, values, motivations and life-style of the poor" and to "develop their potential productivity." Similarly, Sugrue confirms that the programs "focused on behavioural modification as the solution to poverty" (Sugrue 1996, p. 264). In other words at the core of the War on Poverty was an assault on the "culture of poverty," understood as the culture of the poor.

- Associated with this, a belief that the "community" itself must be involved in and actively participate in the management of the new programs. Famously (see, e.g. Moynihan 1969), the Economic Opportunity Act contained the phrase "maximum feasible participation" to reflect the new approach and even the (less radical) legislation associated with the Model Cities program included the requirement for "widespread citizen participation" and "maximum opportunities for the employment of residents of the area." Not only did this mean that community representatives had to sit on the key partnership and agency committees (such as the community action agencies) but it was expected to reinforce community commitment to the self-development and self-improvement activities associated with the programs. As the report to the select committee puts it: "Above all it includes the poor people of the community whose first opportunity must be the opportunity to help themselves" (quoted in Marris and Rein 1972, p. 113). Rein develops this point more fully elsewhere, explaining that, "democracy tends to be interpreted as a form of direct participation at grass-roots level. Community competence through self-help becomes defined as a therapeutic process for promoting social integration ... The rewards of participation are defined as civic pride, personal growth and the reduction of community deviancy" (Rein 1970, p. 227).

- Underlying much of this was a rejection of the existing structures involved in the management of welfare and in the programs associated with the alleviation of poverty. A powerful critique was mobilized, which emphasized the "existence of over-centralization; the lack of lateral communication between administrations; their indifference to the effectiveness of their work; and their unresponsiveness to the people they served" (Marris and Rein 1972, p. 278). The problem of "functional and geographically segregated bureaucracies," it was argued, was that they could only be "co-ordinated by an increasingly centralized political authority, or not co-ordinated at all when the power at the centre is stultified by its divisions" (Marris and Rein 1972, p. 289). More pragmatically, as Piven and Cloward note, "city government was defined as major impediment by many federal officials, an obstacle to be hurdled or circumvented if federal funds were to reach blacks" (Piven and Cloward 1972, p. 262). It was in that context that community action agencies were presented as solutions, bringing together policy and implementation at local level, as well as having the capacity to be more open to those the new initiatives were intended to serve.

- A belief existed that the new approach offered a means of delivering major change at relatively low cost. Although the absolute levels of spending rose through the 1960s, at no time did expenditure on the initiatives associated with the Office of Economic Opportunity and the War on Poverty ever rise above 1.5 percent of the federal budget (Marwick 1998, p. 269). Marris and Rein neatly summarize the position: "So the war was to be fought by making savings elsewhere, without raising the national budget by a single dollar" (Marris and Reins 1972, p. 256). The aim was to produce a "more rational, coherent system of services to low income residents that would increase the efficiency with which services were delivered" (Peterson and Greenstone 1977, p. 242). The launch of these initiatives not only presented a fundamental critique of universalist models, which were deemed to have failed in eradicating poverty, but also promised a more cost-effective means of tackling the problem and a way of involving the poor in helping to solve it through their own initiative.

- Above all, of course, within this framework one assumption may have been unspoken but it was nevertheless clear. The development of urban policy was predicated on the understanding that the problems being tackled were not structural, but rather the unfortunate consequence of concentrations of particular (locally specific) combinations of factors. "Thus," as Smith (1988, p. 93) puts it, "black urban poverty was treated largely as a problem of needy places rather than faulty labor market structures." This was an explicit break with approaches that focused on the existence of inequalities of income and sought to counter them with wider (national) redistributive policies (see, e.g. Lehmann 1991, p. 144). The program of reform reflected a belief that the problems which needed to be tackled were essentially technical ones, because the institutions that should be distributing the benefits of affluence were failing to do so effectively (Marris and Rein 1972, p. 1).

The officially stated ambition of these programs was to attack poverty wherever it was and whatever its causes. However, the fundamental linkage between the initiatives associated with the War on Poverty and cities did not take long to become clear. In a sense they were explicitly acknowledged in the creation of the Department of Housing and Urban Development as an executive agency in 1965 and the launching of the Model Cities program in 1966. But in practice the understanding that what was developing was an urban policy was inescapable at a much earlier stage. In part it emerged from the practice of pursuing the implications of the various initiatives – whatever the intent of their progenitors, in practice they could only be taken further in an urban context; in part it emerged from the wider political and social context in which they were launched; and – associated with this – in part it emerged in reaction to the urban riots of the mid 1960s and the overwhelming popular fears of (or moral panic around) urban crisis that were associated with them.

Welfare, urban policy and race

The War on Poverty emerged in the context of major political and social upheavals in the United States. The Civil Rights movement focused attention on segregation and political exclusion in the South, famously mobilizing a remarkable coalition stretching from black church groups in the South to students from universities across the North, and incorporating a range of political views from the visionary appeal of Martin Luther King to the radicalism of Stokely Carmichael and the Student NonViolent Coordinating Committee. 1963 saw the quarter of a million strong March on Washington, at which King gave his inspirational "I have a dream" speech, powerfully highlighting the position of African-Americans in the midtwentieth century. One hundred years after emancipation he said: "the life of the Negro is still sadly crippled by the manacles of segregation and the chains of discrimination. One hundred years later, the Negro lives on a lonely island of poverty in the midst of a vast ocean of material prosperity. One hundred years later, the Negro is still languishing in the corners of American society and finds himself an exile in his own land" (King 1963). In 1964 the Civil Rights Act was passed, declaring discrimination illegal in public places, housing and employment and an Equal Employment Opportunity Commission was set up as an enforcement agency. Between 1963 and 1965 the campaign for civil rights brought conflict to the streets of the American South, as demonstrations against segregation and drives to register black voters were often met with violent responses.

These events helped to reinforce the linkages between "race" and the War on Poverty. Martin Luther King himself called for a Bill of Rights for the Disadvantaged – "with equal opportunity," he wrote, "must come the practical, realistic aid which will equip" people "to seize it" (King 1964, p. 136). For the black populations of the Northern cities, many of whom had themselves only recently come from the South, the lessons of civil rights had equally strong messages (in 1940 only half of the black population of the United States lived in cities; by 1965 it was 80 percent). They too were facing the pressures of discrimination, poverty, and segregation. Black support for Kennedy also created the strong expectation that they "would share in the fruits of his victory," not just in the Southern states but also in the Northern cities, to the extent that it was clear that "racial changes were critically shaping the urban policy agenda at both national and local levels" (Peterson and Greenstone 1977, p. 252). Kotz similarly argues that "there was real political pressure for change that came from a rapidly evolving civil rights movement that already was engaged in the struggle against poverty as well as against segregation and discrimination" (Kotz 1977, p. 49). The civil rights movement also succeeded in constructing a broad alliance linking black people and middle class whites around the notion of "rights" and this undoubtedly played into the way in which urban policy developed as a comprehensive program (see, e.g. McCann 2003, p. 180).

It has been strongly argued that in effect the War on Poverty represented an attempt by the (Democrat controlled) federal government to integrate the growing and politically mobilized urban black population into mainstream politics as supporters of the Democrats, through "the development of place-specific entitlements which could shore up as many Democratic urban regimes as possible" (Smith 1988, pp. 92–3. See also Mollenkopf 1983). Similarly Piven and Cloward (1972) argue that "The Great Society Programs were promulgated by federal leaders in order to deal with the political problems created by a new and unstable electoral constituency, namely blacks – and to deal with this new constituency not simply by responding to its expressed interests, but by shaping and directing its political future" (Piven and Cloward 1972, p. 249. See also Peterson and Greenstone 1977, p. 251).

It is not necessary to agree with the conclusions that Piven and Cloward draw about the intentions of those developing the policies to recognize the significance of these programs in drawing in a new constituency. The War on Poverty in practice provided an uneasy and often contradictory way onto the political stage for people who had previously been excluded or simply not been present in the cities. In 1968, relations between the white and black urban populations were still characterized by fundamental political inequality (Rossi et al. 1974, p. 416). So this was the moment that the post 1945 welfare settlement was extended to include at least some of the African Americans living in the major cities of the United States, as the Great Society measures "created new social programs and liberalized existing ones" (Piven and Cloward 1997, p, 4).

The community oriented programs bypassed the existing structures of municipal government in ways that promised opportunities for black professionals excluded from traditional forms of municipal employment. The new programs did not (initially at least) directly confront the old arrangements and certainly did not undermine those employed in the existing bureaucracies of welfare and local government. In other words rather than heralding direct black challenges to the existing white control of municipal services and jobs, the new initiatives were focused on channelling services and jobs direct to black neighborhoods – a process that has been described as "localizing and particularizing concessions to blacks" (Piven and Cloward 1997, p. 104).

However, the new structures also soon provided platforms for wider protest and mobilization. Community action came to mean (and the community action agencies came to work in ways that were focused) on the mobilization of the community, rather than attempts to coordinate services, and "maximum feasible participation" was increasingly and self consciously directed towards what were defined by the professionals and activists as the "socially subjected population" (Peterson and Greenstone 1977, p. 255). "Maximum feasible participation" may initially have been little more than the usual genuflection towards community involvement, but in the context of the upheavals of the 1960s, even if the extent of the active participation of the "poor" remained severely limited (see, e.g. Edwards and Batley 1978, p. 23), it became a rallying cry around which social and political change was initiated. Whatever the intention of those who used the rhetoric, the advice of the Office of Economic Opportunity gave local activists permission (or, to use language that might have been used today, it empowered them) to take action that challenged the existing rules of the game, in seeking to mobilize communities and access resources from government.

In practice the methods adopted looked a great deal like those used by the old style traditional political machine as it mobilized ethnic and neighborhood support, responding to the rise of new groups by finding (some of them) jobs (Piven and Cloward 1972, p. 261; Peterson and Greenstone 1977, pp. 263–4). So, for example, local welfare rights and related agencies were set up, often in the form of storefront centers; professional staff were appointed to help support these and to help people find jobs, deal with the workings of public welfare and gain access to municipal and other services; ways were found of supporting and building neighborhood leaderships, often through the appointment or identification of community workers, through whom patronage and (admittedly limited) funding would be distributed. Nonprofessionals from the communities being served (or members of the racial groups who lived in them) were recruited to a range of professional or semiprofessional posts, including teaching assistants, consumer protection advisors, health service assistants, as well as neighborhood organizers. Here the link to the civil rights movement was particularly clear – "the war on poverty became the successor to the civil rights movement by providing a sanction for middle class ethnic activists to speak for the poor and to organize them as a constituency that might be used as a pressure on community institutions" (Kramer 1969, p. 25).

"In many cities," argue Piven and Cloward (1972, p. 274), "the Great Society agencies became the base for new black political organizations whose rhetoric may have been thunderous but whose activities came to consist mainly of vying for position and patronage within the urban political system." In other words, "the political progress of the black community during this same period can be most persuasively interpreted not as a "political revolution" – blacks are as yet unequal, even politically – but as an accommodation which has preserved the underlying stability of social and economic as well as political relations" (Peterson and Greenstone 1977, p. 276). By the mid 1990s, Fainstein and Fainstein (1996) were able to record a relative "success" for these policies, in the shape of black incorporation into the formal structures of urban politics, both in terms of political office, such as the mayoralties of major cities, and also in government employment, to the extent that they were disproportionately dependent on public sector employment, particularly for middle class and professional jobs. It is, nevertheless, salutary to be reminded by Kraus (2003) that the working out of urban policy in practice in many cities (his case study is of Buffalo in New York state) has effectively worked to reinforce inequalities and concentrate poverty among the black population (see also Sugrue 1996).

One unintended consequence of the new approach to welfare embedded in the programs associated with the War on Poverty was that the demands made on traditional welfare actually rose dramatically (e.g. through payments under the Aid to Families with Dependent Chidren Program. See Piven and Cloward 1997, p. 139). Effectively the budgets allocated to community action groups were used to lever additional funds from mainstream welfare. One aspect of this could be seen in the role of the legal services program that was embedded in the Office for Economic Opportunity and had local expression in what were effectively neighborhood law centers (of which there were around 850 in 1968). The neighborhood-based lawyers launched campaigns that sought to use the courts to determine universally applicable rights for those they represented – and above all (e.g. in cases relating to eligibility) rights to welfare (see, e.g. Marris and Rein 1972, pp. 288–90 and Piven and Cloward 1972, pp. 302–20, for a discussion of some of the cases pursued, and their wider significance). They sought to use the law to achieve wider institutional change, and not just to support individual cases. It is perhaps not surprising that one of the first acts of Donald Rumsfeld (by 2004 Secretary of Defense in George W. Bush's Cabinet) on the broader political stage in his role as Nixon's appointee as head of the Office of Economic Opportunity was to sack the head of the legal services program in 1969.

Riots and "Urban Crisis"

The identification of the Great Society and the War on Poverty as urban policy was powerfully reinforced by the impact of the urban riots that took place in America's major cities between 1965 and 1967, and to which those programs came to be seen as a response. These riots had a clear racial expression – generally taking place in the African-American areas of cities and often in response to the experience of heavy policing – to the extent that they have also often been described as "rebellions" rather than riots. Riots took place in Watts in 1965, in Chicago and Cleveland in 1966, and in 150 cities in 1967 (the most violent being in Newark, New Jersey and Detroit). The riots were important catalysts for change, which "particularly highlighted urban issues, many of which overlapped with racial ones" (Gurr and King 1987, p. 128), since, as Smith notes, "The black urban rebellions of the 1960s" were seen by elites both as proof of the existence of an urban crisis and confirmation "that it was a social crisis" (Smith 1988, p. 91). It was an "urban crisis" to which the new (urban) policy tools might be applied.

A *New York Times* editorial in August 1964 following the first of the urban riots made it clear that, "The anti-poverty bill … is also an anti-riot bill. The members of the House of Representatives would do well to bear that in mind when the time comes for a vote" (quoted in Peterson and Greenstone 1977, p. 253). In the wake of the riots, the Kerner Commission (set up to explore the causes of the riots, or "civil disorders" as they were labeled) was quite explicit in arguing that "programmes on a scale beyond anything hitherto envisaged were vital: there must be a commitment, compassionate, massive, and sustained, backed by the resources of the most powerful and richest nation of this earth" (US National Advisory Commission on Civil Disorders, 1968, p. 1). While the scale of the programs never reached anything like that envisaged by the Commission, this conclusion was consistent with the dominant understanding that helped to sustain the poverty programs as an urban policy.

By the end of the decade, the relationship between "race" and urban policy (and indeed the urban in the United States) was taken for granted, because race was simply understood to be "an urban 'problem'" (Rossi et al. 1974, p. 57). As Piven and Cloward indicate, the language of legislation and policy-makers that referred to the inner cities, slums or the urban core, "were only euphemisms for the ghetto, for it was ghetto neighbourhoods that these programs were chiefly designed to reach" (Piven and Cloward 1972, p. 260). The equation between race and urban policy has, for good and ill, cast a continuing shadow over future development of policy and the commonsense frameworks within which such development takes place. At the start of the twenty-first century, even the application of "urban" to a whole genre of popular music was universally understood as a code for contemporary "black" music. By 2002 Davis confirms that the word "city" had become "color coded," which also meant that any policies directed towards the city were not attractive to suburban voters (Davis 2002, p. 241) – "the semantic identity of race and urbanity within US political discourse is now virtually complete" (Davis 2002, p. 255). This is particularly significant at a time when the main political and business elites not only reside in but draw their support from the suburbs and see their main task as defending those suburbs from the perceived threat of the cities (Goldsmith 2000).

Transatlantic drift

Many, although not all, of the characteristics that have come to be associated with urban policy (and particularly urban policy as social policy) can be identified in the policy developments of 1960s America, to the extent that it sometimes seems as if little or nothing has been learned from the past. It looks as if each newly minted initiative has been tried before and found wanting before, but somehow the memory banks of policy makers have been wiped clean so that they are persuaded that this time it really will work. In this context it is perhaps just worth returning to the main features of the policy approaches developed at this time and in these places. They include:

- A commitment to coordination in policy and practice
- A belief that universalism no longer works and that targeting needs to be more sophisticated
- A desire to reduce welfare spending
- An emphasis on community development – so that communities take on responsibility for their own well-being
- A conviction that existing public service structures are bureaucratic, cumbersome and self-serving, which means they have to be bypassed
- A belief that current electoral structures (at least at local level) are unrepresentative and exclusionary
- A fear of crime and disorder and the search for ways of minimizing threats to social stability
- Associated with this, an often coded concern about race and the ways it plays out on the streets of the cities

Of course, missing from this list are those aspects of policy that relate to economic regeneration, urban competitiveness, urban regeneration, and urban renaissance. Their arrival at the table is not far in the future. But their absence at this stage reflects the extent to which in its first incarnation urban policy is probably best seen as part of a last ditch attempt to save the Keynesian welfare state – finding ways of integrating, and managing sections of the community that were previously excluded – even if was later to slide almost seamlessly into moves to restructure, reshape, and supersede that particular welfare settlement, with an increasingly powerful statement of the extent to which welfare flows from the success of the private economy, rather than the provision of state welfare. Although Barnekov et al. (1989) argue persuasively that there was a strong element of privatism in policy development throughout this period (particularly in the United States) the evidence they mobilize shows still more clearly how the emphasis shifted dramatically over the years after 1970, as the leading role of the private sector was stressed more and more explicitly (see also Chapter 6). Indeed (and despite the survival of the Department of Housing and Urban Development) the high point of national – federal – urban policy in the United States had already passed by the early 1970s. As Vidal and Keating (2004) note, "By the early 1970s place-based approaches to urban problems had largely faded from the federal scene." Instead – with just a few exceptions – local initiative, civic or metropolitan, became the norm, often encouraged by federal and state governments.

The relationship between the rise of a distinctive urban policy in the United States and its development in other countries is not a straightforward one. The discovery of "area based initiatives" in Britain had its own precursors in a series of reports published in the 1960s, including the Milner-Holland Report (1965) on *Housing in Greater London*, the Plowden Report (1967) on *Children and their Primary Schools* and the Seebohm Report (1968) on *Local Authority and Allied Personal Services*. Each pointed to the benefit of concentrating intervention in particular neighborhoods in order to counteract deprivation of one sort or another. So, for example, the Plowden Report argued that "As a matter of national policy, 'positive discrimination' should favour schools in neighbourhoods where children are most severely handicapped by home conditions" (Plowden Report 1967, p. 464).

Nevertheless the role of the United States experience in shaping policy developments in the United Kingdom has been widely acknowledged. This may not be a simple case of policy transfer (see Hambleton and Taylor 1994, Dolowitz et al. 2000) but there was certainly an active process of learning, as senior civil servants visited their US counterparts and explicitly referred to transatlantic models (even if, as Loney 1983, pp. 25–31 notes, members of the policy community had only a very superficial knowledge of the situation in the United States). A British-American conference was held at Ditchley Park in 1969 whose purpose was specifically to bring together the lessons of the US experience for the more modest British programs (see, e.g. Community Development Project 1977b, p. 52). Despite the learning process, however, the differences between the two countries remained significant, with the United Kingdom following a much more centralized process of managing projects (perhaps learning some lessons from the US experience, but also reflecting more fundamental differences in approach, as part of a more centralized welfare state). The scale of the urban program was also much more modest than the ambitious program launched in the United States in the 1960s. In 1968 in the United States, $3 billion was being spent annually, in the United Kingdom, the Urban Programme promised to spend £20–25 million over four years (Loney 1984, pp. 22–3. See also Edwards and Batley 1978, pp. 24–5).

Britain's Urban Programme, launched in 1968, promised "expenditure mainly on education, housing, health and welfare in areas of special need." These areas were defined as "localized districts which bear the marks of multiple deprivation, which may show itself, for example, by way of notable deficiencies in the physical environment, particularly housing; overcrowding of houses; family sizes above the average; persistent unemployment; a high proportion of children in trouble or in need of care; or a combination of these" (Home Office 1968). Educational Priority Areas were a related but separate initiative, also launched in the late 1960s (following the Plowden Report and in emulation of Headstart) and were set up as action-research projects in five deprived areas, with the expectation that lessons could be learned which would help to bring underprivileged children more productively into education. The initiatives included the development of community schools, training for teachers, attached social workers backed up by researchers (based at Oxford University) whose task it was to draw out the lessons for further policy development – "to discover which of the developments in educational priority areas have the most constructive effects, so as to assist in planning the longer term programme to follow" (Plowden Report 1967, p. 466).

In practice the Urban Programme (which survived until the early 1990s, although the emphasis of inner city policy shifted dramatically in the late1970s) funded a series of relatively small-scale locally based (often described as community) initiatives, in partnership with local authorities (Edwards and Batley 1978, Higgins et al. 1983, pp. 47–85, Atkinson and Moon 1994, pp. 44–6). In retrospect the "traditional" Urban Programme, before its refocusing on economic development in 1977, has been described as "modest in scale and intent and has in practice proved to be a small scale social and educational welfare program" and it was noted that "while it talks of poverty and unemployment it spends money on projects that, however worthwhile, are not directly aimed at these issues" (Edwards and Batley 1978, p. 225). That the program was initially based in the Home Office (with responsibility only transferring to the Department of the Environment in 1977), rather than any department directly involved in the funding or management of welfare services, was itself significant, because it reflected the origins of the policy in concerns about the integration of "immigrant" populations and because it was intended to overcome threats to social order in cities, as well as an orientation which stressed self-help and renewal, rather than the provision of universal services or even services to the disadvantaged.

Possibly more significant in the process of transatlantic policy transfer was the strength of a popular and political ideology in which the United States represented the future, whether positively expressed in visions of economic success and individual affluence, or more negatively in fears of disorder and visions of dystopia. The US experience of riots, particularly as filtered through the interpretations of overseas observers, helped to provide a dystopian narrative of the inherent threats and insecurities of urban life. For some, the fear of black takeover took on an almost parodic expression. So, for example, Blair (Thomas not Tony) produced a popular text on what he called the international urban crisis, in which he quotes Stokely Carmichael with some trepidation – "Let me tell you, baby, when we get 52 per cent of the voters in the city, we own that city – lock, stock and barrel" (Blair 1974, p. 132). Here, of course, it is not just the electoral success of black people that is worrying the author, but the attitude summed up in the scare figure of Stokely Carmichael and the language he uses. Later Blair also lists ways in which black radicals may take advantage of urban locations – so, for example, "In Chicago's South Side every fourth street is commercial. Arsonists could set off fires in the principal white-owned businesses, thereby occupying the fire and police departments while well-trained saboteurs spread out over the city to blow up power plants, despoil water systems, and derail trains – most of which run through the ghetto" (Blair 1974, p. 133). This was a message intended for consumption far beyond the boundaries of the United States.

The threats associated with modernity, as well as its excitement and promise, were inherent in the complex social construction that constituted the "United States" from the perspective of the United Kingdom. As Hall et al. (1978) argue of the role of the United States in helping to frame British politics and policy development: "It does not simply set the pattern which Britain like all other 'modernizing societies' will follow, but may actively impose aspects of that pattern on our society by force of imitation and example if not by direct cultural influence" (Hall et al. 1978, p. 26). This provided an important context for the way in which – as Halsey noted – urban policy was influenced by "ideas drifting casually across the Atlantic, soggy on arrival and of dubious utility" (Halsey 1973, quoted in Edwards and Batley 1978, p. 24). Even the rediscovery of poverty was given its British (in this case English) equivalent by Coates and Silburn (1970) in the graphically titled "Poverty: the Forgotten Englishman." In this case, however, the focus on the inner city (and specifically on St. Anne's in Nottingham) was still more explicit than in Harrington's evocation of poverty in the United States (Harrington 1962). The policy program that was adopted might turn out to be a pale copy of the US model, but there is little doubt that the United Kingdom eagerly followed in US footsteps in developing its own urbanized "war" on poverty.

A racialized urban pathology was a crucial element in generating Britain's urban policy, too. In a series of speeches in 1968 Enoch Powell (then a leading right wing Conservative politician) prophesied that Britain's inner cities would be transformed into "alien territories." "Like the Roman," he said, "I seem to see the River Tiber foaming with blood" (Smithies and Fiddick 1969, p. 43). And he explicitly called on imagery from the United States, since he predicted that the "tragic and intractable phenomenon which we watch with horror on the other side of the Atlantic … is coming upon us here by our own volition and our own neglect" (quoted in Loney 1984, p. 21). The response of Harold Wilson (then Prime Minister) was to promise the introduction of an Urban Programme alongside increasingly tight immigration control. So Britain's Urban Programme was a direct response to fears about racial tensions in British cities albeit with their own specific post-imperial spin. And these fears were reinforced by the imagery of urban "race" riots – the US experience was presented as a frightening warning of what would follow unless action was taken. As late as 1977, it was suggested in official reports that developments in Britain's inner cities offered:

> a sinister caricature of the urban crises in the United States. The parallels are striking, are the inner areas of London, Glasgow, Liverpool, Manchester and Birmingham to go the same way as those of the USA? Is "poverty in the midst of plenty," as President Johnson put it, also to be a chronic malaise of British urban society? (Lambeth Inner Area Study 1977, p. 2).

The very concentration of households with members whose origins were in the so-called New Commonwealth was identified as evidence of multiple deprivation. The 1968 Home Office circular on the Urban Programme concluded that: "a substantial degree of immigrant settlement would … be an important factor, though not the only factor, in defining the existence of special need" (quoted in Higgins et al. 1983, pp. 52 and 54). Alex Lyon, Minister of State at the Home Office in 1974, was explicit about this: "a great many of those who suffer in these areas are black and immigrant and, therefore, add to the deprivation felt by the indigenous population of these areas" and he emphasized fears about riots like those which took place in Watts and Los Angeles, to justify the need for an urban program targeted on areas with relatively high proportions of black people among their population (quoted in Community Development Project 1977b, pp. 47–8). Members of minority ethnic groups were defined "either as generators of problems or as special needs groups" (Higgins et al. 1983 pp. 53/4). In their discussion of the Community Development Projects, Marris and Rein similarly note the extent to which they were launched "out of a concern with the assimilation of newcomers to the city" (Marris and Rein 1972, p. xvi).

However, even at this stage the formal politics of "race" in Britain ensured that any direct reference to the provision of additional services or targeted resources to black or "immigrant" communities was avoided. The language adopted was one that used apparently universal terms such as urban deprivation and community (Higgins et al. 1983, pp. 53–4). Care was taken in drafting legislation and the guidelines flowing from it to avoid identifying particular groups directly, for example, through a stress on multiple deprivation and its concentration in particular areas (what would now be described as neighborhoods), highlighting a "different kind of social need" rather than explicitly focusing on the social effects of Commonwealth immigration, even if that was the unspoken agenda (Edwards and Batley 1978, p. 139). In other words, the area base itself became a surrogate for "race" based intervention, since it was assumed that the concentration of black and minority ethnic populations (or, indeed, "immigrants") in inner city areas meant that implicit targeting was likely to be effective, even if many of those being "targeted" in this way actually lived outside such areas. Not until the mid 1970s did Urban Programme funding guidelines explicitly endorse a focus on support for voluntary organizations representing and reflecting minority ethnic communities.

By the time England's own urban riots actually arrived in 1981 and 1985, the political context had changed once more (for a discussion of more recent riots, see Chapters 4 and 5). The language of "race" had been downplayed as urban policy developed through the 1970s into the 1980s. It only had a minor part in the 1977 White Paper (HMSO 1977), which emphasized economic regeneration, and was denounced as inherently "racist" by Rex because it did not take the needs of black communities into account. He argued that by incorporating a strategy of "population replacement carried out in the name of 'dispersal and balance'" the new strategy effectively meant clearing the black population out of the inner city, even if it was never directly expressed in those terms (Rex 1988, p. 3). The urban riots of 1981 and 1985 helped to force the issue of race explicitly back onto the agenda, particularly in the wake of the Scarman Report on the Brixton riots (Scarman 1981). But they only seem to have done so temporarily. The "traditional" elements of the Urban Programme (focused on voluntary/community initiatives which were taken up by members of minority ethnic groups, particularly in the years after 1974) were given a brief reprieve, only to disappear later in the decade. Spending on the "traditional" Urban Programme became a very small element in the overall inner city program.

As in the United States, however, Atkinson and Moon (1994, pp. 229–52) acknowledge, the issue of "race" has been like a thread running through urban policy in Britain (from Enoch Powell to Scarman and beyond). It underpins many of the specific understandings reflected in particular policy initiatives, often as an unspoken sub text. "Race" has been a central element in the discourse which has constructed the image and *idea* of an inner-city crisis or problem in English cities. And it is still there as an important undercurrent, reflected, for example, in government guidelines on the involvement of representatives of a range of ethnic groups in inner city partnerships of one sort or another (see, e.g. Maginn 2004, who suggests that "race" is more significant in policy statements than in the practice of community based partnership working). Even where formal urban policy programs are presented as color blind "everybody knows" that the inner city, the urban equals black (see, e.g. Faith in the City 1985). Similarly, although there has been an increasing reluctance to develop "racially" targeted initiatives, it is assumed that members of racialized communities are likely to benefit disproportionately from initiatives designed to improve access to training and education. Paradoxically, the construction of urban policy as "color blind" has helped (as in the United States) to ensure that the label "urban" is widely understood to mean "black." As Keith and Cross note in another context: "What appears at first glance to be missing, the centrality of race … turns out on closer inspection not to be missing at all, only unspoken" (Keith and Cross 1993, p. 8) (see discussion of community and its management in the next two chapters).

Beyond the US Model

Despite the important similarities between their rhetorics and the cross-national borrowing of policy (evidence for which runs through this book), however, unlike the position in the United States, urban policy in Britain has remained a national program, or – following devolution – a series of national programs in England, Wales and Scotland, reflected in a series of white papers and policy initiatives (see, e.g. Scottish Executive 2002, DETR 2000). Local partnerships have underpinned these developments and individual city governments have also actively pursued their own forms of urban policy, but they have generally done so within the frameworks given by national policy, for example, competing for government grants as much as following an independent or autonomous line (see, e.g. Jones and Ward 1998; Cochrane et al. 2002).

Urban policy emerged in the context of the crisis of the nationally based welfare regimes of the Fordist era. From the start, however, as we have seen, there was extensive borrowing between national systems (particularly between the United Kingdom and the United States) even where the nature of the urban problems being tackled was rather different.

Indeed the emphasis on the "inner city" translated uneasily into some contexts with differences even within the United Kingdom. The notion of the "inner city" fundamentally builds on a US-based image of urban development (rooted in the ecological models of the Chicago School). The "inner city" is what is left over after the extensive suburbanization, which has characterized the United States and some urban areas in England (particularly in the South East). So, for example, in England from the 1960s to the 1990s the policy emphasis was overwhelmingly on the "inner cities" (see, e.g. Lawless 1981, 1988, 1996; Robson 1988; Lewis 1992; Mossberger and Stoker 1997).

However, the notion has much less of a resonance in Scotish (as well as other European cities) where suburbanization (although significant) has been much less extensive and the break between "inner" and "outer" city is less clear-cut. In the case of Scotland large scale slum clearance in the 1950s and 1960s had effectively removed many of the classic inner city slums left over from the nineteenth century (largely relocating them to the periphery where they soon recovered their roles as symbols of social disorganization) (see, e.g. Checkland 1976, Ch. V, Scottish Office 1988, p. 6) while its built form, particularly as reflected in the proportion of people living in flats or apartments, is closer to that of European than English cities (Scottish Executive 2002, p. 88). Although it is possible to argue that the "inner city" was a *"problem locale"* in Scotland in the 1960s and 1970s, particularly in Glasgow's East End (Middleton 1987), the imagery of a specifically *"inner city problem"* was largely borrowed from the US and English contexts.

Similar points could be made about the urban structure of many major European cities, where housing for the migrants and the poor has often been located on the outskirts of the cities, and the notion of "suburb" can take on a different meaning. While the French urban riots of 2005 were clearly spatialized (and racialized), the spatialization was the reverse of what might have been expected from the traditional rhetoric of inner city crisis (Dikec 2006) (see also Wacquant 1993b, who powerfully brings the US inner city crisis and that of the French periphery together). In Australia, too, it has been strongly argued that a policy focus on urban consolidation on revitalizing the "inner cities" fits uneasily with an urban model in which it is the suburbs which face "urban" problems (see, e.g. Johnson 2003). The issue of "race" also fits uneasily in or needs to be interpreted differently in different contexts. In Australia, for example, while Sydney's suburban race riots in 2005 suggest that this issue may need to be revisited, it has been strongly argued that an assimilationist model remains persuasive even for recent migrants and that the segregation of neighborhoods along racial lines which has been identified in British and US cities is not reflected in the Australian urban experience in the same ways (see, e.g. Forrest and Poulsen 2003; Poulsen et al. 2004). While the Aborigines and Torres Strait Islanders have continued to face significant problems and these have sometimes found an urban expression they have not generally been defined in urban policy terms (see, e.g. Wiseman 1998, pp. 150–51).

In neither in the United States nor in the United Kingdom can urban policy be reduced to any simple representation, summarized in a set of documents or the responsibilities of a particular government department. On the contrary, urban policy is a dynamic process being produced at different levels of the state and involving a range of nonstate actors, from the voluntary – non-statutory or third – sector as well as the private sector. The focus of urban policy is continually changing in ways that reflect the dominant ideologies and discourses of public policy, but the development of urban policy itself plays its own part in shaping those understandings and the initiatives that flow from them. It is this process that is explored more fully in the chapters that follow.

Chapter 3

Managerialism and the City

Sometimes discussions of managerialism in the public sector imply that it is a phenomenon of the 1980s and 1990s associated with the rise of the global new right (in the form of the "new public management"), before in turn being incorporated, in slightly different form, into the third way politics of Clinton and Blair (see, e.g. Hood 1991, 1996; Osborne and Gaebler 1992; Dunleavy and Hood 1994; Newman 2001). But – even if they have more recently crystalized around a particular political project – many of the issues that have come to be associated with the new public sector managerialism in its various forms were prefigured in the experience of urban policy. Indeed the development of urban policy itself could be seen as offering different ways of managing (and substituting for) welfare provision.

Even in the 1960s, the new approaches directly challenged or sought to challenge what were seen to be the underlying assumptions of public service, and, in particular the existence of departmentalized structures supported by specific professional expertise. Since poverty was understood to be multi-causal and systemic, only a coordinated attack could work effectively. However, centralization was also seen to be a problem in its own right, likely to lead to inflexibility and conflicts between central departments, rather than responsiveness to the needs of the communities and individuals they were supposed to serve. So, what was needed alongside a holistic and comprehensive understanding of the problem, was the breaking up of the bureaucracies through more area-based, targeted and participative projects. It was said to be necessary to move beyond the boundaries created by professional disciplines, bureaucratic structures and government divisions (see, e.g. Marris and Rein 1972, p. 113).

A focus on urban problems appears to offer the possibility of working across the traditional divisions associated with the professions and organizational structures of the welfare state – in health, social services, social security, employment services, education, housing, planning, and even economic development. The way in which this was attempted in the United States in the late 1960s was discussed in the previous chapter, and in Britain, the government has noted the way in which urban regeneration initiatives have sought to work "across traditional programme and subject boundaries to achieve an holistic impact – the horizontal approach – in contrast to main programmes, which have tended to operate vertically" (DETR 1998, para 4.6).

The relationship between the new managerialism and urban policy has been focused around some key points of intersection: an emphasis on coordination and holistic or joined up thinking; the rise of "partnership" working; the making of new urban managers and new urban professionals; and a concern for evidence-based policy and the mobilization of new technologies of management.

The Search for Coordination

The familiar refrain, criticizing the "old" professional and departmental structures of the welfare state as incapable of tackling urban problems, has reemerged on a regular basis and found echoes in a range of policy contexts. Even in Australia, where the definition of "urban crisis" focused on the suburbs rather than the inner city, the early 1970s saw the creation of a new Department of Urban and Regional Development which was committed to taking "a rational 'management' approach to urban policy and practice," with a strong emphasis on coordination between departments and levels of government, because it was "believed that the traditional fragmented institutional practices had contributed to the unequal spatial distribution of resources and infrastructure throughout the built environment" (Oakley 2004, pp. 303–4). Troy, who was Deputy Secretary of the Department until its demise in the mid 1970s, describes its staff as being "totally committed to changing bureaucracy" (quoted in Oakley 2004, p. 301) and argues that "we were trying to find devices to decentralise the administration not only decentralise it but open it up . . . we were out to try to change the administrative culture in the nation" (quoted in Oakley 2004, p. 302). The challenge went beyond any narrow definition of urban policy, because as Troy notes, "DURD was always about distribution and access to services right from the beginning" (quoted in Oakley 2004, p. 305). In other words it aimed to transform the delivery of welfare in Australia.

The search for coordination in a more complex world has been central to policy development in the United Kingdom, too. From the inception of the Urban Programme in the late 1960s to the introduction of the Single Regeneration Budget and the launch of New Deal for the Communities in the 1990s on to the Urban Renaissance and then the Sustainable Communities plan of the early 2000s, one aspect of the rhetoric of urban policy has consistently been couched in these terms – often combining the identification of areas for targeted attention with the promise of coordination.

Through the 1970s, the Community Development Projects were succeeded by the Comprehensive Community Programmes and those in turn were overtaken by the Inner City Partnerships spawned by the Inner Urban Areas Act. Each promised area-based coordination, albeit of a different sort and often at a rather different spatial scale. An area focus was in itself assumed to foster coordination by cutting across functional professional boundaries through the working of multifunctional teams within the specified area. One of the justifications (alongside arguments emphasizing the importance of private sector led property development, discussed in Chapter 6) for setting up the Urban Development Corporations in the 1990s (particularly in London's Docklands) was that because the existing local authorities had proved unable to develop a coherent and comprehensive set of policies a dedicated single purpose authority was required if any progress was to be made (see, e.g. Imrie and Thomas

1999). In this vein Robson et al. (1994, p. 52) approvingly report the comment that "Urban problems are multi-faceted: departments are not." Following a comprehensive scrutiny of the published aims of urban policies, they conclude that "well over 100 programme objectives" could be identified with little or no overall attempt to link them together (Robson et al. 1994, p. 5; see also Audit Commission 1991). They stress that more "interagency collaboration" is needed, pointing to what they see as the success of schemes "operating within defined areas," where "there has been scope to develop more integrated programmes involving training, job creation, environmental and infrastructural improvements" (Robson et al. 1994, p. 52).

This area-based emphasis (sometimes uneasily) exists alongside wider beliefs in the value of coordination, which generally find their expression in national (and now supposedly regional) mechanisms of coordination. The Urban Programme itself was conceived as an interdepartmental initiative, with the Home Office acting to coordinate the program as a whole, working with other departments, even if in practice this meant that the individual departments retained their dominance in the areas for which they had prime responsibility, with the Home Office doing little more than providing a gloss of coordination (Edwards and Batley 1978, pp. 73–5). Even in the Thatcherite 1980s, the Action for Cities program was launched with the (unrealized) promise of ensuring that the range of initiatives launched from central government were made complementary, instead of existing alongside each other, sometimes duplicating and sometimes even conflicting with each other.

One of the most comprehensive statements of the ambition to coordinate and integrate policy is probably to be found in the Social Exclusion Unit's report on neighborhood renewal which stresses that it is "a joined up problem that has never been addressed in a joined up way" (Social Exclusion Unit 1998, Summary. See also Parkinson et al. 2005, para 6.8). So the challenge taken on by the Social Exclusion Unit (set up in 1997) was to find ways of bringing the relevant parts together. The report identifies three main strands through which it was hoped change could be achieved – the various New Deals (Ch. 3), a range of area-based initiatives (including the Single Regeneration Budget, SureStart, the Employment, Education Action and Health Action Zones, New Deal for Communities) (Ch. 4), and the refocusing of mainstream programs with the help of eighteen cross-cutting Policy Action Teams drawn from ten Whitehall Departments (Ch. 5). The action teams were organized under five main headings: getting the people to work; getting the place to work; building a future for young people; access to services (work with private sector); making government work better. So, for example, the cross-departmental team concerned with skills (and training) was led from within the Department for Education and Employment, that concerned with business from within the Treasury, neighborhood management and learning lessons (to make government work better) were led from within the Social Exclusion Unit itself, while the team concerned with community self-help was led from within the Home Office.

A series of reports was prepared by the action teams, which were intended to show how mainstream services might be redirected as part of the process of neighborhood renewal. In this context, a government website on "Information on Programmes Relevant to Urban Policy" (admittedly rather loosely defined) prepared by the Urban Policy Unit within the Office of the Deputy Prime Minister listed 87 separate programs, ranging from "VAT Relief for Listed Buildings that are Places of Worship" and "Sport Action Zones" to the "New Deal for Communities," but now the intention was to show how they reinforced each other, even if only through the process of listing (ODPM 2001. See also Imrie and Raco 2003a, pp. 14–16).

The logic of this broad approach is incontrovertible, and echoes the arguments of Blackman (1995) in his attempt to define urban policy as a sum of those policies that affect people living in cities. Many of the policies clearly have affinities with urban policy. So, for example, SureStart was initially launched as a major program which focused on the provision of nursery and related support for children in their early years in areas that were deemed to be deprived. In other words, it seemed to be targeted on issues of urban deprivation, as expressed through educational underachievement. And it is analytically helpful to bring programs such as this together so that (in principle at least) it becomes possible to make some overall assessment of the extent to which they collectively impact on the lives of those in urban areas.

Unfortunately, however, the major difficulties associated with adopting such an ambitious and all-encompassing approach cannot simply be wished away. It is difficult not to be sceptical about the attempts to bring urban policy together at national level, since each of the initiatives listed is also driven by the priorities of its home department and there is no overarching authority focused on urban policy that is capable of bringing them together. If SureStart began as a targeted ("urban") initiative it was later transformed into a more or less universal policy for "early years" provision, which makes it more extensive even as each individual project is less heavily resourced. Health, education, and employment all have their own specified targets (whether in terms of waiting time, qualifications, or skills targets) and new initiatives (such as foundation hospitals, city academies, or Job Centre Plus) which may turn out to have significant urban impacts, but do not emerge from any explicit urban policy. Even strategies such as Excellence in Cities (which is explicitly targeted at raising standards in schools in urban areas) are driven more by the wider achievement targets identified for young people than any specific ambition for urban regeneration or renewal.

Lawless (2004) notes the dramatic expansion in the number of area-based initiatives since the 1980s, each with its own particular professional bias (from education to health; early years to employment; physical redevelopment to crime and social order), and according to one recent report, nearly two-thirds of the United Kingdom is covered by some form of neighborhood level organization (Prime Minister's Strategy Unit 2005, p. 65). Lawless suggests that this growth may be because "Complex difficulties and constraints within deprived areas are likely to require complex solutions" (Lawless 2004, p. 384). But another interpretation might suggest that the generation of still more semi-autonomous schemes, each ultimately responsible to a different branch of the state, is as likely to encourage incoherence as complex solutions.

Each new proposal offers the prospect of working together on particular schemes, even if it also implies the generation of a range of schemes that may not fit together very well. The Prime Minister's Strategy Unit sets out the broad issue particularly clearly by outlining a view of multiple deprivation (largely assumed to be in urban areas) as an interlocking process – a cycle of decline in which each part reinforces and feeds into the next. They stress both the need to understand the problem holistically and – in a fine example of what Harvey (2000) has identified as utopian thinking – seek to identify key moments in which to intervene in the system in order to shift it from a self-sustaining cycle of decline to a self-sustaining cycle of success (Prime Minister's Strategy Unit 2005). More modestly, this understanding has been translated into statements which emphasize the importance of "joined-up" action at the "community" level along lines like those set out in a report prepared for the Scottish Executive, which argues that "Integrating delivery is achieved in homes, streets, neighbourhoods and cities" (Scottish

Executive 2002, p. 17). Like many other reports, this one also repeats the mantra that, "In a joined-up world, linked places need not just holistic policies, but also integrated planning" (Scottish Executive 2002, p. 125).

One consequence of the search for integration on an area basis – and indeed on a policy initiative by policy initiative basis – is that urban policy in practice is characterized by extensive fragmentation. While policies for urban regeneration promise the possibility of working across the departmental and professional divisions of the welfare state, the practice of urban regeneration has generated its own fragmentation, since each area-based project exists alongside other projects, some of which may even overlap at local level, Although a particular area may be defined and clearly bounded for the purposes of one program, there is no guarantee that other programs will not define the borders rather differently. In early 2000 it was possible to identify 11 government area-based initiatives and a further 31 regeneration related initiatives in England and Wales, as well as four other programs associated with Lottery funding (DETR 2000).

At best units like the Social Exclusion Unit or the Neighbourhood Renewal Unit are left trying to construct an overarching policy (or an overarching commentary) out of those that already exist. This is reflected, for example, in the production of a report published in 2001 which purports to be an "audit" of the work undertaken in response to the reports of the policy action teams, and to "join up" their findings, but which in practice simply lists the initiatives in separate departmentally led chapters, within which each responsible minister claims that the policies being implemented are contributing to the delivery of neighborhood renewal (Social Exclusion Unit 2001b). A more "joined up" and glossier review of progress was produced by the Neighbourhood Renewal Unit in 2005 but it, too, brought together a series of relatively discrete initiatives to confirm (perhaps in preparation for the general election taking place later in the year) that some progress had been made, while acknowledging that more was needed (Neighbourhood Renewal Unit 2005). Another government report produced at the same time (and also with a foreword by the Prime Minister) went further in not only explicitly identifying the number of area-based initiatives (in this case put at 71) as excessive, but also emphasizing the continued incoherence and duplication involved in supporting a whole series of different monitoring arrangements and lines of accountability (Prime Minister's Strategy Unit 2005, p. 65). While the lead department (in the case of urban policy generally, but not always, the Office of the Deputy Prime Minister, now Department for Communities and Local Government) may have a clear commitment to a "joined up urban" policy it is less clear that other departments share that commitment (Parkinson et al. 2005, p. 53; Prime Minister's Strategy Unit 2005). A report prepared for the "Delivering Sustainable Communities Summit" in 2005 notes, with respect to area-based initiatives, that there are "consistent concerns about their conflicting or overlapping priorities, boundaries, resources, flows and targets" (Parkinson et al. 2005, p. 53).

The comments of Edwards and Batley (1978), following a consideration of the initiatives of the 1960s and 1970s, remain apposite 30 years later. They warn that an emphasis on comprehensive approaches and coordination may simply serve to mask the lack of an effective policy (Edwards and Batley 1978, p. 245). And it is also worth bearing in mind Fairclough's warning that the language of joined up government may be mobilized to mask the difficulties of developing a coherent (or "holistic") program capable of dealing with the challenges of managing a complex society made up of people with a wide and changing range of ambitions and interests (Fairclough 2000).

The challenge for the policy makers and the professionals supporting them is that "the networks of control that snake their way through cities are necessarily oligoptic, not panoptic: they do not fit together" (Amin and Thrift 2002, p. 128). It is this, which makes the effective management of communities so important within the new urban policy, as well as undermining the more ambitious claims of "joined up" government. Because urban change is not predictable, Amin and Thrift argue that the state requires an approach to governance that is capable of drawing on the skills and understanding of those being managed. As Amin and Thrift put it: "nearly all systems of governance in effect acknowledge that they are dealing in part with the unknown and ungovernable; they do not just tell their inhabitants what to do, they learn from them" (Amin and Thrift 2002, p. 129). The tensions and ambiguities within the governance of urban policy suggest that this summary of governance practice may be overoptimistic, as "holistic" and "joined up" approaches are translated into centralized targets, even as responsibility is delegated downwards.

Making Up Partnerships

One of the key roles for the new managers is to find ways of working through and mobilizing partnerships of one sort or another. Partnerships are seen as "a search for efficiency within an organisationally fragmented and fiscally constrained government landscape" (Lowndes 2001, p. 1962) but they are also seen to offer new opportunities to bring in additional human as well as financial resources and to build the capacity of the partners. The notion of partnership is – of course – itself an elusive one, but it implies that no single agency is capable of tackling urban problems effectively. Partnership has been presented as a panacea – whether it is between statutory agencies of one sort or another, between statutory and voluntary agencies, between community and state, or between public and private sectors. So, for example, in the words of a Discussion Paper on regeneration programs prepared by the Department of the Environment, Transport and the Regions: "The advantage of partnerships is that if properly constituted and run they are more suited to implementing the bottom-up approach to regeneration than a single central or local government organisation. They can help to promote ownership of regeneration activity within local communities" (DETR 1997, para 5.2.1). The official consensus increasingly sees "cross-sector, inclusive partnership working as itself inherently preferable to the narrower, outmoded styles characteristically pursued by local government" (Deas 2005, p. 205).

This process can be traced back through British urban policy (the Inner City Partnerships arising from the Inner Urban Areas Act 1978 promised much the same) but was rediscovered in the launch of City Challenge in the early 1990s, when partnerships between the public and private sector were invited to bid for regeneration funds through a competitive process. The Single Regeneration Budget which followed (and was launched in 1994) similarly relied on evidence of partnership (as well as community involvement) as the basis on which funding would be released for particular projects. Despite complaints about the bidding process, the existence of funding was seen by those involved as "an important stimulus" and "glue" in underpinning the development of partnerships (Davies 2004, p. 578). The process was taken further in the New Deal for Communities, launched in England in 1998 with a specific focus on the building of "community partnerships" with responsibility for the regeneration of local neighborhoods (of between 1,000 to 4,000 households) in a limited range of areas.

Despite the ubiquity of "partnership" as an urban policy nostrum, as Ball and Maginn (2005) point out, it is not always easy to see what the positive outcomes of partnership have been in practice. They identify several major inner city property development projects where the "partnership" approach helped generate failure, precisely because of the extensive negotiation that was involved. In itself the formation of a partnership cannot eliminate fundamental causes of conflict, particularly in the overheated policy environment of the inner city where development gain, community benefit and even government priorities sit uneasily together.

In the New Deal for Communities areas, the expectation was that by working together with other agencies (in this case particularly other public sector agencies) it should be possible to mobilize significantly more resources – using the average £50m (over 10 years) project budget to lever an equivalent sum from other providers (in health, police, education etc.). In other words, the aim was to use the dedicated funding to find ways of mainstreaming the priorities of the New Deal (see Social Exclusion Unit (1998, Ch. 5) for a more developed argument about the need for mainstreaming). In practice, however, the available evidence suggests that mainstream agencies (themselves "partners" in the process) have reacted rather differently and have cut back their own spending on core activities in the New Deal areas, because those areas are perceived as already receiving additional funding, and thus it becomes possible to redirect mainstream funds to other areas in need (Lawless 2004).

The assumption seems to be that the emphasis on partnership reflects the emergence of a new world which is characterized by networked governance, rather than state hierarchy (see, e.g. Stoker 2004). However, partnership building is not so much the inevitable outcome of wider societal shifts in this direction, as the outcome of dynamic (and even top-down) processes of state restructuring. The search for forms of partnership has become the dominant "common sense" of urban policy in ways which make it a taken-for-granted element of urban governance (see, e.g. Mayer 1992; LGMB 1993). So, for example, Atkinson suggests that the process has been one in which those involved have been drawn into (and accepted as their own) a new policy discourse – the "linguistic market and products which dominate urban regeneration" (Atkinson 1999, p. 67). From this perspective, partnership working could be seen as becoming a "habit" – as Davies puts it, "The practice of partnership-working is becoming culturally ingrained among local political and officer elites and a few business leaders. This habit is reinforced by, and in turn reinforces, the ideological predisposition towards market-led regeneration" (Davies 2004, p. 578). In other words, it could be argued that the rise of partnerships in urban policy represents another form of self-discipline through which the different agencies in the process come to accept a particular (managerialist) approach to tackling problems (instead, for example, of identifying more fundamental problems associated with the ways in which cities – and the inequalities within them – have developed).

In Britain, the most developed institutional expression of partnership working has come through the launch of local strategic partnerships. Following the Local Government Act 2000, all local authorities in England and Wales now have a specific duty to prepare community strategies and there is a similar requirement for community planning in Scotland. These plans would normally be prepared through local strategic partnerships (community planning partnerships in Scotland), although there is only a requirement for the strategies to be prepared through local strategic partnerships in 88 areas specifically identified as eligible for funding from the government's Neighborhood Renewal Fund. Community strategies are intended to prepare long-term shared visions for their areas and to outline the ways in which agencies will work together to tackle problems and achieve the vision in partnership with local residents and communities. According to the Government Guidance Summary, "These partnerships will bring the key organisations together to identify communities' top priorities and needs and to work with local people to address them" (DETR 2001a, para 3). The membership of Local Strategic Partnership Boards is supposed to reflect the local community, with involvement of key stakeholders from business, community, education, health, and the voluntary sector, as well as local government.

Local strategic partnerships are expected to have overall responsibility for neighborhood renewal activities in their area. However, Johnson and Osborne (2003) note the tension between the twin role of Local Strategic Partnerships as bodies aimed at ensuring the coordination of services between agencies and bodies delivering "co-governance" (that is in providing structures through which community participation can be achieved). They suggest that in practice an emphasis on coordination is likely to dominate, with central government more concerned about the meeting of targets specified in government sponsored local area agreements and the delivery of key outcomes. But there may be a danger of exaggerating the extent to which local strategic partnerships can be significant political drivers. Following a review of the findings of a major ESRC research program, for example, Deas (2005) suggests that they are expressions of "retrospective strategy building," rather than having a more dynamic role. In other words they are more significant within the process of political legitimation, than one seeking to achieve effective coordination of policy making (Deas 2005, p. 208).

At neighborhood level, the New Deal for Communities boards have been expected to plan over a 10 year period, with the aim of identifying broader "pathways of change." In practice, however, this has proved rather more difficult to achieve – it has been difficult to incorporate community representatives into the ethos of corporate planning so familiar to the professionals of local and central government (and even to private sector managers). Community representatives, have instead tended to focus on immediately achievable outcomes (e.g. relating to street cleaning and environmental improvement rather than health or education) (see Lawless 2004, p. 392, who notes the extent to which decision making was "ad-hoc reactive" rather than based on rational planning). According to Davies, "Resident activists frequently perceive that statutory agencies are hijacking the programme, while regeneration professionals feel that residents find strategic thinking difficult" (Davies 2004, p. 580).

So, as the New Deal projects have developed, the managerializing process has taken on a different shape. There has been a shift away from a model based loosely on "decentralisation, local negotiation, and introversion" to one more clearly rooted in "centrally imposed, locally effected, performance management," and an "increased emphasis has been placed on a performance management system stressing themes such as leadership, robustness of partnership, interagency working, and, crucially, results" (Lawless 2004, p. 396). The problem of seeking to combine an approach that seeks to encourage innovation and creativity through the mobilization of community resources with one which is obsessed with the achievement of a series of closely specified targets has been widely noted (see, e.g. Turner and Martin 2004). Yet this is precisely the approach that has been adopted in a range of policy areas as New Labour has apparently both passed responsibility downwards (often bypassing existing hierarchies of authority) and at the same time sought to impose new controls and measures against which the newly "empowered" may be evaluated. It is a recurrent problem associated with attempts to build community participation since those being managed and invited to participate may respond in ways that are unacceptable to those issuing the invitations. In the case of Ferguslie Park (an area in Paisley) at the end of the 1980s and in the early 1990s, for example, the newly created Scottish Office sponsored Partnership not only set up its own organizational structures rather than building on existing community organizations, but, in the face of disruption from community activists, set up alternative forms of community participation which bypassed or incorporated them (Kintrea 1996; Collins 1997).

Managerializing the Urban Professionals

The principles of the new urban policy imply the need to build a different understanding of the role of the public sector professional – the postbureaucratic official. The rise of an urban policy which combines a community (or neighborhood) emphasis at one end (discussed in Chapter 4) alongside a more explicit emphasis on urban competitiveness or salesmanship (discussed in Chapter 6) has at the same time reinforced the need for a professionalism of a new (or at any rate different) type – more "entrepreneurial," more skilled in the management of complex governance and partnership arrangements, able to work with the private and voluntary sectors. Even the more recent attempts to build the creative city (or to enable its construction) have led to the call for a new breed of professionals more in tune with the ethos of the new creative class said to be defining the successful cities of the twenty-first century (see, e.g. Landry and Bianchini 1995; Florida 2002).

The emphasis on these new urban managers has to be understood in the broader context of managerialization in the public sector, which stretches back to the early 1970s. Benington's analysis of the process (summed up in the title of his pamphlet as "Local Government becomes Big Business"), and its relationship to urban policy, predates the arrival of the Blair government by two decades. And in the United States, too, as early as 1970 Moynihan was suggesting a new model in which: "a primary mark of competence in a federal official," he said, "should be the ability to see the interconnectedness between programs immediately at hand, and the urban problems that pervade the larger society" (Moynihan 1970, p. 9). In both countries, the old public administration or civil service models were being challenged through the 1970s and 1980s with a growing emphasis on "the public sector's emulation of the private sector as a model of efficient performance" (Barnekov et al. 1989, p. 4), and as Hood notes, a similar model was being adopted across the countries of the OECD, with a lead being taken in New Zealand and Australia (Hood 1991, 1995).

But the promise of managerialism increasingly goes beyond narrow issues of financial efficiency, particularly as it has been combined with the notion of leadership (see, e.g. Stoker 2004, Ch. 7). Clarke and Newman (1997) and Newman (2001) have explored some of the ways in which since the mid 1990s a new managerialism has challenged the bureau-professionalism that characterized the welfare professions of the postwar period. They chart the complex process by which a "managerial state" was constructed across the public sector in the 1980s and 1990s, both building on the neo-liberal agenda of privatization and markets, and on the need to manage more complex mixed economies of care. Clarke and Newman (1997) remind us of the importance of managerialism as an ideology with which many professional and organizational actors are actively engaged, to the extent that its features have been increasingly internalized in the organizational structures of government. Pollitt (1993), too, highlights the power of managerialism as an ideology because of the way in which it emphasizes the importance of managers in all organizations, whether in the public or private sectors. It links the public and private sectors in ways that help to give public sector managers external and personal legitimacy in the current (neo-liberal) climate.

In the US context, Osborne and Gaebler (1992) construct a vision for the new public sector and its management (endorsed by the Clinton administration), based around a simple mantra – steering, not rowing – which questions what they see as the traditional models of public administration and became a global bestseller among public administration managers. They argue not only that bureaucratic arrangements and professionals are standing in the way of change, but also that ways need to be found to mobilize (or empower) social or community entrepreneurs to act. They maintain that forms of "community-owned government" (which they favor) represent a move away from the notion of "serving" people (the old model) towards one in which the emphasis is on "empowering" them (Osborne and Gaebler 1992, pp. 49–75). "Professionals and bureaucracies deliver services" they say, while, "communities solve problems . . . Communities focus on capacities; service systems focus on deficiencies" (Osborne and Gaebler 1992, pp. 66 and 70) (the discussion of community and its significance for urban policy is taken further in the next chapter).

A similar critique is presented by Euchner and McGovern who emphasize "the tendency of bureaucrats to protect and expand their turf" (Euchner and McGovern 2003, p. 29) which makes them reluctant to innovate because of the need to protect (and grow) existing programs along traditional lines, and point to the importance of "street level bureaucrats" (Lipsky 1979) who work more closely with service users and local communities, and (where effective) tend to work outside the bureaucratic rules and hierarchies they are supposed to uphold. There is, say Euchner and McGovern (2003, p. 30), little communication between these "street level bureaucrats" and their superiors which means that the system is unable to learn about how it might work better. It is in this context that looser forms of governance ("steering not rowing" in the language of Osborne and Gaebler) are seen to provide a potential way forward.

Following the model of management text books and consistently with the shift away from presenting any unified set of government programs, Osborne and Gaebler (1992) present a series of case studies of community success and seek to identify community leaders in the same way as writers of popular management texts often focus on business leaders. Their stress is on finding a ways of working through a decentered and fragmented policy field – held together by the exchange of best practice between social (and public) entrepreneurs, rather than any regulatory framework or overarching national policy.

In the case of the United Kingdom, a rather different, but no less managerialist, approach has been adopted, which seeks somehow to combine the development of a national (centralist) urban policy with space for local initiative – and in particular the possibility of generating innovation, dynamism and commitment from within the communities where change is needed. The growth in the number of large professionalized "voluntary" organizations involved in the provision of (social) services of one sort or another has been accompanied by increasing claims by them to be able to deliver those services more effectively than the state (see, e.g. Aldridge 2005). Alongside a stress on the importance of "joined up" thinking – the need to move beyond traditional professional and departmental boundaries – is the attempt to find some means of doing so both "locally" and nationally. In other words, the task of the new professionals becomes that of finding ways of "joining up" policy locally, while also "joining" local initiatives "up" with the aims of national government. And the search for social or public sector entrepreneurialism is central to this. So, for example, in the context of the Sustainable Communities plan (ODPM 2003a), whose purpose is to generate urban development on the edge of the South-East of England, the nationally appointed local delivery vehicles are akin to, if not quite as powerful as, the urban development corporations or their new town predecessors (see, e.g. Schaffer 1970; Imrie and Thomas 1999; Raco 2005a), and are expected to work as public entrepreneurs, manipulating property markets to deliver economic growth and social infrastructure.

There is an increasing emphasis on the importance of training (and retraining) for those involved in the development and implementation of renewal strategies, since it is agreed that existing professional skills fit uneasily with new market aware, partnership-based, and interagency ways of working. Diamond (2001) notes that the role of locally-based regeneration managers is essentially that of a broker, whose task is to "sell" the priorities of the program to communities – and where necessary to negotiate around those priorities. The scope for negotiation may be limited, but this is nevertheless a very different role from the one to which most government officials are accustomed, and the rise of text books and teaching programs for the training of regeneration professionals is only one indication of the extent to which the process is being taken further (see, e.g. Diamond and Liddle 2005).

As well as pointing to the need for mainstream staff in public sector and welfare agencies to learn to work with others and interact with communities, there have been explicit calls for training directed at those involved on the informal side and in voluntary sector organizations. This is recognized in the United States, too, where the absence of more professionally trained management in community development corporations (CDCs) is seen as a weakness. As Steinbach notes, "Entrepreneurial leaders, not managers dominate the ranks of CDC directors . . . Investments by CDC supporters in broad management capacity building . . . could significantly leverage the field's performance" (Steinbach 2000, p. 5). In the United Kingdom, Lawless also identifies the problems of recruiting and retaining suitable staff within community-based organizations (Lawless 2004, p. 393), while Rallings et al. (2004) point to the need to provide support to those elected to New Deal partnership boards. In England and Wales, a "community empowerment fund" whose purpose is to help community representatives to prepare for (and gain a better understanding of) their representative roles, has been set up under the aegis of the Department for Communities and Local Government.

Unsurprisingly perhaps the professional claims of community workers have also been raised in this context. By this time of course, their radical roots in the United States of the 1950s and 1960s (summarized in Alinsky 1971, 1989, but also reflected, for example, in Cowley 1977) with their stress on mobilizing the previously unorganized and marginalized to challenge those in power and build community power as an alternative seem to have been long forgotten. It is hard to believe that any of the new breed of community development workers would follow Alinsky's thirteenth rule, which was to "Pick the target, freeze it, personalize it, and polarize it" (Alinsky 1971, p. 130).

By contrast, Chanan (of the Community Development Foundation) makes claims for community work as "a continuous movement with a coherent philosophy and established working methods" (Chanan 2003, p. 68) which supports communities in working together and in work-ing with other agencies. In this context, Gilchrist (2000) explicitly identifies what she describes as a "meta-networking" as a fundamental professional skill within community development: "The purpose of community development," she says, "is to support and shape social net-working in order to facilitate the emergence of flexible, effective and empowering forms of collective action" (Gilchrist 2000, p. 273. See also Gilchrist 2003). Chanan is concerned about the continued insecure status of the profession: "Skilled non-directive support to multi-level community organising and involvement is the unique stock-in-trade of this discipline. But its deployment is very unstable, and as a profession it is poorly and haphazardly resourced" (Chanan 2003, p. 7. See also Sn. 4.9).

Evidence-Based Policy and the New Technologies of Management

Urban social policy relies on the clear understanding that it is possible to manage more effec-tively through area-based initiatives and the assumption that it is possible to map deprivation, and specifically "multiple deprivation." In other words it is assumed that more or less objec-tive – and certainly "technical" – criteria can be identified on the basis of which the targeting of additional resources or particular forms of intervention on one area (neighborhood) or another can take place. The concept of multiple deprivation implies that if a person is disad-vantaged in one way or another, then he or she is also likely to be disadvantaged in several other ways. If a family lives in slum housing, it is also likely to have a low household income, the children are likely to have low levels of educational qualification and family members are also more likely to suffer ill health. "Area effects" (i.e. the impact of living in areas whose population was poor and within which access to services was also restricted) simply help to reinforce the disadvantage of individuals living within what were labeled multiply deprived areas.

Harrington graphically summarizes this notion in confirming that in such areas, "Each disability is the more intense because it exists within a web of disabilities" (Harrington 1962, pp. 158–9), and in the United Kingdom a similar point was made by Coates and Silburn: "All these different types of deprivation mesh one into another, to create for those who must endure them a total social situation shot through and through by one level of want after another" (Coates and Silburn 1970, p. 38). This has been summarized in the view that not only are "People living in deprived areas more likely to be worse off than similar people living in more prosperous areas. They are less likely to work, more likely to be poor and have lower life expectancy, to live in poor housing in unattractive local environments, with high levels of anti-social behaviour and lawlessness and to receive poorer education and health services" (Prime Minister's Strategy Unit 2005, p. 27), but also "People living in deprived areas have a lower quality of life than otherwise similar people in less deprived areas" (Prime Minister's Strategy Unit 2005, p. 41). More recent academic discussions have been reluctant to make such big claims for the impact of these "neighborhood" or "area" affects, but they continue to underpin the development of area-based urban policy initiatives and to be seen as significant in the development of urban policy (see, e.g. Glennerster et al. 1999; Buck 2005; Meegan and Mitchell 2001; Deas et al. 2003; Noble et al. 2004, p. 12).

If, as Rose (1999, p. 175) suggests, one of the key features of the process of making up "community" as a subject for intervention is to map and classify it, then the arena of urban policy is one of the key areas within which this takes place. The rise of the language of "community," says Rose, helps to specify "the subjects of government as individuals who are also actually or potentially, the subjects of allegiance to a particular set of community values, beliefs and commitments," which will provide the expected self-disciplinary mechanisms (Rose 1996, p. 331). But the official rediscovery of community (discussed more fully in the next chapter) also offers another means by which the subjects of intervention may be redefined: "Communities become vectors to be investigated, mapped, classified, documented, interpreted, their vectors explained to enlightened professionals-to-be in countless college courses and to be taken into account in numberless encounters between professionals and their clients, whose individual conduct is now to be made intelligible in terms of the beliefs and values of 'their community'" (Rose 1996, p. 332). In other words, as well as offering the prospect of self-management (ideologically/discursively), the notion of community also offers new ways of management, through new managerial technologies and new professional styles. The mapping of poverty is just one part of this, so that as Baeten notes (reflecting on the case of Brussels), even the apparently "neutral" or "objective" process of constructing a poverty atlas has to be seen as part of managing the poor (Baeten 2001, p. 60).

In Britain, this was implicit from the start, even if the basis on which deprived areas might be identified was recognized to be inadequate (reflecting political priorities as much as "objective" data) (see Edwards and Batley 1978, pp. 50–3). Today, however, the mapping takes a technical form in the shape of an index of deprivation (or local deprivation) which is reviewed and reframed from time to time. This index makes it possible to rank areas (at ward level) by the extent of deprivation within them. It provides part of the basis on which state funding is distributed to local authorities through calculations that are intended to reflect the relative cost of service provision in different areas. It underpinned the identification of the 88 local authority districts eligible for funding under the Neighbourhood Renewal Fund. The Index of Deprivation 2004 (Noble et al. 2004) is a vital element in constructing the official map of deprivation in England, lending apparent objectivity to distributive decisions, freezing dynamic social relations within the administrative boundaries of the state and expressing them in technical terms (see also Noble et al. 2003 for the Scottish equivalent). It promises to make it possible "better to identify and target areas where small pockets of deprivation exist" (Noble et al. 2004, Preface). Nevertheless, while the attempt to find ways of mapping and defining communities may be real enough, the extent to which it can be achieved (and "calculability" finally delivered) is more questionable.

In part the debates around the construction of the indices are technical ones. So, for example, Deas et al. (2003) in discussing an earlier Index of Multiple Deprivation (produced in 2000) suggest that underlying the statistical certainties – the objective realities represented in the index – there are assumptions and calculations that work to understate the problems of big cities – so for example, no account is taken of the absolute size of deprivation, of neighborhood effects, of fear of crime, or of the physical environment, while too much emphasis is placed on accessibility, defined as distance, and on the numbers in receipt of benefits (so excluding those who do not take up benefits to which they may entitled, as well as those informal workers who may have no entitlements).

However, they also note that the construction of the Index in 2000 was not simply the result of some technocratic decision – a search for more accuracy – but reflected a decision that the previous Index of Local Conditions published in 1998 did not adequately capture "deprivation" outside the urban areas (e.g. in mining communities, declining holiday resorts, and rural areas), as well as "more nakedly political pressures for government to divert resources beyond the major cities, the most potent of them centring on the influential arguments proffered by a disparate coalition of rural interests" and a desire to reflect "what was seen as a more intricate geography of deprivation than had previously been assumed" (Deas et al. 2003, p. 891). In other words, even the most apparently technical of processes may reflect the outcomes of significant political decisions, only being given the apparent objectivity of indexation at a later stage.

Similarly the production of a revised index in 2004 reflected a policy shift that was expressed in the new emphasis on "neighbourhood renewal" (Social Exclusion Unit 2001a). So, although the authors of the Index quite rightly note that, "The identification of deprived areas may be necessary if area-based solutions to deprivation are to be pursued, but identifying deprived areas in no way assumes that such solutions are the right one," the production of the Index was itself predicated on just such a view (Noble et al. 2004, p. 13). The ability to identify and track what are called "super output areas" (i.e. information on deprivation for areas with resident populations of between one and three thousand) has been celebrated as offering ways of "making sure that local plans and activities are really focused on neighbourhoods and types of problems that need most attention" (Neighbourhood Renewal Unit 2005, p. 44. See also Prime Minister's Strategy Unit 2005, p. 125, where it is argued that this data will make it possible – and necessary – to more effectively target the use of the Neighbourhood Renewal Fund).

A second aspect of evidence-based policy making in urban policy is reflected in the continuing commitment to learning from the success of individual projects, aiming to replicate them or to translate them into locally relevant practice. Area-based projects, it is believed, provide an excellent base for identifying what works and then looking for ways of generalising it. This underpinned the approach developed in the United States in the 1960s discussed in Chapter 2, but was also taken up directly in the United Kingdom. So, for example, each of the Community Development Projects of the 1970s was made up of an "action" team and a "research" team attached to a university: the intention was for the research team to evaluate the work of the action team, highlighting its successes, as well as learning from its failures, feeding in and influencing (Loney 1983). Similarly the Inner Area Studies were just that, studies whose findings were to feed into more general policy development, and it could be argued that their findings fed directly into first the White Paper on the inner cities (HMSO 1977) and then the Inner Urban Areas Act 1978. The Urban Development Corporations have all been evaluated independently by major consultancy companies (see, e.g. Roger Tym and Partners 1998). Nevertheless, the lack of a sound evidence base about the effectiveness of urban area-based initiatives was identified by government once more in the early years of the twenty-first century (DETR 2001b) and the New Deal for Communities program has been accompanied by a major evaluation project (involving a large consortium of academic and consultancy organizations) which has the "twofold function of support and evaluation" (Lawless 2004, p. 385).

It is, of course, hard to argue against what appears to be the obvious common sense of statements like those of the Social Exclusion Unit which define the value of evidence-based policy making in straightforward terms as the "better use of available research to design policy, but also extending our knowledge through pilots and robust evaluation studies" (Social Exclusion Unit 2004, p. 31. See also, e.g. Solesbury 2002).

Even such apparently modest claims, however, may still need to be assessed carefully. In the early 1970s Marris and Rein (1972) were already highlighting some of the challenges faced by policy makers and professionals in trying to learn the lessons of research. They note that capturing what would have happened without intervention is often impossible, because social processes are fluid and some change would have taken place without the intervention. More important, perhaps, the intervention being evaluated is itself likely to change over time, as those engaged in "action" themselves modify what they are doing in response to feedback. Since they do not wait for the outcome of the evaluation before undertaking those modifications, and may even modify their objectives over time, there is never any completed process to analyze (Marris and Rein 1972, pp. 191–207). They argue that, "Research requires a clear and constant purpose, which both defines and precedes the choice of means; that the means be exactly and consistently followed; and that no revision takes place until the sequence of steps is completed. Action is tentative, noncommittal and adaptive. It concentrates upon the next step, breaking the sequence into discrete, manageable decisions . . . Research cannot interpret the present until it knows the answers to its ultimate questions. Action cannot foresee what questions to ask until it has interpreted the present" (Marris and Rein 1972, p. 205). In other words it is not possible to escape from the messiness of political decision making through the promise of greater technical proficiency and the accumulation of "evidence." Even if it is clearly preferable to have some evidence which can inform the process of adaptive action, the nature of that evidence will always itself be uncertain and subject to challenge and reinterpretation.

In their comprehensive review of the research literature on the effectiveness of community involvement in area-based initiatives, Burton et al. (2004) similarly identify a series of methodological problems, which make it difficult to make informed judgements on the role (and form) of community involvement. They, too, highlight the problem that it is difficult to assess what would have happened without intervention, particularly since the local contexts in which actions take place are likely to be significantly different. And they go on to point to the difficulty of determining which among a series of interventions has any particular effect – an issue of particular concern in a policy field that seems to attract new and overlapping initiatives from a wide range of sources and with an ever changing set of ambitions. There can be no guarantee that the combination of initiatives that works well in one area will be equally successful in another. Evaluative research focused on any particular area-based initiative also needs to take into account the way in which the areas have been defined since where the boundaries around them are placed also determines who is included or excluded (Burton et al. 2004, p. 7).

Nevertheless, the search for a more "rational" evidence-based way of making policy and delivering implementation continues to influence the making of urban policy (and Burton et al. make their own suggestions for improving the process). It has, for example, been suggested that it is possible to evaluate "comprehesive community initiatives" through what has been called the "theory of change" approach – that is one involving "a systematic and cumulative study of the links between activities, outcomes and contexts of the initiative" (Connell and Kubisch 1998, p. 15). This is a fundamentally holistic and qualitative approach, in which stress is placed on the need to understand the core principles underlying the initiatives concerned, the intended outcomes as well as the strategies being mobilized to achieve change. Emphasis is placed on working with those who planned the initiative as well as stakeholders in the implementation process to identify the different elements of the program and the ways in which they are expected to, and might best, work together to deliver the desired outcomes.

Despite the broader base underpinning such an approach, it is consistent with the rise of new professionals and the process of defining decision making as a technical process, rather than a political one or, indeed, one defined through the traditional expertise of professionals (whether in medicine, teaching, or the civil service). Evidence-based policy making provides the new professionals in government and in the practice of urban policy with an ideology around which it is possible to mobilize or a discourse which effectively undermines the securities of the bureaucracies of welfare with their reliance on the old certainties of professionalism. But, of course, that does not mean that it provides the answers which they so desperately seek (see, e.g. Young et al. 2002; Hammersley 2005).

The process of evidence-based policy making has, however, also been revisited to suggest ways in which it might be mobilized in a more creative way by activists and community workers. Davies et al. (2002), for example, question the extent to which it clear and generalizable policy answers to a series of research questions can be provided and then rolled out through centrally determined initiatives. Instead they emphasize the value of taking an incremental approach, learning from particular initiatives and building on them. Similarly, while pointing to the "near impossibility of producing the clear cut evidence that politicians require," Taylor builds on the arguments of Marris and Rein to argue that, "It is important to combine different forms of knowledge production and sharing that can complement each other and create dialogue rather than prescription" (Taylor 2003, p. 219). In other words, she emphasizes the importance of seeing the learning process as a political one based around a continued process of communication between those involved in community action (Taylor 2003, Chapter 7).

Some Tensions of the New Urban Managerialism

The new professionals are being tasked with developing or implementing policies that cannot easily be captured in the templates of rational decision making. The tensions that have to be managed, the changing problem definition, and the dynamic nature of the city make it impossible to achieve some of the ambitions that have been set for them. This point was made long ago by Marris and Rein (1972) who identify a fundamental tension, or dilemma (as they describe it), between a process that seeks to develop policy (rationally) on the basis of research or evidence and the requirement to integrate members of local communities into the decision making process. There is, they point out, little guarantee that those who participate will necessarily agree to the implementation of policies (however "rational") that undermine their existing position, however poor that currently is.

In this context, managerialism helps to move the focus away from "the causes of poverty and inequality" towards more technical issues, whether related to output targets or capacity building (Southern 2001, p. 267). In some respects this could be seen as consistent with

Rose's stress on the shift from the political to the technical in defining the nature of what he calls "advanced liberal governmentality" – in other words the politics of urban development is increasingly reduced to the ability of the new professionals (including the "community professionals") both to determine what the problems are and to identify how they might be resolved (Rose 1999). Rose may understate the provisional and contested nature of the shifts he identifies – the spaces for alternative responses – but the professionalization of urban policy has been fundamental to its development, not only in constructing a new set of professionals and a new set of expertise, but also in involving a much wider range of participants as potentially self-policing professionals (as has also been discussed in the previous chapter).

There is a continuing tension between attempts by the professionals to carry out policies drawing on evaluative evidence and strategic priorities, and the attempt to involve residents or community members whose priorities may be rather different. The process of managing urban policy through more decentralized and fragmented arrangements is a complex and uncertain one and the positioning of the new professionals is itself not unproblematic, not just a technical process. As Larner and Craig note in their review of community activism and local partnerships in New Zealand, "community organisations increasingly became a site for de-centralised professional and technical capacity" (Larner and Craig 2005, p. 409).

One possible consequence of this might be that local activists themselves become incorporated into wider state agendas through professionalization. The danger of this is powerfully summed up in strong language in the response of one woman to a newly professionalized community activist (about to move out of the local area): "You've fucked up the estate and now you're carrying a briefcase" (McCulloch 1997, p. 51). But the tensions underlying the process may be more significant. The dramatic spread of "professionalism" both into "community" and voluntary organizations and into those areas of the state that have the responsibility of managing them creates new sets of relationships and defines new sets of "obligations," which also generates the risk (from the perspective of state policy) of professionals "becoming over-identified with the client, at the expense of organisational loyalty" (Clarke 2002, p. 11).

In this context, Larner and Craig more positively explore the ways in which the rise of state sponsored local partnerships has generated the need for what they call "strategic brokers," that is people with "an ability to network and promote change" (Larner and Craig 2005, p. 404). They suggest that such people are frequently drawn from the ranks of community activists (and particular from women) providing "new roles for those who were oppositional voices" (Larner and Craig 2005, p. 418). It is they who have the key soft skills as "advocates for both their organisations and more relational forms of practice" with both "knowledge *of* communities" but also, as they develop their professionalism, "knowledge *about* communities" (Larner and Craig 2005, p. 415 and 418). While the relationship between the growing professional role and the community role is not an easy one (Larner and Craig describe it as "fraught") they reject the notion that this is simply a question of incorporation, because it also provides them with the scope to pursue their own visions of social justice in (local) practice.

Chapter 4

The Meaning(s) of Community

Traditionally, "community" has been associated with pre-industrial rural life, and has been sharply contrasted with the anomic, materialist life of the cities. This was famously summarized in Tönnies' distinction between *Gemeinschaft* (community) and *Gesellschaft* (society). According to Tönnies, the former "is the lasting and genuine form of living together, in contrast to *Gemeinschaft*, *Gesellschaft* is transitory and superficial. Accordingly, *Gemeinschaft* should be understood as a living organism, *Gesellschaft* as a mechanical aggregate and artefact" (Tönnies 1887/1963, p. 35). In some ways, therefore, it is deeply ironic that the notion has come to play such a big role in the language and practice of urban policy, particularly as the transfer has carried with it many of the same associations. Community is deemed to be "good," to have been stronger in the past, to provide a "moral" basis for behavior, and to provide ways in which individuals may come together in stable forms of mutual support, such as the family or the church. As Williams summarizes it: "Community can be the warmly persuasive word to describe an existing set of relationships, or the warmly persuasive word to describe an alternative set of relationships. What is most important perhaps is that unlike all other terms of social organization … it seems never to be used unfavorably, and never to be given any positive opposing or distinguishing term" (Williams 1983, p. 76).

In the context of urban policy, in practice the word "community" is generally used to mean one of two things – a territorially delimited neighborhood, within which there is deemed to be some sort of shared identity or set of interests, or some identifiable ethnic group which is also often understood to have its own "community" leaders. So, for example, a local community might also be seen as a site of shared social responsibility and a place within which a community of interest (particularly one associated with ethnicity) finds its expression. While in urban policy practice (as Chanan 2003 suggests) a community is generally simply understood to incorporate those who live in a particular locality (or "neighborhood") somehow the related positive connotations still often seem to be associated with the notion. Indeed, if community meant no more than the population of a particular area, it is unlikely that it would have quite the same (almost iconic status) in the language of urban policy. Above all, perhaps, we need to recognize the ways in which "community" or "communities of place" is produced as an "imaginary" or "imagined" thing – real enough, but not pre-given (Anderson 1983; Burns et al. 1994, p. 227).

In its contemporary interpretation it is widely acknowledged that the notion of community is not only elusive, but also ideologically slippery. In the past I have argued that it has often been used "as if it were an aerosol can, to be sprayed on to any social programme, giving it a more progressive and sympathetic cachet" (Cochrane 1986a, p. 51). Levitas is equally critical, suggesting that: "The role of community is to mop up the ill-effects of the market and to provide the conditions for its continued operation, while the costs of this are borne by individuals rather than the state" (Levitas 2000, p. 194). In practice, too, as Hoggett notes, "For policy makers and street-level bureaucrats within the state the idea of community has been used as a form of shorthand for the socially excluded" (Hoggett 1997a, p. 11). And in some respects, of course, "community" simply plays the role of being "not the state" or "not local government," reinforcing the rejection of traditional models of government, state provision, and bureaucracy discussed in the previous chapter (Everingham 2003, pp. 15–17; Foote 2001, p. 36).

The notion of "community" has a chequered history within urban policy. In this chapter three aspects will be considered in turn: the way in which it may be mobilized as part of a process of moralization or remoralization; the way in which it has been redefined as economic agent, particularly in generating or sustaining social capital; and its role as a base for alternative institutional arrangements in civil society, beyond the state. Finally the chapter will turn to a consideration of the ambiguities of community, exploring the ways in which it may be positively mobilized as well as play a self-disciplinary role.

Remoralizing Community

If one aspect of the emphasis on community in the United States of the 1960s was to find a means of integrating the urban black population into the political mainstream (see Chapter 2), another was to find ways of remaking them in the image of the respectable population of the melting pot – another source of powerful myths about community (see, e.g. Gans 1962, 1968). Moynihan (later Democratic Senator for New York but active participant in the development of urban policy in United States under three presidents – Kennedy, Johnson, and Nixon) argued that the urban problem was explicitly tied in with the rise of the number of black families without male heads, which in turn (he believed) led to disorganization and so to a rise in politicization and a growth in those seeking confrontation with white society. As a result, he argued, that "Urban policy must have as its first goal the transformation of the urban lower class into a stable community based on dependable and adequate income flows, social equality and social mobility" (Moynihan 1970, p. 10). The link between family and community was explicit – and the normative message was explicit, too. The rebuilding of traditional family forms and the remaking of traditional communities or the networks that defined them were seen as the means of solving social problems.

In the 1970s Moynihan summarized the views of a group of administrators, academics, and intellectuals brought together by him:

> Among a large and growing lower class, self-reliance, self-discipline, and industry are waning; a radical disproportion is arising between reality and expectations concerning job, living standard,

and so on; unemployment is high but a lively demand for unskilled labor remains unmet; illegitimacy is increasing; families are more and more matrifocal and atomized; crime and disorder are sharply on the rise. There is, in short, a progressive disorganization of society, a growing pattern of frustration and mistrust ... A large segment of the population is becoming incompetent and destructive. Growing parasitism, both legal and illegal, is the result; so, also is violence (Moynihan 1973, p. 76).

At this stage, the argument being presented was quite explicit. These were not communities in the proper sense, so what was needed was to rebuild communities, or perhaps to provide a basis on which a self-sustaining community capable of generating its own internal moral structures might be created. These were the messages that were transmitted to the United Kingdom as it attempted to translate US policy into a different context. In the late 1960s and early 1970s (e.g. in the planning for – if not the operation of – the Community Development Projects and the Urban Programme), there was a clear emphasis on the need to tackle the problems of "individual, family and community malfunctioning," alongside an almost religious fervor associated with the ambition to regenerate communities and encourage individual self-improvement (Higgins et al. 1983, pp. 7–19) This was later caricatured as the "social pathology" approach, that is one which put the blame for inner city problems on the behavior of those suffering from them (see, e.g. "Gilding the Ghetto," a report prepared by Britain's Community Development Project in 1977).

However ambivalent the notions underlying the programs of the 1960s and 1970s, the practice of community-oriented urban policy remained welfarist, in the sense that resource (however limited) was directed towards the poorer areas of cities in the expectation that it would help regenerate communities, while also often providing direct support to individuals. Although there was a systematic shift through the 1970s from these approaches towards a more explicitly economic and infrastructure-led focus, which emphasized the need to tackle the structural problems of the inner cities (discussed more fully in Chapter 6) (see, e.g. Lawless 1981; Higgins et al. 1983; Atkinson and Moon 1994) the notion of community never completely disappeared as a focus of policy attention and it was seriously revived in the 1990s (see, e.g. Atkinson and Cope 1997).

In Scotland – even at the height of Thatcherism in the 1980s – a continued commitment to community-based initiatives in some form was sustained, even in more narrowly defined economic regeneration schemes (see, e.g. Donnison and Middleton 1987). The Scottish difference was confirmed in *New Life for Urban Scotland*, which was published by the Scottish Office in 1988. It focused explicitly on the peripheral estates on schemes (rather than the inner cities) of Scotland's major cities as the location of urban problems and had a strong emphasis on community-based partnership and joint working between agencies as a means of tackling those problems (Scottish Office 1988). The emphasis on peripheral estates, made it possible to explore individual and community "solutions."

Without suggesting that the individuals living there were necessarily to "blame" for their own problems, it certainly was possible to argue that they could go a long way towards resolving them through their own initiative. The Scottish Office's interim report on the initiatives made the position clear: so, for example, it reported that a Trust Fund was to be set up, "to assist Castlemilk youngsters reach their full potential"; a "team is working with the people of Ferguslie Park to unlock their true potential"; in Wester Hailes a Neighborhood

Strategy has been developed "to encourage resident commitment to individual small areas of housing"; and the aim is "to create a new and better Whitfield, building above all, on the sure foundation of the people who live in Whitfield; they are its greatest asset" (Scottish Office 1990). All of this, of course, predated the election of a Labour government in 1997, but it also anticipated the approach that has come increasingly to be adopted towards welfare issues across the United Kingdom.

This approach to social policy is, to use the words of the Commission for Social Justice (1994, p. 224), about finding ways of giving people and communities a "hand-up rather than a hand-out," which might almost have been borrowed from the statement of the US Office of Economic Opportunity quoted in Chapter 2: "Give a poor man only a hand-out and he stays poor, but give the same man a skill and he rises from poverty" (quoted in Friedman 1977, p. 37). "Community" has increasingly been reintroduced as part of the process of redefining welfare in ways that highlight personal and collective (nonstate) responsibility and this is made explicit in the Commission's report, which suggests that "communities do not become strong because they are rich, rather they become rich because they are strong" (Commission on Social Justice 1994, p. 309). This approach confirms that welfare is no longer about compensating for structural inequalities, but about helping people to operate more effectively in the labor market or in developing their own forms of social or community enterprise (see, e.g. Thake and Staubach 1993).

The arguments developed by the Commission prefigure much of the New Labour program, although it was launched by John Smith, Tony Blair's predecessor as Labour leader and often seen as the last leader to embody traditional Labour Party values. The revival of "community" as a core aspect of contemporary politics in Britain, was, however, symbolically confirmed in the rhetoric of New Labour, as Tony Blair – drawing on US debate about communitarianism (Etzioni 1995) – stressed that "Strong communities depend on shared values and a recognition of the rights and duties of citizenship" (Blair 1998, p. 12). Blair's argument goes beyond the communities of place, which have tended to dominate discussion in the development of urban policy, to wider communities of interest, and above all the relationship of responsibilities as well as rights. From this perspective, it becomes possible to move away from what Etzioni and Blair see as unhelpful and misleading ways of thinking that present us with a stark choice between two extremes – that is between moral authoritarianism at one end and radical individualism at the other. Instead Etzioni suggests that "free individuals require a community, which backs them up against encroachment by the state and sustains morality by drawing on the gentle prodding of kin, friends, neighbors, and other community members, rather than building on government controls or fear of authorities" (Etzioni 1995, p. 15).

Of course, the challenge then becomes then becomes how to make (or remake) the communities that are now defined as a requirement. As Newman notes, the idea of "community" is central to New Labour's rhetoric of modernization and is "strongly linked to very particular notions of civic responsibility and citizenship, notions that informed Labour's attempt to overcome social exclusion and reform the welfare state" (Newman 2001, p. 148). The concept of "community" is used to highlight the interdependence of people and the importance of relationships between them, while also emphasizing the shared responsibilities of those who are members of "communities" and may be "seen to offer the prospect of reinstating social and moral cohesion and releasing resources for inclusion" (Taylor 2003, p. 216). As a result it appears to provide "an alternative both to the untrammelled free market (of neo-liberalism) and the strong state (of social democracy)" (Levitas 2000, p. 191). Although sometimes presented in terms that emphasize increased "empowerment" for communities, Imrie and Raco (2003a) highlight the way in which the discourse of community implies a process of self-management and responsibilization (admittedly a rather unpleasant neologism, but one that summarizes the process accurately enough) (see also Atkinson 1999; Taylor 2003, Ch. 5). Instead of relying on the state (or even the market) as regulator of behavior the implications of highlighting the role of community are that self-discipline becomes equally important (see also Rose 1996).

This sense of "community" has no direct territorial or urban implications, at least in principle. It is a particular view of society – and, indeed, a normative view of society as it should be rather than how it actually is. Nevertheless it has a particular salience in the urban policy context. Its metaphorical power is reflected, for example, in the comments made by Robson et al. (2000): "Even in the most deprived neighborhoods, there are considerable social strengths on which policy could build. Social surveys consistently show that high proportions of residents in deprived areas speak warmly of the 'quality' of the people in their neighborhoods and argue that the problems of crime, dereliction and social disruption are caused by a small minority of residents" (Robson et al. 2000, p. 25). As a result, they argue for "neighbourhood strategies that put local communities at the heart of decision-taking about neighbourhood management and change" (Robson et al. 2000, p. 25). And go on to say that: "The concentration of problems within small neighbourhoods … reinforces the argument for the development of forms of neighbourhood management that may capitalize on some of the inherent community strengths within such areas and can encourage what might be called 'guided community-led' approaches to the revitalization of such neighbourhoods" (Robson et al. 2000, pp. 25–6). Other government reports have gone even further, with one asserting that: "Self-help is an end in itself, as well as a means to an end. It is at the core of the empowerment of communities … about involvement and consultation but also about moving towards self-sufficiency … about communities shaping their own destiny – doing, not being done to" (Home Office 1999, para 1.3). "The level of community and voluntary activity in an area," we are told, "is often a gauge of the social health and spirit of that area and as such is a vital complementary strand in the provision of decent public services and a quality environment in changing people's lives" (DETR 2001b, Annex C, para 12).

It is in this context that the issue has been redefined as one of neighborhood renewal, reflected, for example, in the Social Exclusion Unit's report on "Bringing Britain Together" (Social Exclusion Unit 1998) and the "National Strategy for Neighbourhood Renewal" arising from it (Social Exclusion Unit 2000). Tony Blair expresses the new common sense in his introduction to the "National Strategy," explaining that, "unless the community is fully engaged in shaping and delivering regeneration, even the best plans on paper will fail to deliver in practice" (Social Exclusion Unit 2000). "Communities themselves," we are told later in the document, "ought to be the best advocates of their own interests" (Social Exclusion Unit 2000, para 2.17). The linkage between community, neighborhood and (national as well as local) economic prosperity is also made explicit in the strategy, since, "The waste of potential holds back the country's prosperity" (Social Exclusion Unit 2000, para 3).

Neighborhoods are said to provide spaces of familiarity and a degree of security, helping people to define their own "social identity and social position" (and to define it for them) (Kearns and Parkinson 2001, p. 2108), becoming "part of our statement about who we are" (Forrest and Kearns 2001, p. 2130). But, of course, this can have negative as well as positive consequences. Negatively, it may be expressed through the construction of protected and exclusionary spaces or the emergence of dysfunctional communities – that is those characterized by high levels of social disorder. In other cases, however, neighborhoods and the social networks and community relations that constitute them may provide a basis on which positive development can take place, since it is through "the routines of everyday life ... we learn tolerance, co-operation and acquire a sense of social order and belonging" (Forrest and Kearns 2001, p. 2130). In other words, within the framing concept of "community" it becomes possible to identify both the source of problems and the means of solving them. "Proper" communities deliver solutions, while "dysfunctional" communities work to reinforce and reproduce failure.

The supposed break down of community has itself come to be identified as the problem (or, at any rate, a key problem), particularly as it is redefined through the prism of social exclusion, defined by government as "what can happen when people or an area face a combination of linked problems such as unemployment, discrimination, poor skills, lower incomes, poor housing, high crime, bad health and family disorder" (Social Exclusion Unit 2004, p. 14). Not only are these problems "linked and mutually reinforcing" but, we are told, "they can create a vicious cycle in people's lives" (Social Exclusion Unit 2004, p. 3). At the same time, it is stressed that it is precisely the communities that suffer from social exclusion which are least likely to have the networks of voluntary and community organizations and the volunteering and community involvement that underpins them (see, e.g. Home Office 2002). As a result Gilchrist summarizes the role of community development along similar lines, as being "about the development of the 'community' – the capacity of local populations to respond collectively to events and issues that affect them" (Gilchrist 2003, p. 16). She argues that "robust and diverse social networks are of value in themselves, accelerating people's recovery from disease and trauma, reducing levels of anti-social behavior and fear of crime, enhancing health and happiness generally, and creating a stronger sense of personal identity" (Gilchrist 2003, p. 20).

Urban policy initiatives reflect a continuing ambivalence about the nature of community. In some cases, as we have seen, the emphasis is on trying to find already existing "communities," working with them, generating leaders and developing "capacity" – in other words looking for ways of "responsibilizing" or "remoralizing" existing communities. In others, however, the emphasis is placed on constructing new communities or reshaping existing communities. So, for example, there may be a stress on building areas with mixed tenure, replacing one population with another or inserting new populations into previously industrial or commercial areas (see, e.g. the discussion of gentrification in Chapters 6 and 7). Arthurson (2002) (drawing on evidence from Australia) argues that such strategies often effectively work to destroy existing strong neighborhood-based communities with the promise of a new social mix – which is expected to "help create 'sustainable', 'cohesive' and 'self-sufficient' communities" (Arthurson 2002, p. 251; see also Hoatson and Grace 2002).

There is a long policy tradition in the United Kingdom of attempting to create new communities, which stretches back to the garden cities movement and incorporates the postwar new towns. Its latest incarnation is expressed in plans to develop "sustainable communities," principally on the edge of the South-East of England (the United Kingdom's "growth region") (ODPM 2003a). At the core of the "sustainable communities" agenda is the proposal to develop four new growth areas – in Ashford, the Thames Gateway, Milton Keynes and the South Midlands and the London-Stansted-Cambridge-Peterborough corridor. Major investment will be required to underpin these developments, and they represent a significant shift in ways of thinking about urban policy, since the main purpose of the development is to ensure that economic growth in the South-East is not limited by a lack of affordable housing leading to a "tightening" of the labor market (see Allen et al. 1998).

With the possible exception of the Thames Gateway (ODPM 2004), where the integration of regeneration and development is combined and most development is to be on brown field sites, this program clearly owes little to any concern for the inner cities or other traditional targets for urban policy. What is being promised is the creation of new "communities," rather than the organic development of existing communities. David Miliband (then government minister responsible) makes clear that the aim is "to create communities" based around "new neighborhood-level institutions and spaces" in Thames Gateway as much as any of the other growth areas (Miliband 2006). These are communities that promise the space and security of suburbia, alongside the facilities of urban living (with easy access to shops, public services, employment, and entertainment) (a vision that is positively expressed in Schoon 2001). Within this model, "sustainability" is defined to mean economic sustainability (that is the ability to ensure that the economic success of Britain's "growth region" is not undermined because of labor shortages in key areas), denser housing development and the building of "balanced" communities (i.e. communities within which jobs, housing, and services are in balance, and which are not simply suburban dormitory towns).

The language of the "new urbanism," drawn from the United States (see, e.g. Katz 1993; Dutton 2000; Bohl 2002), underpins this vision. In a promotional publication produced on their behalf by *The Guardian* on the occasion of a "delivering sustainable communities" summit, English Partnerships implicitly position their plans for development in this context by publishing an article by the chief executive of the US based Congress for the New Urbanism (Norquist 2005). According to this article, "The new urbanist movement sought to recreate a world where the built landscape encourages community instead of separation and isolation. It sought to increase the value of the city to its citizens by encouraging walkability and respect for local context" (Norquist 2005, p. 10). As well as offering a way of rethinking existing urban developments and so feeding into regeneration (perhaps along the lines suggested by Rogers 1999) the tools of the new urbanism also provide a model for rethinking the form of new – suburban style – development, as "a re-ordering of the built environment into the form of complete cities, towns, villages, and neighborhoods – the way communities have been built for centuries around the world. New Urbanism involves fixing and infilling cities, as well as the creation of compact new towns and villages" (New Urbanism 2005). In other words, this approach offers us a revival of the approach that better "communities" can be built through particular forms of development or urban design, rather than any engagement with the social processes of segregation and exclusion that produce them. This is a language that is being mobilized by developers and state professionals across the globe, so that, for example, Winstanley et al. (2003) explore its impact in Christchurch, New Zealand, offering the salutary reminder that it provides a means of marketing new housing development and creating socially homogenous neighborhoods, rather than fostering community development.

Community and Social Capital: Economizing Community

In its latest incarnation, the notion of community has been given a particular boost from the widespread acceptance of the arguments surrounding the notion of "social capital" as a key underpinning of economic success and social well-being. This draws extensively on the work of Putnam (1993, 2000), rather than that of Bourdieu, for whom "social capital" has rather a different meaning (Bourdieu 1986). Putnam argues that the existence of reciprocity and trust reflected in networks of informal as well as formal relations, and expressed in a range of institutional settings (from bird-watching clubs to local government), is a necessary basis for continuing economic growth. He argues that "social capital refers to features of social organization such as networks, norms and trust that facilitate co-ordination and co-operation for mutual benefit. Social capital enhances the benefits of investment in physical and human capital" (Putnam 1993, p. 35). Putnam emphasizes the importance of trust and cooperation and the creation of networks and shared understandings, which make it possible for people to act together in the pursuit of shared objectives.

For Putnam this form of associational life also feeds back into civic engagement – so it is valuable in itself as enriching civil society, and not just as a factor in economic development. And his arguments have been widely taken up in official urban policy discourses. The "erosion of social capital," that is "the contact, trust and solidarity that enables residents to help, rather than fear, each other" has been identified as one of the main weaknesses facing deprived communities (Social Exclusion Unit 2000, para 8).

Mayer, however, argues that by identifying social capital as providing the "non-market conditions of economic growth" this argument has the discursive effect of re-defining the social as economic (Mayer 2003, p. 111). She suggests that the concept exemplifies: "a more general trend of dissolving social and political perspectives into economic ones" (Mayer 2003, p. 110) and notes the extent to which in the United States and Western Europe, "the work of civic and community organizations," has been identified as an important source, "for the generation of local social capital, as they increase political participation and improve the social and economic conditions in disadvantaged neighbourhoods – either through capacity building and complex public-private partnerships, or by mobilizing public pressure on political representatives and administrations" (Mayer 2003, p. 116). The broader shift has been helpfully summarized by Harloe, who argues that: "The urban problem has been redefined in terms of a supposed lack of social cohesion, leading ultimately to social and economic exclusion … now cast less as symptoms of urban failure than as potential obstacles to competitive success" (Harloe 2001, p. 889).

Mayer goes further to suggest that the social capital approach favors "consensus organizing, displacing advocacy or conflict orientations" (Mayer 2003, p. 119) because it effectively excludes those community-based groups that challenge the accepted norms or take an adversarial stance from consideration. Yet – as Perrons and Skyer (2003) suggest – in deprived neighborhoods this may make it impossible for demands to be made for the resources required to challenge structural forms of inequality, although in many cases, it is the existence of poverty and not a lack of social capital that is the problem (see, e.g. Forrest and Kearns 1999). There is a danger that community groups may get trapped in "ghetto economies, where they contribute to isolating disadvantaged communities further by drawing them into a localized circuit of capital disconnected from the mainstream economy" (Amin et al. 1998, quoted in Mayer 2003, p. 120). While "gaining more voice and representation in the new structures of governance, the movement and other third sector organizations simultaneously find their input restricted to local capacity building and productivity competition" (Mayer 2003, pp. 124/5).

By focusing on the marginalized and their organizations, argues Mayer, such an approach fails to engage with what made them that way. Instead it is implied that everybody has access to capital, although admittedly of different sorts. As she graphically puts it, it is "as if the resources embodied in community organizations can mend what finance capital has torn" (Mayer 2003, p. 125). She charts the way in which a rhetoric of radicalism (e.g. solidarity groups, empowerment zones, mobilization from below and so on) is used to underpin not challenges to poverty, but, rather, incorporation through "inclusion," since it is suggested that, "A judicious combination of mobilization from below and capacity building from above can solve the problems of uneven development and marginalization, and create the virtuous circle of social capital, economic growth and social cohesion" (Mayer 2003, p. 126). In other words it becomes the task of communities to adapt to external pressures (such as the impact of economic globalization, or the effects of neo-liberal restructuring) by drawing on or building social capital to remake themselves effectively. In other words, within this frame, urban policy, like other forms of social policy, is reinterpreted – moving "from unproductive burden to capacity building" (Smyth et al. 2004, p. 609; see also Cuthill 2003).

As a result, it is argued, "community" itself is given an economic inflection, so that transforming community is also about finding a more secure economic base and community involvement is directed towards infrastructural and even explicit economic development. So, for example, the Urban Affairs Association in the United States argued in 1998 that, "As cities have responded to new economic, political, and policy contexts, they have begun to develop a portfolio of strategies for institution building and community revitalization. These efforts have developed what can be seen as social capital, a partner to financial capital" (http://udel.edu/uaa/ quoted in Mayer 2003, p. 121). More positively, it has been suggested that an emphasis on social capital leads to an approach that focuses on " 'the capacity of communities to act' rather than of 'need' " (Gittell and Vidal 1998, p. 14) and that "building social capital may give people and communities the connectedness they need to face the new realities of devolution" (Gittell and Vidal 1998, p. 13). However, while the discovery of social capital may create "a new framework for dealing with urban inequality and poverty that appears to involve mobilization from below," Mayer convincingly argues that it only "does so in an extremely circumscribed and biased way" (Mayer 2003, p. 110).

Once the potential of "community" to deliver forms of self-help and self-management, to enable the identification of collective rights and responsibilities, and to generate social capital is added to the mix then it might be argued that "urban policy" is almost the perfect social policy for the present period. Not only does it provide a means for integrating those who are currently excluded (for remoralizing communities) but by doing so, according to this approach, it also helps to underpin economic competitiveness through the prism of social cohesion (Boddy and Parkinson 2004; Buck 2005; see also Chapter 6). Kearns (2003) charts some of the ways in which the relationship between social capital and community has influenced the development of regeneration policy in Britain, potentially promising more than it can deliver (see also Popple and Redmond 2000, who explore the relationship between New Labour's "Third Way" and the practice of community development and Chapter 8, where the importance of the notion of social capital within the developing urban policy of the World Bank is discussed).

Community as Business: Building the "Third Sector"

The shifts discussed in the previous sections have been reinforced and supported by the active construction of "nonstate" community-based organizations, neither state nor market, but what has come to be described as "third sector." This has perhaps found its clearest expression in US cities where such agencies increasingly undertake activities that would still generally be more directly state sponsored in the United Kingdom and many other European countries.

In the United States community development corporations (CDCs) first emerged in the context of the "War on Poverty," when they were essentially seen as working alongside government to help deliver on federal urban priorities. As Steinbach notes, "Their role was to encourage neighborhood development, promote anti-poverty strategies, and deliver social services" and they were in receipt of significant federal funding to help achieve these aims (Steinbach 2000, p. 2). Around 40 CDCs were funded by federal agencies as part of this first wave, many of them rooted in the popular movements of the time (particularly the civil rights and antipoverty movements). These CDCs were well-funded and had extensive professional support and ambitious development programs (Steinbach 2000).

However, they actually grew in number through the 1970s and 1980s in a more hostile funding environment, even as federal funding for urban programs fell significantly. As Gittel and Vidal note, their growth can partly be explained as a response to the "gradual withdrawal of other entities working on behalf of poor communities" (particularly in the provision of low income housing) (Gittell and Vidal 1998, p. 35). The rise of "municipal federalism" in the 1990s, whose aim was to devolve local government authority to nongovernment organizations like CDCs, gave them a further boost because they were "seen as alternatives to government" by Reaganite conservatives, particularly as potential recipients of funds for low cost housing (Steinbach 2000, pp. 2–4; see also Reingold and Johnson 2003, p. 528). The Community Reinvestment Act 1997 which requires banks to make loans in areas where they take deposits reinforced their position, since CDCs offered relatively safe forms of investment for financial institutions (Walker 2002, p. 25). In the absence of any federal urban policy, Gittell and Vidal see them as organizations for the generation of social capital in areas and among communities where there is none (Gittell and Vidal 1998, p. 13).

By the 1990s, CDCs were being described as constituting an "industry" (see, e.g. Walker 2002) and there are nearly 4,000 of them throughout the United States. The new CDCs may be more modest in size and ambition than those of the first wave, but the model enabled them to access funding from a range of agencies (private, state, city, federal, and foundations) to undertake investment in mainly inner city areas. In that sense, they provide a model of community entrepreneurialism with an emphasis on finding ways of generating funding from many sources to pay for initiatives and investment in poorer communities. They have been described as "among the most entrepreneurial institutions in the entire civil society sector" (Steinbach 2000, p. 1), since CDCs are said to be able to "respond quickly to the development opportunities offered by a changing marketplace ... CDC improvement efforts can make neighborhoods better in ways that are recognized by the market" (Walker 2002, pp. 8–9). Success is effectively measured in commercial terms, so that the evidence of their success is measured by the extent to which "CDCs are proving that market potential exists" (Ford Foundation 1998, p. 3).

Most (over 90 percent) of them are involved in the provision of low income (rental) housing (and collectively they have responsibility for 13 percent of federally subsidized housing units coming onto the market each year) (Gittel and Vidal 1998, p. 35), and it is their housing activities that draw in the bulk of their funding, from private as well as public sources and foundations, since they generate recurrent income. However, many of them also take on a wider range of responsibilities, including economic (and commercial) development, the provision of community facilities, advocacy and advice. They cover a range of scales (from small neighborhoods to areas of cities and clusters of settlements) as well as varied types of community, from ethnically concentrated to highly diverse.

Although CDCs generally have some direct community (i.e. local resident, tenant, stake-holder) representation on key boards, they are professionalized organizations, sometimes employing hundreds of people, even if only a quarter have staff of 23 or more (Walker 2002). In some cases they have been transformed into major free standing organizations. So, for example, the New Community Corporation is the largest employer of Newark residents. It employs over 1,400 people, has real estate assets of over $250m and owns a major shopping center (Steinbach 2000). The rise and fall of one large community development corporation – Eastside Community Investments, Inc. – in Indianapolis is an object lesson both in what is possible and in some of the risks associated with the model of urban renewal through grassroots capitalism (Reingold and Johnson 2003).

At the height of its success in the early 1990s Eastside Community Investments had over 115 employees and an operating budget of over $8m a year. In 1994, it "offered the community a sophisticated menu of programs: day care, health care, supportive services for the homeless and the mentally ill, youth development and employment training venture capital, and several bread and butter real estate businesses" (Reingold and Johnson 2003, p. 532). Yet already in the following year it began to move into financial crisis, finally closing in 2001. In large part this failure seems to have been the result of expansion into for-profit areas of activity through subsidiaries (e.g. in construction and maintenance), which were intended to generate income to help meet social aims. Investments were not generating returns. In some respects, of course, this can be explained in terms of bad management, but there is also a broader message, because CDCs "are increasingly subject to the conditions of the private market and the political landscape" (Reingold and Johnson 2003, p. 545).

As active sponsors of home ownership in the neighborhoods in which they are active, CDCs have been accused of undertaking forms of "gentrification," albeit through the sponsorship of low cost home ownership, rather than the recolonization of areas by the middle class (Newman and Ashton 2004). The effect is similar, however, it is suggested, because it recasts the areas as homes for the respectable working class, effectively reintroducing the Victorian division between the deserving and undeserving poor.

In the United Kingdom, too, there has been a marked shift away from state or council housing towards the provision of social housing through the "third sector," in the form of housing associations, with funding channeled through the Housing Corporation (see, e.g. Malpass 2000). Although the rise of housing associations has not been directly associated with the building of integrated community development corporations, there has been a community regeneration movement since the 1970s, which has been given institutional form in the shape of "community development trusts" and community enterprise along similar lines to those developed in the United States. These trusts are defined as "community-based organizations working for the sustainable regeneration of their area through a mixture of economic, social and cultural initiatives" (Ward and Watson 1997, p. 1). As in the United States, the aim is for trusts to be self-sustaining, able to generate their own income from the delivery of services, the sale of goods, the renting of property etc., although it is recognized that it may also be necessary to seek funding from public authorities and charitable funders for particular projects (see, e.g. DTA 2005).

The scale of these trusts either individually or collectively does not begin to approach that of similar initiatives in the United States, but the arguments presented for their further development are similar. It is argued that they are able to work at the points of intersection between the public and the private sectors, and both that they can respond more sensitively to the needs of those living in local communities and also that individual projects are able to have a more focused approach – without having any responsibility for the delivery of multifunctional services (see, e.g. Thake 1995). They are said to offer a basis for the revival of an older collectivist welfare tradition – that of "the mutual not-for-private-gain organization" – and to turn that model towards issues of community regeneration (rather than health insurance or support in old age) (Ward and Watson 1997, p. 8). In addition to the public and the private sectors, it is suggested, such initiatives provide the basis for building a "social economy," within which local people may be mobilized as an asset and not just the target of policy implementation.

It is difficult to make an informed judgement on the significance of these initiatives, because of their limited scale – and they are by no means all focused on the cities (Burton et al. 2004). Some, however – such as the development of the Coin St. area to the south of the River Thames in London (near the growing South Bank cultural space that links the Tate Modern to the South Bank Centre) for housing – have become famous as case studies of community action (see, e.g. Brindley et al. 1988) and have proved able to manage their own niche spaces within property markets very effectively. And for a time notions of community were strongly mobilized around the community enterprise movement and that continues to be an element in community regeneration through development trusts (see, e.g. DTA 2002). Self-help through the market was presented as a way forward, particularly for those areas unlikely to attract investment from the outside. The growth of community businesses in Scotland in the 1970s and 1980s has been widely documented and the Scottish example has been taken up to underpin the case for the development of community enterprise throughout the United Kingdom (see, e.g. Hayton 1996; Pearce 1993, pp. 5–11) and is reflected, for example, in the Phoenix fund (managed through the small business service of the Department of Trade and Industry) which was set up to provide support for community finance initiatives and for the development of ("innovative") small businesses in disadvantaged areas.

The more extreme claims for the success of community enterprise have, however, increasingly been questioned – because many "businesses" have found it difficult to survive without continuing local authority subsidy, because many "community" businesses turn out to be more conventional small firms, because they have tended to reinforce existing employment patterns of low pay, casualization and job insecurity and because – in some cases – there is evidence of corrupt relations between community businesses and the agencies which commission work from them. Coin St. itself was in a particularly (possibly uniquely) favorable position, protected by a radical urban council (the Greater London Council) itself abolished in the mid 1980s, and then able to benefit from wider shifts in property markets and the redefinition of the wider area of which it was a part – away from office development towards a global cultural space. "Community" involvement and empowerment remain powerful aspects of the rhetoric of community enterprise, but as Hayton (1996) notes, it is rather more difficult to discover their significance in practice.

The Ambiguities of Community

One of the challenges faced by those seeking to work through communities to achieve change is, of course, that the communities (and their leaders) first have to be identified. Although the rhetoric often implies that the existence of communities is unquestionable, in practice they often remain elusive and, where they appear to exist, are less homogenous than might be expected. As a result "communities" are being constructed as subjects (at least provisionally) through the working and language of state policy. There is, in other words, a strong emphasis on the need to build the communities (or generate community representatives) with which central (and sometimes regional or local) government can work.

For some this is simply understood as a matter of providing the opportunity: "why not," ask Osborne and Gaebler, "create more opportunities in poor communities and see how many leaders emerge?" (Osborne and Gaebler 1992, p. 72). So, for example, in their case study of community development in Kenilworth-Parkside (a public housing area in Washington) the role of Kimi Gray as community leader (and social entrepreneur) is celebrated, as is the success of the move towards tenant management and the creation of a resident management corporation, to replace the old public housing model of management by the city (Osborne and Gaebler 1992, pp. 60–5). "Before they took control of their own environment," we are told, "people at Kenilworth-Parkside expected things to happen to them." Now by contrast, it is argued, they can make things happen (Osborne and Gaebler 1992, p. 65).

In this context, Robert Woodson of the National Center for Neighborhood Enterprise is quoted as saying: "Only when you overcome the crisis of self-confidence can opportunity make a difference in your life" (Osborne and Gaebler 1992, p. 65). The argument is that neighborhood people lack confidence and that this form of renewal can help create confidence which in turn leads to renewal. "The empowerment of communities like Kenilworth-Parkside not only changes expectations and instils confidence – it usually provides far better solutions to their problems than normal public services" (Osborne and Gaebler 1992, pp. 65–6).

Similar arguments have underpinned the development of British urban policy since the mid 1990s, because it is increasingly predicated on a belief that "empowering" communities and giving them direct responsibility for their own well-being will make it more likely that any gains will be sustained over the longer term, even when particular projects have come to an end. As John Prescott (then government minister with overall responsibility in England) puts it in the Introduction to the Urban White Paper (DETR 2000) "our policies will empower communities to determine their own future." In England, the Neighbourhood Renewal Unit (currently located within the Department for Communities and Local Government) has the task of ensuring that there is community involvement in the preparation of community strategies and within local strategic partnerships (DETR 2001a). In order for this to happen, however, communities have to have their own "leaders" and in this context in England, the Home Office Active Community Unit has been given the responsibility of seeking to generate strong and active communities with a target of ensuring that one million people are actively involved by 2004. The aim is to help generate and identify community "leaders" who are able to encourage community cohesion and to take responsibility for their own areas (see, e.g. LGA, DTLR, HO, CRE 2002).

This has been turned into a model or template of "best practice" in neighborhood management, which includes the need for: an action plan and a means of monitoring it; the oversight of a "champion" leading a team; a community development fund for pump-priming; and neighborhood forums for local involvement (Robson et al. 2000, Box 6). Diamond links the search for "social entrepreneurs" to a "strategy of co-option and inclusion" in which key professionals are empowered "to act as a local neighborhood catalyst or 'supremo' " (Diamond 2001, p. 277).

There was already extensive reference to the involvement of the community in guidance developed for the Single Regeneration Budget (SRB) (initially launched in 1994) which invited bids for area-based projects from local government (and, potentially, other agencies). Guidance stressed that the community should be involved "in setting up and running these programmes" and those who were intended to benefit from them were expected to "have a continuing say in the management, further development and implementation of the scheme" (DoE 1994). There were six rounds of SRB program and for the last two it was explicitly stated that 10 percent of any funding allocated should be used to build community capacity. Similar approaches underpinned the cluster of community-based policies that were launched in England in the late 1990s, and particularly the two major national initiatives – the New Deal for Communities (NDC) (launched in 1998) and the Neighborhood Renewal Fund (NRF). NDC projects are expected to run for 10 years, and 39 have been funded.

The focus of these is on a relatively small number of areas, so that the individual budgets are significant (between £35–61m) and can be mobilized in a targeted fashion. The NRF focused on the 88 most deprived local authority districts in England, with the aim of generating neighborhood renewal strategies in those districts. In both schemes, the aim was to encourage the creation of community-based partnerships, drawing in business, public service providers, and active members of the community, whose role would effectively be to take responsibility for the regeneration of particular neighborhoods (of 1,000–4,000 households). In Scotland, as indicated earlier, a similar approach had been taken for some time with the development of neighborhood-based initiatives focused on self-help and community renewal. This was already reflected in the strategy outlined in *New Life for Urban Scotland* (Scottish Office 1988), whose four partnership area initiatives had unmistakable echoes of the genesis of the Community Development Projects.

The emphasis on community "capacity building" reflects the ambition to create new institutional spaces of "community." So, for example, the partnership boards set up under the aegis of New Deal for Communities have community representatives but – unlike many other partnership bodies (within which organizations are represented or community leaders invited to join) – in around half of the boards these representatives are elected, in principle giving them a stronger legitimacy (and an alternative legitimacy to that of elected local government) (Rallings et al. 2004).

However the extent to which this ambition is likely to be realized has been widely questioned. One concern is that representation is effectively self-selecting, since only some activists are prepared or able to give the time (see, e.g. Perrons and Skyer 2003). Lawless notes that the involvement of members of black and ethnic minority communities in partnership bodies is lower than might have been expected in over two-thirds of the partnerships, despite the stated ambition to gain such representation (Lawless 2004, p. 389). Evidence from elections to the neighborhood boards sponsored through New Deal for the Communities also suggests that the extent of political (or community) engagement remains uncertain (Rallings et al. 2004). In a few areas turnout has been high, apparently confirming the view that community engagement will be greater when members of the community can see that decisions are being made that will affect them directly (i.e. within the area where they live) (Perrons and Skyer 2003). But in most of these elections, despite the almost universal use of all-postal ballots, turnout has been low and often lower than in local elections (where turnout is regularly criticized as failing to provide adequate legitimacy for local government) (see, e.g. Stoker 2004). The professionals responsible for partnerships are more likely to feel that community groups are engaged than are the community groups or local residents (Burton et al. 2004, p. 40; Lawless 2004, p. 387).

Often, too, those elected as community representatives become identified as part of the local authority, rather than as representatives of the community and in one survey "were not felt to be any more interested in people's views than some of the public services" (Chanan 2003, p. 48). Following his review of the role of community leaders in local regeneration partnerships in nine British cities, Purdue similarly notes the difficulty faced by those identified as "community leaders" in connecting "to their grass roots supporters in the neighborhood," while, the "fragmentation of community networks and a low level of trust in government initiatives made it hard to gain the trust of a wide range of local residents" (Purdue 2001, p. 2221). The "community leaders" faced the problem of co-option – engagement without tangible gain. Their active engagement in partnership sometimes made it more difficult to communicate with other local residents" (Purdue 2001, p. 2222).

A case study of "Shoreditch Our Way," a New Deal for Communities partnership in East London, highlights key issues arising from community involvement in such projects (Perron and Skyers 2003). The complex nature of the procedures is largely alien to community representatives, and the (sophisticated) debates that dominate also fit uneasily with their expectations, while the extent to which local decisions can be made are in any case severely constrained by centrally determined parameters. Similar points are made by Lawless who lists a series of commonly identified obstacles in the way of longer term involvement by community members. They include: "burnout, declining interest, intracommunity strife, disquiet at the operation of formal board, lack of remuneration, formidable time commitments, lack of confidence, lack of perceived skills and so on" (Lawless 2004, pp. 387–8).

In practice, too, the management of the partnerships and the community involvement in them limits the potential for effective engagement. In most cases the partnerships work to targets set by government agencies, so that the " 'success' of these projects is dependent on meeting externally fixed outcomes" which means that the "actual 'space' for local negotiation or variation is limited" (Diamond 2004, p. 180). Perrons and Skyers (2003) argue that community participation only works if it gives access to "decisions over allocation of material resources," which most community initiatives do not. There remains some justifiable scepticism about the extent to which excluded groups really will be given significant influence or involvement in the new arrangements (see, e.g. Brownill and Darke 1998; Diamond 2001; Geddes 1997).

In this context it is worth recalling community work's colonial prehistory, when it was a means of managing and working with communities of which the managers were not a part. Certainly, there was an emphasis on "capacity building," both because there was an assumption that ultimately the colonial power might withdraw to be replaced by a local and suitably trained political elite, but more important, it was essential to generate a "community" with leaders with whom it was possible to work, and who would be able to deliver a degree of political and social stability (see, e.g. Mayo 1975). As Clarke puts it: "The colonized peoples were grasped (physically and imaginatively) by the colonial power as communities, as cultures, as specifically localized 'ways of life' in contrast to the colonial 'civilization' that traversed and transcended space and localization" (Clarke 2002, p. 5). Clarke explicitly places the politics and policy practice of "community" in its postcolonial context, highlighting the ways in which they engage with notions of "multiculturalism," so that communities of difference become spatialized and suitable sites for intervention, for targeted management and the building of normality. The aim is to construct "normal" communities as part of what he describes as a (national) community of communities (Clarke 2002).

The advice given in the 1997 edition of *Involving Communities* (DETR 1997) could have been lifted from guidance given in the colonial era. It emphasizes the need to consult each identifiable ethnic group and to "Show you have the support of accepted leaders but are not in their pocket" (quoted in Chanan 2003, p. 34). However such positions are themselves highly fragile and subject to challenge. Jahn-Khan argues that the Bradford riots of 1995 "need to be viewed as a challenge to the established status quo of institutional sole reliance on so-called 'community leaders' to speak on behalf of and 'police' black and minority ethnic communities" (Jahn-Khan 2003, p. 38). Jahn-Khan forcefully questions traditional approaches to community development, as used in working with ethnic minority communities in British cities, because of the way in which government agencies seek to work through recognized "leaders." He suggests not only that these approaches are legacies of the old colonial approaches but also that they help to define the community itself as "difficult" – only to be managed through those leaders (Jahn-Khan 2003, p. 41).

The management of "communities," whether by themselves or through state professionals, is complex and uncertain and it is important not to be seduced by the warm, almost cosy connotations of the term. It is equally important to recognize that it is neither possible simply to dismiss communities (or neighborhoods) as bases for active political engagement with the potential to reshape the lives of those who live in them, nor simply to celebrate their potential as sources of political dynamism (see, e.g. Cochrane 1986a). In this context, too, it is worth returning to some of the implications of community involvement or the involvement of those designated as community leaders in partnerships, policy making and even service delivery. As Colenutt (1999, pp. 244–5) suggests, this may open up opportunities as well as close them down. Taylor et al. (2002) review the impact of the national and local compacts with voluntary and community organizations, concluding that groups may be affected differently. They question simple models of incorporation, suggesting that some groups have been able to gain more, while others have found themselves sucked in, with extra work but little additional benefit. What matters is how the balance between the different agencies is negotiated – in other words, this is an active process rather than one whose outcome is always predetermined.

Community is certainly capable of generating significant political engagement, and this has been charted in a large number of case studies of community activism (see, e.g. among many others, Fisher and Kling 1993b; Greenberg 1999; Hoggett 1997b). One approach highlights the importance of collective or social consumption and also highlights the potential of community politics as the politics of social reproduction (involving new social movements, often led by women). So, although Cockburn (1977) rejects the notion of "community" as an ideological concept, because of the way in which she believes it is used by the local state to categorize and manage people, to integrate them into a shared agenda, rather than enabling them to mobilize independently, she nevertheless highlights the potential for action around issues of "reproduction."

Cockburn identifies three sites for political action: action around what she calls the "point of collective reproduction" – that is state services; action around the "point of employment" of those providing the services – that is the welfare state workforce; and action around privatized reproduction – that is family (Cockburn 1977, pp. 158–9). What is important here is that Cockburn (in contrast to the historically dominant position of the left which stresses the importance of "production" – that is relations in the workplace) identifies the ideological terrain of community as the space within which there is or can be "struggle in the field of capitalist reproduction." And, of course, the active participants in this struggle (in contrast to male manufacturing workers of Fordism) are the woman who are directly engaged with issues of collective and privatized reproduction and are also more likely to be employed by the local state or its associated community organizations. Whether one agrees with Cockburn's particular theoretical starting point or not, there can be little doubt that women continue to play a particularly active part in the politics of the community. So, for example, Campbell (1993) emphasizes the role of women in maintaining the fragile community and family structures of a range of urban estates throughout England and Wales (Campbell 1993; see also McCulloch 1997). From a rather different perspective, research summarized by Robson et al. in 2000, "suggests that almost all deprived communities still retain elements of their traditionally strong community structures. Much of this is maintained by women, and particularly middle-aged and elderly women" (Robson et al. 2000, p. 25).

There is a danger of seeing this a relatively passive and secondary role (providing the infrastructure on the basis of which the important matters of the urban economy can be sustained), but it may be more appropriate to see it as part of a wider politics of the everyday, which are of far greater significance. In the United States' context, Gilbert suggests that an approach drawing on "feminist conceptualizations of multiple power relations, agency, daily life, politics, community and place can enhance our understanding of the daily lives of poor women in cities as well as their contribution to the production of urban space and politics." In particular, she argues it "provides the basis for a progressive urban politics, based on place-based communities, to respond to the devastating attacks on poor women and their children and the material conditions in inner cities that poor people are currently experiencing" (Gilbert 1999, p. 107). Staeheli (2003) charts the different ways in which women working in community-based social care organizations interpret the meanings of the community. More important, perhaps, she also explores a range of strategies developed by some of these women "as a basis for building an inclusive society in which social justice can be achieved through an ethic of care" (Staeheli 2003, p. 816). In other words they are engaged in an active process seeking to deliver change and not simply to manage survival in a relatively hostile environment.

Byrne stresses the double edged nature of "community." For him a community exists where people are "conscious of the communality which derived from common spatial experience and were willing to act communally" (Byrne 1999, p. 119). Communities cannot simply be squeezed into templates which promise sanitized interaction and networking, through which social capital is constructed. As Taylor (2003, p. 213) notes "All communities tend to organize most easily against those they see as enemies."

However, it is also necessary to recognize the sharp tensions that may exist within places that are understood as communities – or more modestly as "neighborhoods." So, for example, Perrons and Skyers (2003) point to the existence of real, material, differences within "communities" which mean that it is not possible to generate a simple and unified "vision" capable of bringing them together (see also Hoggett 1997b on contested communities). Similarly, Chanan argues that it is important to acknowledge that that each community or voluntary organization is identified with by a part of the community, "not by the community *en masse*" (Chanan 2003, p. 48). In her consideration of the impact of the riots and disturbances (mainly involving young white men) that shook a range of urban areas in Britain in 1991, Campbell puts this particularly forcibly, suggesting that "Crime and coercion are sustained by men. Solidarity and self-help are sustained by women. It is as stark as that" (Campbell 1993, p. 319).

By contrast, while the 2001 "race" riots (mainly involving Asian youth) in Oldham, Burnley and Bradford, also reflect divisions within communities (as well as between neighborhoods), it has been argued that they represent something rather different, namely a claim to citizenship rather than what Amin has called "folklorized" representations of their community (Amin 2003, p. 462). He argues that they involved not merely a reaction to the pressures emanating from their economic marginalization, the activities of white racists and the processes of policing, but also a rejection of their own community leaders. They were making "the claims of full British subjects, without qualification and freed from the politics of community and consensus practices by their community leaders" (Amin 2003, p. 462).

These riots were, says Kundnani, neither self-defense, nor directed against the police, but should rather be understood as the violence of hopelessness – "the violence of the violated" (Kundnani 2001, p. 105). Jahn-Khan goes further to suggest that it is important to recognize that those involved had a "right to riot" to get a voice, citizenship, since it was an "act of desperation by those denied any sense of legitimate participation within the decision-making process" (Jahn-Khan 2003, p. 34). The dominant official response to the riots, however, found its expression in a rather different interpretation of community, with an explicit call for the development of greater "community cohesion." So, the team set up by the government, under the chairmanship of Ted Cantle, to review the tensions between different ethnic communities of the towns where the riots took place utilized a notion of community cohesion. This incorporated a number of key indicators, ranging from shared values and a civic culture to the existence of "effective informal social control" and a high degree of tolerance and respect for differences, the existence of social solidarity, "a high degree of social interaction," civic engagement and involvement in associations, as well as a strong relationship between personal identity and identity with the place within which people live (Cantle 2001, p. 13; see also LGA, DTLR, HO, CRE 2002). Inherent in the approach is a model which seeks to work across local (in this context described as "micro") communities to construct a wider whole. Community cohesion is summarized in Appendix C as being, "about helping micro-communities to gel or mesh into an integrated whole. These divided communities would need to develop common goals and a shared vision. This would seem to imply that such groups should occupy a common sense of place as well. The high levels of residential segregation found in many English towns would make it difficult to achieve community cohesion" (Lynch, in Cantle 2001, p. 70). The emphasis is, therefore, on breaking down borders between "micro-communities" and challenging existing forms of social segregation.

The notion of community cohesion builds on a view of community as a relatively bounded and stable set of relations and is used to undermine some of the divisions between actually existing "communities" in order to build a more stable community at a wider level. By contrast Amin (2004) fundamentally questions this approach, instead suggesting that it is important to focus on the processes of: "local liveability, that is, the micropolitics of everyday social contact and encounter" (Amin 2004, p. 959). He argues that it is important to see places as processes, fragile and temporary settlements, rather than finished sites (as fixed communities) (Amin 2004, p. 972). Clarke (2002) similarly argues that communities are "weakly bounded" which means they fit uneasily with ambitions to generate community cohesion because "people have multiple identities and linkages" (Burns et al. 1994, p. 228). As Clarke puts it, the understanding that underpins the drive to community cohesion "seems a peculiarly archaic view of communities in practice" since communities often (and particularly the communities of multiculturalism) "are also formed as part of transnational imaginaries" closely linked into relationships of solidarity with people located far away (nominally, presumably, in other communities) (Clarke 2002, p. 10; see also Amin 2004), even if some communities can be narrow, conservative, defensive and racist, as well as "empowering" and open (see, e.g. Burns et al. 1994, p. 229ff).

As a result, the search for cohesion is likely to be a hopeless one, and its achievement double edged if it simply generates conflict at a wider spatial scale, and in a sense this is already the message of those dedicated to recreating it at the level of the city. Cantle's report bemoans the existence of socially cohesive (neighborhood-based) communities, arguing instead that what is needed is cohesion at the urban level (Cantle 2001). Not only is such cohesion likely to be impossible to achieve, but – equally important – were it to be achieved it would not necessarily be any less divisive. So, for example, in some cases the socially cohesive communities of the South-East have been able very effectively to exclude the "undesirable" through the mobilization of planning policy against proposals for housing development (Charlesworth and Cochrane 1994). As Raco (2003, p. 241) notes, even in their strongest formulations, communities are "exclusionary in their inclusiveness." In other words what matters with communities is how they are bordered, who is defined as being in and who is defined as being outside particular local, ethnic (and even "national") communities.

The notion of community is an ambivalent and ambiguous, but politically (or "rhetorically") very useful, one, particularly – as we have seen – for those seeking to construct a politics combining moral responsibilization with the drive to economic competitiveness (Everingham 2003). In recent years, it has been reimagined to provide the basis on which social capital may be built as a means of delivering economic success, so that – as Mayer (2003) suggests – as a policy object community is redefined as an economic factor. Instead of seeing community as an aspect of welfare, it becomes a basis on which the economy may be strengthened. At the same time, however, it has provided a set of arguments that underpin new approaches to the management of diverse populations, as well as a means to target forms of welfare intervention more effectively and to mobilize members of the community to take on new social responsibilities.

But the process is not straightforward – attempts to mobilize notions of community (and, indeed, actually existing communities) to manage particular populations more effectively have also generated challenges to those doing the managing: while the emphasis on community may have been intended to encourage a higher degree of self-discipline and self-policing among those populations the tensions between those being managed and the managers have also generated challenges to the arrangements being pursued. The strategy of community development as a form of incorporation is one that has been pursued consistently, but rarely with complete success. Taylor graphically presents an alternative vision in which the task is "to find creative ways of equipping those who are politically, socially and economically excluded to find and exploit the cracks and tensions within the system and the windows of opportunity they create" (Taylor 2003, p. 224). As Clarke puts it: "Community remains a peculiar place to govern, because people consistently refuse to 'know their place'" (Clarke 2002, p. 13). Communities remain highly "contested" (Hoggett 1997b) (and often provisional) sites of popular definition and redefinition, imagination and reimagination as well as objects of policy.

Chapter 5

Managing Disorderly Places

Some of the most powerful writing about the city has seen it as a place of disorder and disorganization. The image of the "slum" – frequently prefaced by the term "Dickensian" – continues to have a powerful resonance, not only in the cities of the West and North, but also – and today possibly still more – in those of the developing world (see, e.g. UN-Habitat 2003; Davis 2004). This negative understanding has underpinned some of the most dramatic proposals for rational planning through design and social reform, for example, expressed in the visions of Howard (1902/1965), for whom the alternative was the development of garden cities, and Le Corbusier (1929/1987), for whom the alternative was the orthogonal grid of high rise development, best viewed from the air. Such understandings have been widely criticized, for example, by Jacobs (1961) who berates the view that "sees only disorder in the life of city streets and itches to erase it, standardize it, suburbanize it" (Jacobs 1961, p. 460), and Mooney (1998) who fundamentally questions the underlying principle, emphasizing the extent to which even the supposedly most disorganized parts of the city (the inner city or the peripheral estates) are actually ordered and organized, albeit along very different lines to those favored by the critics. Even in supposedly dysfunctional neighborhoods, residents may understand the rules and ways of surviving within them, while outsiders simply see disorder (see, e.g. Evans 1997) (for discussion of the "slum" as focus of regeneration, see Chapter 7).

However there can be no doubt of the power of the dystopian visions and – even – the extent to which they influenced the planning of cities at least until the early 1970s (Merrifield 2000; McLeod and Ward 2002). In a sense, however, urban policy (particularly as it has been defined in this book) can be seen as a reaction to such visionary (or utopian) thinking. Urban policy is about dealing with the here and now, the practical, whether defined through community initiatives, economic development or property development, even if, as Harvey (2000, pp. 133–81) notes, even the most apparently practical experiment is often underpinned by its own form of utopian vision.

Nevertheless, urban policy – particularly in its recent reshaping – has also been shaped as a response to similar fears, and indeed as offering a means of more effectively managing the dangerous classes (or the "underclass") in the postwelfare era. There can be little doubt (as discussed in Chapter 2) about the extent to which urban policy (as far back as the 1960s and 1970s) was a response to fears about the city and its unmanageability – specifically the perceived threat from the black population in America's inner cities (and by some form of transatlantic osmosis, apparently also those of the United Kingdom and even France) (see, e.g. Wacquant 1993a,b). Alongside race, and often in combination with it, young people have been identified as a source of urban threat at least since the sixties. The definition of young people – and particularly young men – as "out of control" has fed into the imagery of cities as dangerous places. This has been reflected in a whole series of "moral panics," summed up, for example, in a Campbell's powerful description of "young men on the rampage" in her discussion of the urban disorders which seemed to spread across England in the early 1990s (Campbell 1993). Whatever the precise formulation or the precise location of the "problem" (inner or outer city) the message is clear enough: there are areas which, and people who, are dangerous and from whom the respectable classes need to be protected (see Graham and Clarke, 1996, for a review of the longer history of the relationship between cities and fears of crime).

Blair's (Thomas not Tony) vision of the future of the city from the perspective of the early 1970s is just one particular example of a powerful dystopic (and highly racialized) understanding of the urban that reflects the recurrent fears, albeit in extreme form:

> At the moment it looks to some political observers that cities will be composed of fortified enclaves. Central business districts, surrounded by decaying and increasingly black neighbour-hoods, will be constantly under siege for fear of terrorists and marauding gangs of youths. Streets and residential neighbourhoods will be unsafe. Ghetto slums areas will be "free territories" per-haps out of police control during night-time hours. Armed guards will protect all public facilities such as schools, libraries, and playgrounds, and deputized security police will "ride shotgun" on all public transport. High-rise, high-income apartment buildings and residential compounds will be protected by private armies, savage guard dogs, and electronic devices. The ownership of guns will be universal in white suburbs; home defences will include window grills, audio-visual scanning devices and infra-red cameras to spot night-time intruders; armed citizens in cars will supplement inadequate police controls (Blair 1974, pp. 134–5).

Making Up Policy

One explanation of urban disorder and social disorganization clearly identifies the people living in the cities as themselves constituting the problem which has to be solved. So, for example, Banfield (1970, 1974) argues that the urban problem is largely to be explained by the behavioral patterns of those who live in the inner cities – for him, the poor will always be with us, because they are "present-oriented" and not prepared to plan for some indefinite future. As he puts it: "the lower class individual lives from moment to moment. If he has any awareness of a future it is of something fixed, fated, beyond his control: things happen to him, he does not *make* them happen" (Banfield 1974, p. 61). The poor, he says, are unable or unwilling to "sacrifice immediate gratifications in favor of future ones" (Banfield, 1974, p. 126). This means, according to Banfield, that nothing much can be done about the lower class "slum-dwellers," so his policy nostrums focus instead on those affected by their behavior – the children of lower class parents, middle class people trapped in the inner cities, and middle class people in other (neighboring) areas. One way of saving lower class children, he suggests, would be to lower the school leaving age, so that they can enter paid employment earlier; welfare payments can be used to help the deserving poor, and most of them would be well advised to move away from the inner city; but above all he argues that the key task is to manage the criminal and potentially riotous behavior of the lower class in ways that ensure that it does not adversely affect the lives of the middle classes living elsewhere in the city.

Murray's evocation of an "underclass" (separate from "normal" society) is consistent with and builds on the interpretation developed by Banfield, but he explicitly links its growth with the rise of the welfare state (Murray 1984). He effectively blames state policy for encouraging the development of an underclass rooted in a dependency culture from which it was unable to escape. Murray sees crime as a key indicator of community breakdown and social disorganization: "To the extent that many people in a community engage in crime as a matter of course, all sorts of the socializing norms of the community change, from the kind of men that younger boys chose as heroes to the standards of morality in general" (Murray 1990, p. 31). Debates about the "underclass" have often been used to raise concerns about the parenting practices of members of some minority ethnic groups (in the United Kingdom particularly those from African-Caribbean backgrounds, and in the United States particularly those with African-American backgrounds) (see, e.g. Moynihan 1973; Wilson, J. 1975; Murray 1990) but they have also underpinned debates about urban policy, with their focus on community, neighborhood, and security.

More structural (and more sympathetic) interpretations have also led to the identification of an underclass, although the policy conclusions to be drawn are rather different. So, for example, although Wilson, W. (1987, 1992) identifies the fundamental causes in the deindustrialization that creates the ghettoes of the old industrial cities of the United States rather than any inherent psychological or behavioral failing among the local residents, nevertheless some of the symptoms identified seem similar. Wilson, too, focuses on the creation of a social formation, which he calls the underclass, which is isolated from mainstream society (with its sets of shared understandings) and highly individualized with little collective solidarity (see also Wacquant 1993b).

This critique is taken still further by Wacquant, who argues that the creation of ghettoes in Northern cities initially provided an important source of "abundant and cheap labor willing to ride along its cycles of boom and bust . . . while keeping black bodies at a safe distance, to the material and symbolic benefits of white society" (Wacquant 2002, p. 48). Wacquant defines the ghetto as "a distinct *space* containing an ethnically homogeneous *population*, which finds itself forced to develop within it a set of interlinked *institutions* that duplicates the organizational framework of the broader society from which that group is banished and supplies the scaffoldings for the construction of its specific 'style of life' and social strategies. This parallel institutional nexus affords the subordinate group a measure of protection, autonomy and dignity, but at the cost of locking it in a relationship of structural subordination and dependency" (Wacquant 2002, pp. 50–1). He argues that changes in the US economy (towards "a suburban service economy" and away from "an urban industrial economy"), alongside the rise of a new immigrant work force, made possible a fundamental shift in the way in which the "ghettoes" and their black populations were to be managed, particularly in the wake of their success in achieving political citizenship. In particular, he draws attention to the shift away from social welfare programs and towards crime control and penal policies which substantially changes the ways in which people are able to live in those areas, generating, particularly for young people, "a self-perpetuating cycle of social and legal marginality with devastating personal and social consequences" (Wacquant 2002, p. 53).

As articulated by Wacquant, this vision is quite specific to the US experience, but popular variants are presented as if it were a universal one – whatever happens in (or is predicted for) US cities is frequently presented as the future for all, whether living in the *favelas* of Brazil, the *banlieues* of France, the inner cities of England or the peripheral schemes of Scotland. Castells argues that there is a global geography of social exclusion, which, "is also present in literally every country, and every city . . . It is formed of American inner-city ghettoes, Spanish enclaves of mass youth unemployment, French banlieues warehousing North Africans, Japanese Yoseba quarters and Asian mega-cities' shanty towns. And it is populated by millions of homeless, incarcerated, prostituted, criminalised, brutalised, stigmatised, sick, and illiterate persons" (Castells 1998, pp. 164–5).

There is also little doubt, for example, that similar fears about the challenge from Britain's rather smaller black population have underpinned policy developments in Britain. Gilroy quotes Sir Kenneth Newman (at the time Commissioner of the Metropolitan Police) as identifying the areas where (particularly black) young people congregate as having symbolic importance – "The youths regard these symbolic locations as their territory. Police are viewed as intruders, the symbol of authority – largely white authority – in a society that is responsible for all their grievances about unemployment, prejudice and discrimination" (quoted in Gilroy 1987, p. 108). Similarly, Hall et al. (1978) chart the discovery or "invention" of "mugging" as a specifically inner city (and "black") phenomenon in the Britain of the early 1970s, and highlight the extent to which it was held to represent the existence of a much wider social – and, in practice, specifically urban – crisis of law and order.

There continues to be a very strong shared (almost taken for granted) understanding that cities are places of disorder (or places within which disorder is more likely). And this seems to be confirmed by the extent to which they have been the sites of riots and "uprisings," even in the countries of the prosperous West. So, for example, Rogers and Power explain that, "Cities collect strangers. Major population movements concentrate vulnerable people in the places where other people choose not to go. Crime exploits this phenomenon. As social cohesion and informal controls weaken, so our ability to contain disorder and violence declines . . . Where social controls are weak, policing inadequate and levels of fear high, matters can get completely out of control" (Rogers and Power 2000, pp. 43–7). This understanding is also reflected in the reports of the Social Exclusion Unit (1998, 2001) where the solution is presented in terms of rebuilding communities and delivering joined up government, linking social improvement with more effective forms of punitive intervention or social control (see, e.g. Social Exclusion Unit 2001a, Paras 4.25–4.34). Tackling "concentrations of crime and poor living environments" (in which "poor living environments," too, tend to be defined as places with high levels of crime) remains one of six key priority areas in the British government's policies for challenging social exclusion (Social Exclusion Unit 2004, p. 73).

The development of policies directed against social exclusion (discussed more fully in earlier chapters) is not simply reducible to the arguments of Banfield and Murray. But the echoes are unmistakeable. In his first set piece speech after coming to power in 1997, Tony Blair made this clear when he identified "what we all know exists – an underclass of society cut off from society's mainstream" and argued that "fatalism, and not just poverty, is the problem we face." He reflected on a world of social disorder, crime and dereliction in Britain's urban estates.

"Behind the statistics," he said, "are people who have lost hope, trapped in fatalism" so that in this context the greatest challenge facing government is "to bring this new workless class back into society and into useful work" (Blair 1997). Although in one sense the notion of social exclusion avoids the charge of "blaming the victim," since the victims are positioned by an active process of exclusion (see Byrne 1999, p. 120), in practice it is clear that the "culture" of which they have become a part fits uneasily with the renewed emphasis on "an ethic of mutual responsibility or duty ... A society where we are playing by the rules. You only get out what you put in. That's the bargain" (Blair 1997). Since the government role is redefined in terms that mean it helps people who help themselves, then those who (for whatever reason) are not responsive are once more in danger of marginalization. As Haylett (2003) points out, those labeled as socially excluded are clearly not viewed positively, since to be validated as a full citizen, it is necessary to achieve "inclusion in the cultural mainstream of consumption and labor market participation ... the discourse of 'social inclusion' alongside a lack of positive namings and valuations around working class people and places is, at least, contradictory" (Haylett 2003, p. 69). And, of course, it is the places as well as the people of social exclusion that are the targets of urban policy.

If such visions of the urban and the threats it represents are widely accepted (as well as being actively produced) the question then becomes what policies emerge in response to them.

Creating defended spaces

The most powerful response is itself dystopic and may be individualistic – expressed in the form of a privatized search for security. It has been suggested that, "Increasing ghettoisation is occurring in a bifurcated manner with groups at both the top and bottom increasingly concentrated together in socially homogeneous areas" (Atkinson and Blandy 2005, p. 180). Calling on imagery from the film *Blade Runner*, Davis (1998, Chapter 7) has gone further to identify an "ecology of fear," in which a range of protected enclaves is constructed by the middle classes to exclude those who may challenge their security. Davis (1990) vividly describes the creation of protected enclaves in Los Angeles:

> The security-driven logic of urban enclavization finds its most popular expression in the frenetic efforts of Los Angeles' affluent neighbourhoods to insulate home values and lifestyles ... new luxury developments outside the city limits have often become fortress cities, complete with encompassing walls, restricted entry points with guard posts, overlapping private and public police services, and even privatised roadways. It is simply impossible for ordinary citizens to "invade" the cities of Hidden Hills, Bradbury, Rancho Mirage or Rolling Hills without an invitation from a resident ... In the once wide-open tractlands of the San Fernando Valley, where there were virtually no walled-off communities a decade ago, the "trend" has assumed the frenzied dimensions of a residential arms race as ordinary suburbanites demand the kind of social insulation once enjoyed only by the rich (Davis 1990, 244–6).

Even in its most extreme form – that is the literal creation of gated areas, accompanied by private policing – Los Angeles is not unique. Similar arrangements are emerging in most of the world's major cities, in luxury developments in London, as well as Detroit, Santiago and Johannesburg (Robinson 1999; Salcedo and Torres 2004). Amin and Graham (1999) note how "physical proximity" increasingly coexists with "relational difference." In other words, the connected live alongside the disconnected – the favelas and shanty towns, and informal living survive and develop alongside the gated homes of the rich. They use the example of Sao Paulo in Brazil, where they depict "luxury enclaves rising above the roofs of the surrounding shanty town" (Amin and Graham 1999, p. 19).

Atkinson et al. (2004) summarize the English experience, confirming that fear of crime is a powerful driver in fostering the development of gated communities, and elsewhere Atkinson and Flint (drawing on the notion of "splintered" cities developed by Graham and Marvin 2001) argue strongly that the segregation is not restricted to the gated communities themselves (as protected places) but goes much further to produce protected spaces for elite and middle class groups in the city that link work, home, and leisure, effectively enabling them to "escape from the urban realm" (Atkinson and Flint 2004, p. 889). Instead, it is suggested, that they "are linked by patterns of movement which are detached from their social contexts, promoting a cognitive map of the city inhabited by like-minded individuals that generate socially homo- geneous contact absent of potential threats and encounters. The dependence on, and use of cars can be seen as an extension of gating and 'bubbling' – the orchestrated management of perceived risk spaces and social contact while moving around the public realm in shielded corridors" (Atkinson and Flint 2004, p. 889).

However, this is not just a process affecting or involving social elites. So, for example, Young (1999) describes the city as a space "of barriers, excluding and filtering," much of which he suggests can be seen as "defensive exclusion" rather than the deliberate exclusion by the powerful of those who might threaten them (Young 1999, p. 18). At its simplest and most mundane this is reflected in the spread of suburbia (see, e.g. Clapson 2003; Schoon 2001). Increasingly – perhaps in the face of increased uncertainty and risk (Bauman 2000; Beck 1992) – cities are "imagined as landscapes of risk" (Back and Keith 2004, p. 59), which leaves urban residents seeking to build their own forms of security and protection and to buy into others, as a taken-for-granted part of their daily lives.

There has been a significant rise in the use of private security services, particularly in the United States, but also more widely. Today there are more private than public police in most Western states (Nellis 2000, p. 116). In the United States there are over 1.5 m privately employed security staff compared with only 500,000 police officers employed by public agencies (Euchner and McGovern 2003, p. 277). It has been argued that the broader shift away from an emphasis on finding ways of integrating different social groups through welfare leads to an emphasis instead on the generalized containment of crime, which effectively means it can be privatized, creating a sense of security for those being protected or protecting themselves, rather than the identification and pursuit of criminals (Lea 1997, p. 53).

Euchner and McGovern comment that, "Many cities now resemble checkerboards, with certain high-profile neighborhoods protected by private security, and other neighborhoods protected by public cops" (Euchner and McGovern 2003, p. 277). Security is also privatized in a range of consumption places, from the clubs and pubs of the "24 Hour" city to the large and inclosed shopping malls. Processes of securitization help to create spaces within which it becomes possible to "pursue pleasure" (Rose, quoted in Raco 2003, p. 1871), through the pursuit of a "strategy of 'controlled spontaneity'" (Coleman 2003, p. 32). Indeed, the apparently clear cut division between state policing and private suppliers is itself increasingly unsustainable since the relationships between the two are increasingly close, overlapping and interconnected. So, for example, the use of CCTV (Closed Circuit Television) as a technology of surveillance in the United Kingdom, effectively draws other agencies into the process of policing, since it is often managed by (civilian) local authorities or by private companies (Fyfe 2004, pp. 50–2).

The fundamental aims of these initiatives are to reduce opportunities for criminal behavior and, through architectural design, to create an environment that will encourage people to behave well. Developers seek to design out features such as climbable drainpipes, vulnerable skylights, blank walls and dead spaces, that is, spaces with no ownership. The intention is to remove potential hiding places, so that, for example, green spaces are also planned with low trees which provide no cover (Raco 2003, pp. 1881–2). And CCTV also helps to design out undesirable people through surveillance and (possibly more important) the threat of surveillance. One critical commentator powerfully summarizes this to suggest that "the accelerative trafficking of shoppers and pedestrians can now be freeze-framed and dissected down to the tiniest pixels . . . where both public and private police forces treat you as potentially guilty until proved irrelevant" (Fitzpatrick 2001, p. 224).

Some of the consequences of the apparently insatiable search for "defensible space" (Newman 1972) are rather paradoxical. Instead of creating greater feelings of security in suburban areas, in gated areas or in areas with neighborhood watch schemes, or even in shopping malls overseen by CCTV, the creation of more protection seems to have been accompanied by increased concerns about crime and increased insecurity, potentially reinforcing "a decline in communal trust and mutual support" (McLaughlin and Muncie 1999, p. 135. See also Low 2003 on the new fears of those living in the gated communities of the United States).

Those captured on CCTV become redefined as somehow threatening, or at any rate "different" or "other," in part because the technical process of reproduction means they lose those identifying features which define them as "human" and sympathetic. Nowhere is this more apparent than in the ubiquitous television programs that ask us to respond to the images of criminal behavior by identifying those committing it – or, still more powerfully, in the images of both the failed and successful suicide bombers who hit London's public transport system in July 2005. If the camera as a form of "gaze" generally provides a means "through which we are socially ratified or negated as spectacle" (Silverman 1996), then CCTV is a particularly powerful means of negation, even if it can also be subverted to produce images suitable for creating spectacle out of the apparently ordinary – four men with rucksacks preparing to board a train in Luton.

The use of CCTV and the development of private shopping malls helps to create "safe" spaces, but it also helps to confirm the existence of other places as unsafe, even as certain behavior is defined as unacceptable (see, e.g. Fyfe 1997, pp. 257–8). Signs of disorder are effectively removed to other places, where CCTV works in other ways – it operates to discipline those who live in disadvantaged neighborhoods and removes disorder from high status places of spectacle and consumption (Johnstone 2004, p. 88). The main effect of the use of CCTV is that it moves rather than reducing crime (NACRO 2002). Coleman describes the use of CCTV as part of a *"normative strategy of spatial ordering"* (Coleman 2004, p. 200), suggesting that what he calls a process of urban reclamation is taking place, one in which issues of social order are redefined in spatial terms (Coleman 2003).

The wider use of new technologies of law enforcement can be seen to generate new "landscapes of domination" (Nunn 2001). Nunn highlights the existence of techniques relating to locational monitoring, including the use of ankle bracelets and video surveillance, and points to the way in which processes of monitoring help to define the "other" as problematic, noting in particular the way in which they are able to characterize one neighborhood as more "criminal" than another. The operation of the new technologies of surveillance highlights and emphasizes the differences between neighborhoods, since that is why they are monitored.

This helps to reinforce understandings of the problem as one of "place management" as a means of "representing and maintaining order within the city" (Coleman 2003, p. 24). The focus, suggests Coleman, is on the rehabilitation of space, rather than people, "seeking out the forces of urban 'degeneration' and contaminants of the urban civic aesthetic" through processes of surveillance and the power of inspection (Coleman 2004, p. 204). Using the case of Brussels, Baeten (2001) similarly explores the ways in which "mainstream urban planning" has attempted "to tame the urban wilderness" and notes the extent to which "the unwanted city is suppressed through displacement, surveillance and control" (Baeten 2001, p. 55). It is, of course, in these areas of crime management and the taming of the "urban wilderness" that the echoes of Rose's visions of the technologizing of politics, the mapping of social processes and individual behavior and (even) the rise of self-discipline through privatized forms of security, are at their strongest (Rose 1999; see also Chapter 3).

Managing Disorder

The emphasis is on creating forms of self-management, alongside punitive policing where necessary. As Back and Keith put it, "The project of community safety and crime reduction through self-government contains within it both a moralizing reinvention of individual selves and also some straightforward disciplinary measures" (Back and Keith 2004, p. 59). The direct criminalization of previously legal behavior may be avoided, as the emphasis is placed on finding ways of encouraging more "responsible" behavior, often giving the organizational role to agencies not previously identified as part of the criminal justice system. But the corollary of this seems to be that in practice wider processes of criminalization take place, with particular groups (and particular spaces) being specifically identified as more likely to cause or experience crime and disorder.

So, the identification of individuals undertaking actions which are seen to be inappropriate may serve to "irresponsibilize" particular targets as a first step towards "their criminalization and/or exclusion from public space" (Coleman 2003, p. 28). Coleman (2004, p. 207) argues that these processes not only do not protect the vulnerable – such as homeless people and small time traders – but in practice serve to further stigmatize them. And he also goes further to suggest that by identifying these places (and these behaviors) as antisocial (or criminal) other places of crime are hidden – particularly those of corporate crime, which may be pursued in the very buildings being protected by CCTV, but also in other spaces that are deemed to be private (e.g. domestic space, where violence against women or children remains hidden).

In his discussion of the US "war on drugs" Goetz (1996) highlights the ways in which actions which are not strictly responses to crime nevertheless have to be understood as crime management, making it possible to target those thought likely to commit crime, even when no evidence of a crime has been discovered. So, for example in cases he considers using drug raids as a basis on which to evict tenants, even when no drugs are found. A similar point might be made about the development of Anti Social Behavior Orders (ASBOs) in the United Kingdom – while ASBOs themselves do not immediately draw individuals into the criminal justice system, once an ASBO is breached individuals are liable to legal sanction pursued through the criminal courts. They are orders that may be imposed by police or the local authority on anyone whose behavior is thought likely to cause alarm, distress or harassment. Breaches of such orders (like other civil orders) can be dealt with by criminal sanction (nearly one-third are breached and around half of those are punished by imprisonment), so the slide into criminalization is direct. The technology itself is part of this process – for example in the decisions taken in several UK shopping malls to exclude those wearing hooded sweatshirts and other headgear that makes individual identification by CCTV more difficult.

In a sense, this approach is characteristic of the methods adopted more generally by the New Labour government – seeking to find ways of using law, but not criminal law, to target "potential" offenders, as part of the attempt to find ways of changing behavior – to find ways of making people responsible for their own behavior, "defining problems in advance and clamping down on any hits of abnormality" (Fitzpatrick 2001, p. 221). So, for example, legislation has introduced a range of possibilities – child safety orders, local child curfews as well as antisocial behavior orders. The first makes it possible to identify a child as being at risk and placing him or her under the supervision of a social worker, and has been reinforced by the responsibility now placed on Youth Inclusion and Support Panels (multiagency planning bodies involving social services, police, health, schools and sometimes community organizations) to identify the 7–13 year olds most at risk and engage them in "programmes" (Muncie 2006, p. 10). Individuals are referred to these panels by a range of agencies and an individual support plan is agreed. Youth Offending Teams have been set up in all local authority areas in England and Wales to tackle young people's antisocial behavior, and not just those identified as "offenders" (i.e. those found guilty of criminal acts) but also to ensure that those at risk are diverted from crime and antisocial behavior. The second gives councils the power to apply a curfew on children in specific areas after 9.00 PM, but it is, perhaps, ASBOs that have attracted the most attention. Although ASBOs are more broadly applied, young people in urban areas have been their main target in practice (summarized from Muncie 2006).

What has come to be called Zero Tolerance Policing (even if the specific term is often avoided by the police themselves) is used to help clear the high status streets of undesirables, moving them to other places (see, e.g. Atkinson 2003, pp. 1836–9). The argument is that dealing with low level social misbehavior is part of the process of making it unacceptable, removing the evidence of disorder (what Douglas so evocatively has called "matter out of place") (Douglas 1966) in order to make it less likely that other forms of misbehavior (and criminal behavior) will take place, as well as to attract back ordinary or respectable people into the use of previously threatening places. This is, perhaps, most famously captured in the argument that the first step is to make sure that broken windows are no longer tolerated, since evidence that no one cares is itself likely to foster or encourage further disorderly behavior (Kelling and Coles 1996). If the window is repaired, then the "message is that the community notices and cares about any threat to stability and order," whereas, if it is not "the community advertises its vulnerability to future breaches of order and respect" (Euchner and McGovern 2003, p. 257). In this context, as Mitchell (2003) notes, disorder is identified as "the primary threat facing urban neighborhoods" and broken windows are taken to be "a metaphor for 'disorderly behavior' "(Mitchell 2003, p. 199–200). The key task is to ensure that those likely to be responsible for "disorderly behavior" (even where it is not strictly illegal) are disciplined and, where possible, removed.

The prime model used as a global example of best practice has been New York in the 1990s, when Rudolph Giuliani was Mayor and William Bratton was Police Commissioner (and the two have become iconic symbols of success). It has been argued that by creating "a more attractive public realm," that is one in which the "vague sense of unpleasantness" associated with a reluctance to deal with petty crimes and disorderly behavior on the streets, in the parks and on the public transport networks of the city was explicitly challenged, people themselves became more confident about challenging such behavior, themselves becoming "eyes on the street." In other words, "once the city's public spaces look more inviting and safe, people repopulate public spaces – and bring even more surveillance by ordinary people on the streets" (Euchner and McGovern 2003, p. 260).

The basis of this approach is that it is for the good of us all – it appeals to the "public," that is those of us who will use the space responsibly – so it helps to define the users in those terms, too, with the expectation that we will discipline ourselves and, indeed, others using the space. So, for example, a proposal to create a Business Improvement District in the center of Liverpool effectively promises the privatization of a series of streets (although they remain open for public uses of consumption) and is summarized by its proponents as "developing a series of quarters for the area which will have security staff making sure that people maintain reasonable standards of behavior" (Indymedia 2003, quoted in Coleman 2004, p. 207). The clear expectation is that the maintenance of "reasonable standards of behavior" is something on which we can all agree – indeed who could disagree?

The precise form taken in securing private and public spaces for commerce and acceptable forms of social interaction may be negotiated differently in particular cities and areas within cities, but the drive for the creation of secure spaces is unquestionable and is unquestionably associated with major regeneration and renewal projects in cities across the globe (e.g. in the case of China, see Wu 2004, pp. 419–20), as well as with the rise of the entrepreneurial city (see, e.g. Belina and Helm 2003; Raco 2003). Coleman (2004) quotes a typical document of the municipal entrepreneurs, reporting on the development of an initiative in Liverpool: "Developing a Safer City is an essential element of the holistic approach to promoting Liverpool as a safe, vibrant, regenerating city, which is attractive to inward investors and supports a high quality of life for residents and visitors" (Liverpool City Council 1997, p. 1; quoted in Coleman 2004, p. 203).

This process is not straightforward, however, since as Harvey (1989b) puts it the entrepreneurial city "has to appear as an innovative, exciting, creative, and safe place to live or to visit, to play and consume in" (Harvey 1989b, p. 9). Merrifield asks pointedly: "Why do we feel drawn to things in cities which we hate and which we are battling to stamp out?" (Merrifield 2000, p. 474). Similar tensions are also identified in the official discourses of government policy – so, for example, a report prepared on Scotland's cities suggests that the "different requirements may be contradictory . . . People wish freedom to express themselves and meet new people, but they also want security and safety . . . City centre residents want 'buzz' but they also want to have peace and quiet in their own homes" (Scottish Executive 2002, p. 128).

This is a point recognized by Lees, who comments that, "The rhetoric of urban renaissance yearns for heterogeneity, but in practice harmony and stability are often emphasized over other forms of urban experience" (Lees 2003a, p. 630). Along similar lines Mitchell (2003) asks whether "designed diversity has so thoroughly replaced the free interaction of strangers that the ideal of an unmediated political public space is wholly unrealistic" (Mitchell 2003, p. 142). He charts the way in which public space has been redefined within America's cities through soft as well as hard approaches. The clearance of the homeless and "aggressive" beggars from the streets has largely been justified in terms which emphasize the extent to which they interfere with the use of the same space by "normal" people – that is those engaged in shopping or travel to work – as well as the use of the space to support more productive activities. He forcibly notes the paradox that public space is the only space to which the homeless have access to pursue activities others might pursue in private spaces (including the most basic and mundane, from sleeping to urinating), arguing that the public policy being espoused is inappropriate to the problem being identified – at least, if it is expected to reflect the needs faced by the homeless.

In practice, Mitchell argues, the securitization of the city (reinforced by reactions to the attacks on New York in 2001 and in a series of European cities since then) limits the opportunities and quality of life of those being protected as much as those from whom they are supposedly being protected: "through these laws and other means, cities seek to use a seemingly stable, ordered urban landscape as a positive inducement to continued investment and to maintain the viability of current investment in core areas (by showing merchants, for example, that they are doing something to keep shoppers coming downtown)" (Mitchell 2003, p. 177).

The tensions that exist in seeking to manage disorder are apparent in these arguments, since they seek to hold in balance the "cityness" of cities (with all the "buzz" and even "spectacle" implied by such a notion) with security for those who live in and use the cities. Zukin (1995, p. 276) discusses the process of using "aesthetics to banish fear" to construct public spaces (or hybrid public-private spaces) in which certain behaviors simply become unacceptable, but – of course – this promises exclusion as well as inclusion. This is "their" city as much as "ours," but only as long as "they" accept the rules of the game, or only reinterpret them in ways that are deemed to enrich it, to reinforce the spectacle through forms of transgression that are themselves incorporated into the spectacle, whether they take the form of "unconventional" architecture or space for skateboarders on London's South Bank. As a way of summing up the tensions, Zukin introduces the notion of hybridity, suggesting that the same space may (at the same time) be capable of interpretation "as both a safe and attractive urban space and one that forcefully imposes a specific vision of security and civility" (Zukin 1995, p. 294). Making a space safe (in this case Bryant Park in New York) for some users (office workers, women) may also result in the expulsion of others (the homeless, drug dealers) (Zukin 1995, p. 275).

Lees' study of the conflict between youth and local businesses in downtown Portland, suggests that the outcomes may sometimes be rather more ambivalent. She records a series of complaints from shopkeepers, which can be summed up in the words of one of them: "These kids scare off my customers. It shouldn't be allowed" (Lees 2003a, p. 624). The young people, by contrast, see the public spaces of downtown as spaces within which "they can meet without adult interference" and argue that their behavior should not be seen as threatening. While the overall balance of public policy and the policing of the area tends to favor the demands of the local businesses, the uneasy experience of not so peaceful coexistence also seems to survive.

The process of managing disorder may, in other words, be more ambiguous than either its proponents or its severest critics recognize. One attempt to explore this distinguishes between different forms of Zero Tolerance Policing suggesting that "zero tolerance of particular incivilities may actually enhance the confidence of some groups in using the city," while other forms "may severely inhibit freedoms in the city" and seeking to pursue the latter may also undermine trust in and support for those doing the policing (Fyfe 2004, p. 48). Similarly, it is suggested that CCTV might be mobilized positively through the determination of behavior to be scrutinized and when intervention should be allowed. The ambiguity of CCTV is already widely recognized because of the way in which it both promises greater security but also seems to highlight the existence of danger (and even a new fear of being watched). Fyfe suggests that the possibilities of the new crime control technologies are more open than is sometimes believed, since there is scope for more extensive popular engagement in their management (Fyfe 2004, pp. 52–3). Merrifield is more fundamentally critical of the new arrangements, commenting that "One can't help wondering whether the baby of disorder might be getting ditched with the criminal bathwater [since] While it is evident that disorder can lead to crime it is also evident that not all disorder is criminal" (Merrifield 2000, p. 484). He might also be rather more sceptical about the democratic potential of existing arrangements, but, from his rather different perspective, he, too, stresses the need to build cities of tolerance which require the construction of spaces within which it is possible to negotiate about what is "good" and what "bad," what can live side by side with other activities and what may need to be criminalized (Merrifield 2000. See also Mouffe 1993 for a discussion of some of the principles on which a pluralist democratic order based on forms of nonantagonistic – or "agonistic" – negotiation might be based).

Towards a Punitive Urbanism or Constructing New Moral Spaces?

Dominant understandings of urban rioting draw from a powerful mix of images – Detroit in the 1960s, Paris in 1968 for the romantics, the streets of Belfast and maybe even Beirut in the 1970s, Brixton in 1981 and 1985, Los Angeles in 1992, the *banlieues* of Paris in 2005, burning cars, bricks, broken glass, Molotov cocktails, rubber bullets, and young people with their faces covered by scarves. Such events are interpreted as explosions of rage, often racialized, always pored over for the bigger messages they seem to contain about the state of society. The reality is often more mundane, as much to do with the particular failures of those seeking to manage disorder – the police and other agencies. But it is also clear that all the events that are labeled as riots are not the same.

So, for example, in her review of the riots that took place in a number of British cities in 1991/2, Campbell discusses a particular case of young people on one housing estate whose behavior (in taking over public space for off road motorbiking) had for some time been seen as unpleasant and about which older residents had complained. And (in an echo of Wright Mills) asks why "a public order problem of ten years' standing became a major public order crisis" (Campbell 1993, p. 286). She argues that the problems were effectively ignored at first, because "they happened on *estates*, in *class communities* overwhelmed by *unemployment* and *crime*" (Campbell 1993, p. 302). Power and Tunstall (1997) make similar points: the areas in which the riots took place were council estates, but mainly characterized by traditional houses and gardens (rather than high rise blocks or inner city locations). Those involved were mainly young white men and the areas had higher than average concentrations of young people, among whom unemployment levels were high. As Campbell also noted there had been high levels of violence and other criminal behavior before the riots, with little action having been taken to deal with it. When the police finally became involved the 'riots' took the form of running battles between police and young men over who controlled the area, leading to significant damage of community facilities including shops and other businesses (Power and Tunstall 1997).

The riots that took place in a number of England's northern cities in the early years of the twenty-first century expressed a rather different dynamic, since (as discussed in Chapter 4) they took place in predominantly "Asian" areas of the inner city. However, they, too, raised fears about the young, since the main participants were young "Asian" – and "Muslim" – men, who were challenging the "traditional" structures of authority within "their" communities, questioning the role of those that had been identified themselves as "community leaders." In echoes of colonial practice, such "leaders" had also been identified by urban managers as the routes into managing these, potentially troublesome, communities, so it was this relationship, too, that was being questioned (Amin 2003).

Davis (2002) forcibly contrasts the response of Johnson to the US riots of the 1960s (when the Model Cities Program was pushed through Congress) with the response to the Los Angeles riots of the 1990s. He argues that instead of a policy response focused on the needs of those living in cities and facing the challenges of poverty, unemployment and social disorganization, the response of Bush (the father, not the son) (largely endorsed by Clinton) was to introduce "Weed and Seed" as a policy through the Justice Department – the problem was redefined as a problem of the "gangs," disorder and drugs. The gangs were to be dealt with by heavy policing ("weeding" out the leaders getting them off the streets and into prison) and this was to be coupled with job training and community development (aimed at providing "seeds" of positive opportunity to those left) (Davis 2002, p. 240). Although the legislation promised that 80 percent would be spent on "seeding" and 20 percent on "weeding," in practice the proportions were reversed with the vast majority of the funds going to criminal justice (Goetz 1996, p. 540).

Davis concludes that this approach effectively prefigures the "ultimate absorption of welfare state by the police state" although he also concedes that in practice spending was too low to make such a policy work effectively (Davis 2002, p. 244). We may, as he says, be seeing the end of 'urban reformism' – but it seems that the cities (or some of them) have been so completely written off, that there is not even enough of a policy drive to replace that reformism with an alternative comprehensive framework. As Goetz puts it, US "urban policy is less about revitalizing cities and neighborhoods and combating the disinvestment of capital, and it is more and more about controlling the dangerous classes" (Goetz 1996, p. 539), abandoning "physical rehabilitation and social development policies, replacing them with criminalization of the poor" (Goetz 1996, p. 547).

This argument is taken further by Wacquant (2002) who identifies the rise of the prison as a fundamental element in the new urban policy, particularly as part of the management of the black ghetto populations. Since, he argues, the ghettoes can no longer contain the population which (after the riots of the 1960s) is seen "not only as deviant and devious but downright dangerous," the prison is extended into what he calls "a single *carceral continuum* which entraps a redundant population of younger black men (and increasingly women)" (Wacquant 2002, pp. 52–3). A similar approach seems to have been adopted in Brazil, where the policing of the *favelas* is "more about containing violence in the areas where it was deemed socially acceptable, namely *favelas*, rather than combating it. As a result, members of state and federal authorities . . . have promoted military-style police operations, and have trained army units to intervene to maintain social order," which has effectively " 'criminalized' their residents" (Amnesty International 2005, pp. 1–2).

In the US context, Peck (2003) takes these arguments further to suggest that that there has been a shift from welfare state to penal state – so that instead of neo-liberalism bringing less government, it brings different government reflected in the use of prison as a racialized strategy for "brutally" regulating the urban poor. With a prison population of over 2 million, suggests Peck, this cannot be seen as a marginal issue, particularly when 70 percent of them are black or Latino and two-thirds of African-American men in their 20s living in the North-East cities of the United States are either in prison, on probation or on parole (Peck 2003, p. 226. See also Young 1999, p. 18). Nor, he argues, can the dramatic growth in the prison population be seen as a response to an increased threat of crime, since levels of crime have been falling. He concludes, therefore, that it is an expression of the emergence of a postwelfare state, one in which the state continues to play a major role, but one that is focused on regulating and disciplining the poor rather than seeking to provide them with forms of welfare support.

What such writers highlight is the rise of a postwelfare policy discourse, in which policing and community safety are given the status that welfare rights were given in the Keynesian welfare state. In its most extreme forms, the process has been characterized as one of "revanchism," the revenge of the middle class gentrifiers and developers on those who threaten their security (Smith 1996a,b). This approach blames "the failure of post 1968 urban policy on the populations it was supposed to assist" (Smith 1996b, p. 227). Smith contrasts the confidence of the urban gentrifiers of the 1980s, with the "unabated litany of crime and violence, drugs and unemployment, immigration and depravity – all laced through with terror" which character-ized the 1990s (Smith 1996a, p. 227). He believes that this shift has generated more active attacks on the poor and the homeless, some of which he powerfully explores, charting the active ways in which the streets (and parks) of New York have been cleared of the homeless, highlighting a process of enforced separation, and protection for the middle classes through increasingly harsh policing. The revanchist city is, he says, "a divided city, where the victors are increasingly defensive of their privilege . . . and increasingly vicious defending it" (Smith 1996a, p. 227).

The notion of the "revanchist" city captures one aspect of the security state that it can be argued urban policy has become. However, it is incomplete, in part because it too definitively dismisses what Atkinson (2003), echoing Zukin, summarizes as "Domestication by *Cappuccino*," but more important because it seems to exclude the possibility of more community-based approaches. Some interpretations of such approaches can be seen as repro-ducing the divisions identified by theories of "revanchism." So, for example, Goetz (1996) questions the extent to which "community-based" crime prevention programs are genuinely community-based. He argues both that they are usually initiatives of local government or the police which are then taken up by community organizations and that they encourage a partic-ular understanding of the problems faced by the areas in which they are launched, since they are "essentially top-down policy models that impose upon neighborhoods one interpretation of the problems they face; an interpretation that emphasizes social deviance" . . . and "can easily polarize a community as middle class citizens organize against the 'bad elements' in the neighborhood" (Goetz 1996, p. 541).

However, this may understate the extent to which 'community' can be mobilized to develop self-policing, as much as policing from the outside (see also Chapter 4). Garland (2001) starts from a similar understanding as Smith, in the sense that he believes that it is the threat of crime for the middle classes, which has led to a changed approach to policing and community safety. "The open, porous, mobile society of strangers that is late modernity," he argues, "has given rise to crime control practices that seek to make society less open and less mobile: to fix identities, quarantine whole sections of the population, erect boundaries, close off access" (Garland 2001, p. 165). Garland also acknowledges the "revanchist" aspect of the new urban policing in what he calls punitive segregation as one of two fundamental strategies he identifies as characterizing the new regime. He defines punitive segregation through the expanded use of prisons, but it might equally be applied to the threat and sometimes reality that effectively defines and segregates particular neighborhoods as criminal – that is those where community action has failed to bring renewal, neighborhoods which "are not only seen as a social problem in their own right, but also as a more pervasive threat to the moral order or social cohesion of cities" (Forrest and Kearns 2001, p. 2133). The relationship between punitive segregation and the management of the cities is apparent in the ways in which penal policy and welfare policy interact, determining rights to welfare outside as well as inside prison. So, for example, Haney (2004) charts the way in which US penal policy has also had significant effects on the way in which women have experienced welfare – reducing the rights of those who have committed crimes (including those related to drug use) to forms of welfare payment, reinforcing the message of personal responsibility.

The second strategy Garland identifies, from his review of the United States as well as the United Kingdom experience, is what he calls preventative partnership (i.e. responsibilities beyond the state) (Garland 2001, p. 140). This is, for example, reflected in the BIDS (Business Improvement Districts) programs which have been initiated in the central areas of many US cities and taken up as a model in several UK cities. These initiatives (born in New York, but spreading to other cities in the United States, to the United Kingdom and through Europe) provide ways of mobilizing commercial interests to maintain and protect the areas within which their businesses are located, through "soft" (for example, through street cleaning, the provision of street furniture and decoration) as well as potentially "harder" forms of intervention (through the use of neighborhood patrols). They fund themselves through a voluntary system of taxation on the owners of property and businesses, that is outside the traditional forms of public finance, and in some cases (e.g. in Central Manhattan) are in a position to invest in infrastructural and other commercial development (Zukin 1995, pp. 33–8; 66–7). Zukin highlights the way in which such arrangements construct public spaces and a "public culture open to all but governed by the private sector," that is one that "derives from commercial culture" focused on space that encourages and enables consumption (Zukin 1995, pp. 36–7).

Notions of community have also been mobilized to similarly achieve forms of self-policing. In the United Kingdom there has been a shift of emphasis from policing from the outside, towards policing from within communities, and indeed an emphasis on the management of social order (including acts that are not strictly "criminal") through communities. This approach has its origins in policy developments of the 1980s (expressed, e.g. in the emphasis of the Scarman Committee report on the 1981 Brixton riots, which raised the possibility of community involvement in the planning of policing). The "Safer Cities" initiative launched in the late 1980s explicitly highlighted the issue of urban crime, setting out to mobilize "communities" in the fight against crime (Walklate 1996). The dramatic extension of such initiatives in the 1990s was reflected in the creation of community safety partnerships throughout England and Wales, and the identification of antisocial behavior as a problem that needs to be tackled (see, e.g. McLaughlin 2002, p. 91). As we have seen, the introduction of antisocial behavior orders (ASBOs) in 2003 highlights the understanding that protection by lock and key (individual security measures, but also design features) or active policing are insufficient – what is needed, it has been strongly argued, is to challenge behavior that might in itself not be criminal, but which helps to create an atmosphere in which crime was more likely (McLaughlin 2002, p. 81).

The aim is to build active and responsible communities (see also Chapter 4). The strategy combines self-discipline, with externally imposed policies for neighborhood renewal and the appointment of neighborhood wardens and neighborhood management coupled with CCTV (Johnstone 2004). It is stressed that "People living in deprived areas experience higher levels of disorder and other neighborhood problems," which makes this a specific target of intervention (Prime Minister's Strategy Unit 2005, p. 55). The aim is to find ways in which high crime localities may be " 'disciplined' in order in order to encourage desirable social behavior, thereby recreating or strengthening local communities and families and improving the quality of life" (McLaughlin 2002, p. 92). Walklate (2002) reports from her research on local Crime and Community Safety Partnerships (later relabeled as Crime and Disorder Reduction Partnerships) to suggest that the dominant understanding underpinning their work in practice is that "crime is a local problem to be *managed* locally, not necessarily prevented or reduced" (Walklate 2002, p. 71; see also Hughes 1997).

In contemporary Britain it is hard to escape from the rhetoric that fuels an urban policy focused on crime and community safety or disorder management (sometimes captured under what has come to be called the "respect" agenda), even if, as Johnstone (2004, p. 75) notes, that form of urban policy is pursued through the Home Office, rather than the departments of government that have been given responsibility for mainstream urban policy since the mid 1970s. At local level policies on lighting, traffic management and protected space have all been developed in response to fears about crime. Johnstone succinctly summarizes the arguments that point to the downward spiral that is seen to be associated with crime and disorder in particular neighborhoods, not only, it is argued, increasing "the fear of crime" and reducing "the quality of life for residents of affected areas," but also reinforcing a slide into a world in which, "Serious crime, violence and, in some places, racial conflict, become common currency." As a result, "The demise of the neighborhood is complete" (Johnstone 2004, p. 78). As early as 1983, the Home Office was identifying this process as crucial to urban policy, beginning to endorse "the theory that as neighborhoods decline, those living there become less willing to control the uncivil and anti-social activities of others and that in time this breeds an atmosphere where crime is acceptable" (quoted in McLaughlin 2002, p. 83). It is in this context that Whitehead (2004) argues that the policies of government are determined to locate neighborhood as a "moral space" that is a space within which a moral renewal can be achieved, antisocial behavior reduced and residents protected from crime. He suggests that "certain codes of conduct and social responsibilities are now being constructed around neighborhood spaces" (Whitehead 2004, p. 63).

As Garland (2001) puts it, " 'The community' has become the all-purpose solution to every criminal justice problem" (Garland 2001, p. 123). "The state's new strategy is not to command

and control but rather to persuade and align, to organize, to ensure that the other actors play their part" (Garland 2001, p. 126). From this perspective the vision of urban policy as a policy of crime management and crime control is one that is not merely authoritarian (or revanchist), but also fundamentally "conservative" because of its focus on the building and rebuilding of forms of community, capable of surviving in a hostile (globalizing) environment. The mix of urban policy tools being developed in this postwelfare world is a complex one that brings together a package characterized by forms of punitive segregation, revanchism, the designing out of opportunities for criminal behavior, and a belief in the possibility of making communities responsible for the management of social order within particular local areas. The various forms of policy exist in an uneasy tension, even as attempts are made to reconcile them. The choice seems to be between isolating, managing and policing the disorderly and disorderly areas and somehow seeking to integrate, responsibilize and "domesticate" them. In the new urban policy, the urban is increasingly understood as a key site across which an active process of responsibilization must be pursued. Unfortunately, the urban is also the place where new challenges, new divisions and new forms of disorder are continually being generated.

If the emphasis is on the "unruliness" of cities (see Pile et al. 1999), then urban policy – as a state response – can be understood as the process by which attempts are made to manage that unruliness, and – above all – by which the dangerous populations that inhabit some areas of the city are kept under control. In some cases the areas may be sanitized and in others they are simply policed with their boundaries being carefully controlled. In other words, attempts are made to create order by the spatial policing of heterogeneity (see McLaughlin and Muncie 1999, pp. 117–25). In this context, the pursuit of urban policy through forms of policing supported by the planning system can effectively operate to imprison some people in the dangerous places in which they live, while apparently "protecting" others. It is often accepted that those living in such areas are the biggest victims, but the main emphasis seems to be placed on defining them as the "other" who need to be managed, if the rest of us are to retain a secure environment, even if they are offered the prospect of saving themselves through a process of community engagement and revitalization.

Chapter 6

Competitiveness, the Market, and Urban Entrepreneurialism

In retrospect, it now almost seems as if the whole understanding of what constitutes urban policy was turned on its head in the 1980s. If the approach of the 1960s and 1970s encouraged a focus on struggles in and against the state, around issues of collective consumption and social reproduction, the 1980s saw a shift towards ways of thinking that began to redefine urban policy in terms of economic regeneration and increasingly as an expression of urban competitiveness. In part this shift reflected a widespread disillusion with the promise of the Keynesian Welfare State, which came under attack from both left and right: from the left it was argued that it brought mechanisms of social control without either challenging the central inequalities of class and power or even delivering reforms capable of reducing levels of poverty (see, e.g. O'Connor 1973; Gamble 1985); from the right it was argued that state spending on welfare and state regulation merely served to undermine the efficiency of business, by demanding bigger and bigger shares of the income generated from "productive" investment (see, e.g. Bacon and Eltis 1976; Selsdon 1985).

In other words, from one perspective it was argued that programs whose starting point is the search for social welfare are likely to fail in achieving their ends because they do not challenge fundamental economic inequalities, while from the other it was suggested that they are more likely to undermine a country's (or a city's) economic base than to deliver the hoped for social benefits. Each was underpinned by a shared understanding that the "economic" was paramount, that it was economic prosperity which determined social welfare, even if the policy conclusions to be drawn were sharply different. The problem of the cities was increasingly defined as a structural problem – one of economic decline – rather than one faced by people or communities in need of help.

Echoes of this broad understanding found their expression in the legislative initiatives of the late 1970s, which began to shift the emphasis of urban policy in both the United States and the United Kingdom. Many analysts of the development of urban policy in Britain have argued that there was a dramatic shift in the late 1970s from an approach which stressed the social pathology of urban communities (based around a version of the "culture of poverty" thesis) towards one which stressed structural issues – essentially the need for economic regeneration. It has been strongly argued (e.g. by Lawless 1981, 1988; Higgins et al. 1983; Ginsburg 1999) that there was a systematic shift from people-based and community-oriented or welfarist approaches in the 1970s towards a more explicitly economic and property-led focus following on from the Inner Urban Areas Act of 1978, seeking to deal with what were argued to be the structural causes of inequality and deprivation.

The White Paper *Policy for the Inner Cities* (HMSO 1977) launched the vision that Britain's inner cities required economic regeneration, and promised to achieve this through partnerships across the private and public sectors. In practice this heralded the search for ways of encouraging business to invest in those areas, with the help of state subsidy. It was confidently asserted that, "The intellectual transformation of the debate surrounding the urban problem has been rapid and comprehensive, away from the simplistic assumptions adopted in the late 1960s towards a more economically oriented thesis" (Lawless 1981, p. 8). Atkinson and Moon (1994) similarly see the 1977 White Paper *Policy for the Inner Cities* and the 1978 Inner Urban Areas Act as watersheds. The White Paper, they argue, was the "first serious attempt by a government ... to understand the nature and causes of Britain's urban problems" (Atkinson and Moon 1994, p. 66). The government, it was said, had come up with "a much more valid diagnosis of the problem" than the old "social pathology approach" (Atkinson and Moon 1994, p. 75).

The shift to an economic focus was not at first associated with governments of the right. More radical authors had also increasingly emphasized the importance of the economy in defining the experience of the inner cities. So, for example, although the Community Development Projects were set up in the late 1960s within a paradigm that focused on the revitalization of local communities, by 1977 a collective report was produced which concluded that:

> Until policies are implemented which seriously challenge the rights of industry and capital to move freely about the country (not to mention the world) without regard for the welfare of workers and existing communities – who end up carrying the costs under the present system – the problems and inequalities generated by uneven capitalist development will persist (Community Development Project 1977a, p. 96).

The Inner Urban Areas Act and the Inner City Partnerships that flowed from it constituted one of the last gasps of the 1970s Labour government and sought to bring key players together to construct area-based development or "regeneration" policies. The areas themselves were arranged in a hierarchy through the cities of England and Wales (from partnership areas to program areas to designated areas) with different resources and arrangements for each. The partnership areas were identified as slices out of England's major conurbations (in the case of Birmingham, for example, the Inner City Partnership Area included most of the city apart from a suburban belt, although a "core area" incorporating all the inner city wards was also identified within it) rather than "neighborhoods" or "communities," because it was considered that the journey to work in newly created employment could not be restricted to such small areas, and also that economic decline over a wider area had itself affected particular neighborhoods, even where the industries concerned were not located within them.

There was a heavy stress on the reclamation of areas of industrial dereliction, which meant that the main significant partnership agencies were in the public sector – in addition to local and national government and health authorities they included many of the agencies that were later to be privatized (such as the Water Authorities and other nationalized utilities, such as British Gas and the regionalized electricity companies, as well as British Rail). At the core of the partnership approach was the familiar expectation of coordination, both between the various government agencies directly involved and with other organizations in the state, voluntary and private sectors. Within these areas what was being pursued was "a multiagency planning and implementation process" – a technical process based around the priorities of development, rather than a people-based or community-based set of initiatives (Stewart and Underwood 1982). However, as Atkinson and Moon (1994, pp. 78–81) note, in practice it proved impossible for the Partnerships to persuade key government departments to reorient mainstream spending to the newly defined inner cities, so that the level of resource directed towards the Partnership areas remained limited and cooperation between "partners" at local level was also limited, as each remained jealous of its own autonomy (similar points have been made about more recent initiatives, such as those arising from the New Deal for Communities program which are discussed in Chapter 4).

The structures themselves barely survived into the Thatcher era but that did not mean that economic development based urban policy was left to the tender mercies of the "new right." On the contrary, the first half of the 1980s was also the time of the "new urban left" or the "new municipal socialism" in the United Kingdom, with its promise of different approaches to economic regeneration (see, e.g. Boddy and Fudge 1984; Gyford 1985; Cochrane 1986b, 1988; Lansley et al. 1989). Several councils set up enterprise boards (most notably Greater London and the West Midlands), while others created larger employment or economic development departments (most notably in Sheffield).

The arguments underpinning these developments were clear: if local government continued to restrict itself to operating as provider of social services, picking up the pieces of economic decline and unemployment then it would never be able to meet the needs of local residents. Instead it was important to move actively into trying to manage or shape the local economy, generating welfare through such intervention and not just acting as a "safety net." The enterprise boards (and particularly the Greater London Enterprise Board) saw themselves as having the task of influencing economic change through the negotiation of planning agreements with enterprises (including a range of worker cooperatives) in which they invested or otherwise supported. The Greater London Council developed a series of major plans and strategies for the London economy – most notably in the form of the London Industrial Strategy, but also in strategies for the labor market and the finance sector (GLC 1985, 1986a,b). In Sheffield similar initiatives were developed with the aim of working with businesses and trade unions to develop employment that would guarantee security for city residents and encourage investment in training. A plan was developed for the reclaiming and reuse of the Lower Don Valley, previously a major center of large scale steel production and heavy engineering (see, e.g. Blunkett and Green 1983 and Lawless and Ramsden 1990 for discussions of Sheffield's approach to public policy).

The emphasis of all these initiatives was on the possibility of longer term investment that would enable older industrial communities to survive, through a process of repositioning, rather than a simple (and ultimately hopeless) defense of existing industry. It was argued that the "new right" (or neo-liberal) policies of Thatcherism led to closure of industry and the destruction of communities, without offering any prospect of revival. In retrospect it might be argued, as Eisenschitz and Gough (1996) do, that, even if these initiatives (which they label neo-Keynesian local economic development policies) might have mitigated the effects of neo-liberalism, they also made it easier for the ends of neo-liberalism to be achieved, because of the way in which they encouraged flexibility, sponsoring the creation of new "competitive" enterprises and fostering training programs that fitted workers for the new regime. But this was not how it was understood at the time. And the local authorities taking the lead in developing the new economic policies became the focus of government attention, which led to the abolition of the metropolitan counties (such as the GLC and the West Midlands). As a result the enterprise boards that survived became more narrowly focused and begin to redefine themselves as regional investment banks working closely with other financial institutions, (see, e.g. Cochrane and Clarke 1990), and providing a model of partnership with business that was later taken up by the Regional Development Agencies set up throughout England in 1999.

The Impact of the "New Right"

However, the shift in emphasis towards the economy as defining the limits of individual and social welfare was undoubtedly given its fullest expression in the Thatcher years, embodied in a fundamental move away from public sector initiative towards a public/private/not-for-profit partnership or post-Keynesian model (see, e.g. Solesbury 1993; Atkinson and Moon 1994; Lawless 1996). The argument that only economic success – and specifically market entrepreneurialism on the lines favored by the Thatcher governments – could bring urban regeneration seemed to have been won by the mid 1980s. The problem of the cities was defined as a problem of economic decline, which could only be solved by economic development. The structural problem was reinterpreted as a lack of entrepreneurialism and the need to "free" enterprise from state restrictions (e.g. reflected in the launch of enterprise zones) (see, e.g. Anderson 1990). Just as the Labour strategy for the late 1970s constructed urban areas in terms which fitted well with the government's broader understanding of the "British" problem (i.e. the need for economic modernization and regeneration) so the Conservative strategy of the 1980s constructed urban areas in terms which fitted well with their understanding of the "British" disease (i.e. broader dependency culture, lack of enterprise) (see, e.g. Eisenschitz and Gough 1993, pp. 59–75). The policy emphasis shifted away from helping the poor and seeking to tackle urban poverty, towards a view that such problems would sort themselves out, if the local economy could be made strong enough. Economic success would provide jobs and redevelopment in ways that would also transform the inner cities. This is an urban policy consistent with the broader shift towards what Jessop has identified as the Schumpeterian Competition State (Jessop 2002a, Ch. 3).

This shift in analytical as well as political focus had two main interrelated aspects, which tended to reinforce each other. The first highlighted the ways in which public policy (and urban policy in particular) could be and was being reinterpreted through the prism of the "new Right" (sometimes even then called "neo-liberal") ideology (see, e.g. Glennerster and Midgely 1991) (see also Chapter 7), while the second stressed the significance of competition between cities as a driver of policy development. In their review of urban policy in Britain and the United States, Barnekov et al. (1989) argue that the key underlying (and shared) principle of urban policy in the two countries relates to "an underlying confidence in the capacity of the private sector to create the conditions for personal and community prosperity ... a belief in the legitimacy of market values as the appropriate standard for community choice" (Barnekov et al. 1989, p. vii). Although they sometimes seem to be arguing that this is a universal (and culturally deeply-rooted) feature of policy making in the two countries, they also clearly chart a process of change in both countries which led to an increased emphasis on the economic competitiveness of business as the underlying justification for urban policy. The nature of this shift has been captured in Harvey's identification of a move from what he calls urban managerialism to urban entrepreneurialism, which highlights a move away from the management of cities within a framework of state sponsored planning and the delivery of services to residents to one dominated by competition for economic success (Harvey 1989b).

In the late 1970s and early 1980s, Barnekov et al. (1989) suggest that the aim of governments became to build or support the building of a globally competitive service oriented economy. In order "to accomplish this transition, the urban landscape had to be rearranged to allow for increasing mobility and spatial deconcentration of population and economic activities." The vision underlying this approach was that "of a market-led path to post-industrial society" (Barnekov et al. 1989, p. 5). Historically, it was argued that urban policies had acted as an obstacle to growth and successful economic restructuring, by imposing restrictions on development or by undertaking expenditure that represented an additional cost for business. Insofar as attempts were made to support existing employment or provide financial support to those living in cities who were unemployed, then they simply interfered with the efficient working of the market, undermining the competitiveness of employers and thus also of cities. Instead, it was argued, urban policy programs should be "directed at stimulating local economic development," since the prosperity of cities was seen to depend "on effective competition for industry, jobs and investments in a dynamic national economy that is shaped largely by the spatial and sectoral needs of private enterprise" (Barnekov et al. 1989, pp. 5 and 6). In other words, "As a strategy of urban regeneration, privatism ties the fortunes of cities to the vitality of their private sectors and concentrates community attention and resources on economic development and private investment" (Barnekov et al. 1989, p. 11).

There can be little doubt that what Barnekov et al. (1989) call privatism was the shared philosophical understanding of the Reagan administrations in the United States and the Thatcher governments in the United Kingdom through the 1980s. It is also clear that the new right (or neo-liberal) approaches embodied in this understanding were themselves the product of learning across the two countries between think tanks and political elites (see, e.g. Haylett 2003, pp. 65–6) as well as more widely across the globe, as Larner reminds us (Larner 2003). Private initiative was seen as the answer to a range of social and – above all – economic problems, and the state was seen as the barrier. At the core of this analysis was the view that welfare could only be delivered through economic success. The role of urban policy was to assist with wealth creation and emphasis was placed on the (re)creation of markets in inner urban areas – making those areas work productively again as sources of profitable production (see, e.g. Byrne 1997). Public-private partnership in property development (rather than public sector led and funded initiatives) was seen as the route to economic and social as well as physical regeneration (Fainstein 1995).

Just as in the mid 1970s Britain's problems were largely described in terms which stressed economic failure, so in the United States there was a similar "shift from social and political to economic perceptions of 'crisis'' (Smith 1988, p.115). Smith notes that "by the time Carter proposed a 'New partnership' to conserve American communities in March, 1978, the logic of the policy constituted a redefinition of urban crisis as a mere reflection of the general economic crisis," so that it "served to redirect federal 'urban policy' towards revitalizing not distressed cities but the increasingly footloose private sector" (Smith 1988, pp. 100 and 101). Indeed the logic seems to have been carried further in the United States than in the United Kingdom, to the extent that Peterson (reflecting the direction of change expressed through the 1980s and into the 1990s) argues that federal policies should simply have the task of supporting economic growth by allowing the necessary locational shifts, the necessary economic restructuring, to take place however painful it might be (Peterson 1985, pp. 24–5). Instead the state should simply deal with the frictional problems, enabling them to take place without causing excessive hardship so that "the federal government should concentrate its attention on policies that have no specifically urban component at all" (Peterson 1985, p. 25). A similar approach seems to have been adopted in Australia, where Troy suggests that one argument mobilized against any form of federal urban policy has been that "there is no such thing as an urban problem – you simply have to get the prices right." (Troy 2003, p. 229).

The key argument acknowledged the impact of the shift of employment and industry away from the older industrial cities but concluded that this was a process that needed to be accepted as an economic necessity, a necessary part of the process of economic renewal – "in the long run the fates and fortunes of specific places [should] be allowed to fluctuate" (President's Commission 1980b, p. 65, quoted in Barnekov et al. 1989, p. 102). According to this argument, a national urban policy might even undermine the prospect of fostering more general economic revival. Insofar as there was a role for urban policy, its expression was to be found at local rather than federal level so that the emphasis was placed by the Reagan administration on the need for cities to position themselves so that they could work with the private sector more effectively to meet their needs, to enhance the competitiveness of business and to make themselves more attractive to potential investors (Barnekov et al. 1989, p. 107).

The emphasis shifted, as the problem was reinterpreted: not so much to do with the pathology of residents (or at least not only that) but the failure of cities, particularly the older industrial cities, as productive units and generators of wealth (see, e.g. Lawless 1981, p. 8; Atkinson and Moon 1994, p. 75). The position is well summarized in the comment that from this perspective cities are not deemed to be "valuable cultural, social, or economic units except to the degree to which they contribute to a healthy national economy" (Robertson and Judd 1989, p. 314). Urban policy was transformed to fit with a wider national political rhetoric of economic regeneration, public-private partnership, and infrastructural investment to support development.

Public-Private Partnerships and Property Development

One of the key messages of the new urban policy was that cities needed to help themselves, to show that they could work in partnership with the private sector, to compete for investment from businesses by creating the "right sort" of local environment. Barnekov et al. (1989, p. 130) highlight the rise of "entrepreneurial cities" following the cutbacks sponsored by Reagan in the early 1980s. In this context, they argue, "It was not enough for city government to be responsive to the priorities of local business institutions; it was now necessary for the public sector to take the initiative in promoting business priorities" (Barnekov et al. 1989, p. 75). As a result, the need – or perceived need – for city governments to find ways of strengthening their ability to compete for private investment was taken for granted, particularly if it was accompanied by ways of accessing other sources of state funding. In the United States the search for policy leverage was endorsed in the introduction of the Urban Development Action Grant in 1977 (whose approach was later also taken up in the United Kingdom). Its main objective was "to stimulate private investment in severely distressed communities by providing a capital subsidy for economic development projects where there was a firm commitment of private resources" (Barnekov et al. 1989, p. 73). The local government involved had to show that there was some investment gap that had to be filled, as well as indicate how many jobs would be created and outline the social distress of the area. In practice, a private investor had to be committed in advance if the grant was to be forthcoming (which in practice meant investors had to be directly involved in the development of policy). The local council effectively became the dealmaker on local economic development projects, and – as far as the local community was concerned – its success was measured by the extent to which it was able to lever in federal and state resources to encourage development.

Therefore, for example, although the city-based campaigns for the winning of mega events, such as the Olympics, can be seen as prime examples of urban entrepreneurialism, as part of the competition between places for economic success (and city branding, which is discussed further in Chapter 7) they may be more important as ways of levering resources from public as well as private sources (see, e.g. Cochrane et al. 1996, 2002 and Jones and Ward 1998 for discussions of urban entrepreneurialism as a means of levering grants, rather than private investment). The process of levering in support, particularly from state agencies, has been described as "grantsmanship" and is a fundamental aspect of the politics pursued by many local governance regimes (Savitch and Kantor 2002, pp. 224–52). The winning of the 2012 Olympics for London is predicated on the commitment of large amounts of state resources in the regeneration of parts of East London, as well as investment in public transport infrastructure. The United Kingdom's National Lottery is to be used to generate dedicated funds for the development of sport related infrastructure.

This approach to urban policy is often constructed through forms of local initiative, rather than national policy, but it is reinforced by the competitive grant regimes sponsored by central government (and federal government in the United States) to encourage city councils to compete for the allocation of particular urban initiatives and the resources associated with them (see, e.g. Oatley 1998; Wallace 2004). So, for example, in England, City Challenge required local authorities and their private and community partners to compete for funding and the Single Regeneration Budgets are also based on competitive bidding for project resources (it is unlikely that the absorption of the SRB into the "single pot" to be managed through regional development agencies will change this emphasis), while the allocation of the National Lottery funding to major cultural projects (such as theatres and museums) is based on similar expectations.

Within this policy framework, the role of the "community" as a significant agent was significantly reduced, since – in principle (even if this was not always stated explicitly) – the community or its members might constitute part of the problem that needs to be resolved. Particular communities may stand in the way of development, either because the people concentrated in the inner cities are unlikely to constitute a labor force suitable for employment in the new (knowledge-based or service) growth industries, or because they occupy land that might more productively (and profitably) be used by higher end activities. And, of course, if these areas are characterized by high levels of crime and disorder or even dereliction and poverty, that too is seen to work against any ambitions for reclaiming the cities as generators of wealth. Higgins et al. quote the aims of Urban Programme circulars in the early 1980s as being to make "inner cities places where people wish to live and work" (Higgins et al. 1983, p. 83). The clear implication was that those currently living in the inner cities might not be capable of leading the campaign for renewal, since the inner cities had to be reshaped to meet the demands of business.

It is perhaps not surprising, in this context, that the main emphasis of the urban development corporations (particularly the flagship London Docklands Development Corporation) was on property development and infrastructural spending rather than "community empowerment." Although the urban development corporations were launched with a fanfare that stressed their private sector roots and their role in freeing up places where profitable investment could not easily be undertaken, with the implication that one of the core reasons for this was to be found in the local state's obsession with controlling development, in practice, of course, they were underpinned by major investment by the state, effectively subsidizing those who chose to develop property within them, even if this was sometimes explained in terms that pointed to the amount of private sector investment they succeeded in "levering" in (Imrie and Thomas 1999, p. 25). They were also able to mobilize significant state resources, including a wide range of planning and compulsory purchase powers, that cut across the supposedly simple operation of the market through forms of state entrepreneurship, nominally operating on behalf of the private sector and actively constructing new spaces in which it can operate profitably (see, e.g. Imrie and Thomas 1999). More broadly, Rodriguez et al. (2003) review the spread of large scale urban development projects across the major cities of Europe, concluding that such projects are defining characteristics of the new urban policy. They argue that this form of policy approach brings with it new institutional forms. Since "the goals of urban regeneration cannot be achieved with traditional policy structures and processes, internalizing these goals requires a more proactive and entrepreneurial approach to city governance ... a gradual shift away from distributive policies, welfare considerations , and direct service provision towards more developmental approaches aimed at economic promotion and competitive restructuring" (Rodriguez et al. 2003, p. 37).

Although such urban development projects (like the urban development corporations), are presented as public-private partnerships and judged in terms of their success in delivering development goals, they "are decidedly and almost without exception state-led – even if managed by quasi-private structures – and often state financed" (Rodriguez et al. 2003, p. 40). The urban development corporations promised (and indeed delivered) public-private partnership, but the role of the "public" in partnerships of this sort, while fundamental to the success of the project, is always secondary and success is measured in terms of the success of the private component. In this context, Barnekov et al. (1989, pp. 92–5) and Harvey (2000, pp. 138–41) explore the investment in Baltimore around the Inner Harbor. Harvey notes the extent to which the process becomes self-perpetuating: "Every new wave of public investment," he writes, "is needed to make the last wave pay off. The public-private partnership means that the public takes the risks and the private takes the profits" (Harvey 2000, p. 141).

Like community or neighborhood-based approaches, development-based approaches tend to adopt an area-based focus. Indeed, it could be argued that a spatial dimension is necessarily at the heart of some of the key initiatives. So, for example, the Rogers Report on "urban renaissance" specifically calls for the designation of Urban Priority Areas, within which there would be streamlined planning processes, as well as extra compulsory purchase powers and the possibility of offering financial incentives to developers, investors and residents. It is also suggested that special investment funds might be available for these areas. The report suggests that "spatial masterplans based on a clear development brief" should be developed in these designated areas (Rogers 1999, p. 142). Within those areas, "local authorities and their partners in regeneration, including local people" would be able "to apply for special packages of powers and incentives to assist neighborhood renewal" (Rogers 1999, p. 143).

The tension between these approaches and those developed in another government sponsored report published around the same time and discussed in Chapters 3 and 4 may already be apparent. According to the Social Exclusion Unit report on "Bringing Britain Together," "there has been too much emphasis on physical renewal instead of better opportunities for local people" and what was required was investment "in people, not just buildings" (Social Exclusion Unit 1998, Summary). The rediscovery of the neighborhood as a focus and of community as a social base was seen by some as a clear alternative to "property led" approaches to urban policy like those espoused in the Rogers report with its stress on "urban renaissance" and the claim that "Successful urban regeneration is design-led" (Rogers 1999, p. 49). However, the two apparently inconsistent approaches seemed to have survived alongside each other, with policy borrowing piecemeal from each, without any direct reference to the tension in the urban policy White Paper that followed (DETR 2000).

Although the main proposals of the Rogers Report have not been translated into legislative or operational programs, some of them have nevertheless been adopted. Urban Regeneration Companies (generally funded through regional development agencies, local authorities and English Partnerships or Scottish Enterprise) have been set up in 16 areas across England and three in Scotland, with a focus on physical regeneration projects, and there has, for example, also been a revival of urban development corporations through the working out of the sustainable communities plan in a series of towns and cities across the South-East, each of which has its own "local delivery vehicle," alongside a range of planning powers and powers to generate income from the process of development to cover the costs of infrastructural development. In the Thames Gateway and Thurrock in the Thames Estuary, for example, new bodies are to be given the powers of an urban development corporation along similar lines to those familiar from the 1980s and 1990s (ODPM 2003b). The context within which the model is being reinvented may be a rather different one because of the way in which the new urban development corporations are supposed to work more closely with other development agencies, as well as with local partnerships, local authorities and community organizations. They are supposed to offer additional capacity, rather than to substitute themselves for the existing organizations (see Raco 2005a). Nevertheless, the model of a single purpose agency with an emphasis on property development as the driver of change (and indeed the source of added value to fund any social infrastructure) remains fundamentally rooted in an understanding of urban policy in terms that emphasize economic (and competitive) success.

The Enterprise Zone Experience

The strongest and most explicit expression of the market-based approach to urban policy and urban regeneration probably found its expression in the initiatives clustered under the heading of enterprise zones, which promised to free businesses and developers within particular areas of cities from bureaucratic controls as well as taxation that reduced incentives to invest. The argument for enterprise zones, apparently drawing from the experience of cities such as Hong Kong and Singapore (see Hall 1977, 1982), was based on the assertion that enterprise in inner city areas was hampered by the existence of excessive planning controls, government regulation and local taxation. It was believed that by loosening such controls within specifically identified areas investment would take place and new enterprises be created. The implicit logic (as Anderson 1990 argues) was that these areas were a metaphor for the wider problems of UK industry, hampered by the restrictions placed on it by the workings of the social democratic state (and particularly the development control regime associated with it), and with the Labour controlled inner city heartlands simply being the most extreme example. In other words, enterprise zones were as important for the ideological message they carried as in any practical implications they had as they were implemented.

While the enterprise zones finally introduced in the United Kingdom (and later the United States) did not fully reflect Hall's suggestions (which went further in seeking to replicate some of the "freedoms" in the free trade zones of the developing world) around 25 enterprise zones of widely varying size were designated in Britain the early 1980s. The most important features of the zones were probably the tax concessions available to businesses within them (particularly the exemption from the payment of business rates) but planning controls were also simplified (although not removed entirely). In practice the enterprise zones were unsuccessful in achieving their stated aims of job creation (see, DoE 1987, which confirms that only 13,000 new jobs had been created over five years and that the cost of each job created was greater than through other state sponsored initiatives) and tended to attract investment in from just across the border of the zone so that they were more successful in repositioning where investment took place, rather than in creating new jobs.

Paradoxically, given the stated assumptions of the zones, based around a belief that removing controls and reducing state involvement would themselves generate investment, growth and job creation, in practice it appears that they were most successful when accompanied by significant state investment (e.g. where they were associated with urban development corporations) and where the land involved (as in the case of Medway) was already owned by the public sector (for a brief summary, see Atkinson and Moon 1984, pp. 139–43). Although enterprise zones were only designated for 10 years and most were designated in two rounds in 1981 and 1983, in all 38 were designated and the last came to an end in 2006. Despite their greater significance in crystallizing the views of the new right in policy form than as a means of delivering development on any scale, aspects of the model, coupled with elements of other area-based initiatives (including urban development corporations) remain tools in the armory of urban policy makers (e.g. reflected in the identification of "enterprise areas" within which specific forms of support are available). The transferable lessons for government are summarized in Syms and McIntosh (2004).

The policy exchange between the United States and the United Kingdom has generally tended to be one way, with the United Kingdom sending civil servants and policy makers to the United States to learn from initiatives developed there (see, e.g. Dolowitz et al. 2000). However, in the case of enterprise zones, the learning process worked in the other direction. And in the United States, too, the ideological message was more important than any practical significance the initiative might have. It was noted in *The President's 1982 National Urban Policy Report* that "Governments alone can do little to solve problems without the direct and strong involvement of the people … The administration seeks to build on this positive trend by employing private sector initiatives, creating Enterprise Zones and pursuing other approaches and experiment that can help revitalize urban America and improve the quality of life in all our communities" (USHUD 1982, p. 9, quoted in Barnekov et al. 1989, p. 6). As in the United Kingdom, Reagan's proposal for "enterprise zones" was predicated on the belief that relieving business of taxes and regulations would create employment opportunities. In the proposal, businesses within designated areas were to be exempt from the payment of some taxes while others would be reduced and employers hiring "disadvantaged workers" were also to receive additional tax credits. Within specially designated free trade zones they would be exempt from tariff and import duties.

Although the proposed federal enterprise zone legislation was never enacted, many individual states did adopt the approach. In these initiatives, there was a further shift away from the initial emphasis on deregulation and, instead, businesses were offered incentives, mainly in the form of tax incentives which meant that a large amount of public resource was invested both up front and in the continuing process of sustaining them. So, for example, a series of "renaissance zones" were introduced in Michigan in areas identified as "distressed communities." Within the zones businesses and residents were exempted from a range of state and local taxes. As in the United Kingdom, the impact on development was limited – the targeted communities are still lagging behind other areas of the state. The main success seems to have been the subsidy given to existing businesses through tax relief, which has made it easier for them to stay in business and less likely to relocate (Sands 2003). Nevertheless, the power of the enterprise zone metaphor was also reflected in the program of Empowerment Zones and Enterprise Communities announced by the Clinton administration in 1993 apparently in response to the Los Angeles riots of the preceding year, although the underlying principles of the initial enterprise zones seem to have been left behind, since the emphasis is on various tax incentives and the provision of additional resources. The key principles of funding were evidence of "economic opportunity, sustainable community development, community-based partnerships, and strategic vision for change" (Wallace 2004, p. 597).

Opportunities rather than Problems

The initial focus of urban policy as economic policy may have been on the problems of the cities – that is the extent to which cities were having to cope with the impact of dramatic economic restructuring (see, e.g. Allen and Massey 1988) – but a more positive interpretation of the role of cities has also become increasingly significant as a policy driver. It focuses more directly on the economic role of cities emphasizing that they are central to the economic well-being of the country, and may, indeed, be the drivers of national economic prosperity and competitiveness (these arguments owe a strong intellectual debt to Porter, who for a time was in significant demand by public authorities across the globe in carrying the message of national competitiveness and how it might be achieved) (Porter 1998). It is argued that a new emphasis needs to be placed on ensuring and rebuilding their competitiveness, or rather, the competitiveness of those cities, networks of cities and parts of cities that can be made competitive once more (see, e.g. Begg 2002; Boddy and Parkinson 2004).

This rationale has been spelled out in a wide range of official policy documents. So, for example, in an official *Review of Scottish Cities* it is argued that "We need to raise productivity and competitiveness in our cities, to develop skills and science capacities; the vision has to embrace cities creating change, ready to change," and we are told that cities are "a milieu for the development of new ideas, products and technologies" (Scottish Executive 2002, pp. 18 and 31). As a result, "we have to look again at cities as centres of growth, and that look has to take a linked social and economic perspective" (Scottish Executive 2002, p. 33). The implications of this are further developed in a report prepared by Scottish Enterprise which stresses "the vital role of Place" in delivering wider national (in this case Scottish) economic prosperity. "Successful countries, regions and cities," we are told, "compete as places to attract and retain talent and businesses," since, as the "mobility of capital and labor increases so Place becomes more important" (Scottish Enterprise 2004, p. 3).

Buck et al. (2005) have identified this broad understanding as the "new conventional wisdom" (NCW), both because it is presented as a response to the generalized impact of "pervasive forces in a globalized economy" and because it brings together a series of key features in shaping the urban policy agenda which are now widely shared by practitioners, policy makers and politicians (Gordon and Buck 2005, p. 5). The agenda is, they say, constructed around four principal features: economic competitiveness, social cohesion, responsive governance and (although it is suggested that this has a lower priority in the hierarchy) environmental sustainability. At the core of this understanding is the view that cities are not necessarily trapped in a "vicious circle of development" but may rather be able to position themselves in ways that enable them to move into a "virtuous" circle (Gordon and Buck 2005, p. 13).

In this context (as we have seen) even arguments about social exclusion tend to be reframed within an economic paradigm. Although, as Boddy (2002) and Buck et al. (2005) conclude, there is little evidence that high levels of social exclusion reduce the competitiveness of cities that experience them, there continues to be a dominant policy assumption that it does, both because it is believed to make them less attractive to investors and to limit the development of the local labor force. And notions of environmental sustainability may also be mobilized (and reimagined) in this context because of the new emphasis on making cities attractive to visitors and businesses, as well as the reclamation of derelict places for more productive uses. Even "investment in energy and waste management schemes," it is argued, "not only offers incentives in terms of a green image, but also cost savings for residents and businesses" (While et al. 2004, p. 550. See also Raco 2005b).

Instead of the urban simply being defined as a "problem" this approach suggests that there might also be opportunities and, indeed, that (some) cities (and their populations) will be able to redefine themselves in ways that will generate positive outcomes. The focus is not on providing support for those who are victims of urban processes, but on finding ways of strengthening the competitiveness of key cities and sectors within them. The task of urban policy makers becomes to actively position (or reposition) their cities within the competitive hierarchy. Urban policy is redefined as the task of selling cities to private sector investors (defined as the only group that can generate self-sustaining growth) or government, at the same time as selling a vision to residents and citizens for them to buy into. The danger is, of course, that the treadmill of competitiveness will help to generate what Berry long ago identified as "islands of renewal in seas of decay" (Berry 1985, p. 69), but here the assumption is that economy and welfare are so closely entangled with each other that only competitive success can offer the prospect of social benefit through access to employment, while the construction of palaces of consumption provides new spaces within which people are able to find other forms of satisfaction (Harvey 1989c, pp. 270–2; Zukin 2004).

Within this understanding or redefinition of the problem, instead of being the victims of wider structural forces, cities (and their citizens) become more or less active participants in shaping their futures. Within what is seen to be an increasingly globalized world, cities are given the responsibility to carve out their own economic and social spaces. They become potential sources of growth (see, e.g. Rogers 1999). It is now increasingly recognized that there may be economic benefits as well as disbenefits from some forms of urban structure, so for example, Amin and Thrift stress the significance of what they call "institutional thickness" – networks of interaction which will tend to encourage the development of relations of trust and, when working positively, are likely "to stimulate entrepreneurship" (Amin and Thrift 1994, p.15).

The new entrepreneurialism fosters an approach to urban policy which both encourages a process of public-private partnership (with the public sector underpinning the investment of major private concerns, particularly in the form of large scale property development) and also presents the private sector as a model for the ways in which city governments and other actors should behave (in that sense, it encourages forms of managerialism, discussed more fully in Chapter 3). As Jessop (1997, p. 40) summarizes the position: "the city is being reimagined – or reimaged – as an economic, political, and cultural entity which must seek to undertake entrepreneurial activities to enhance its competitiveness." This, in turn, is, he says. "closely linked to the re-design of governance mechanisms involving the city – especially through new forms of public-private partnerships and networks" (Jessop 1997, p. 40).

Globalization and Urban Entrepreneurialism

The redefinition of urban policy in economic terms is one element in the (tortuous) process through which the US and European post-welfare states are being disassembled and (potentially) reconstituted along very different lines (see, e.g. Clarke 2004). However, it also highlights the extent to which similar policy initiatives are being adopted in a much wider range of countries than the traditional homes of the Keynesian Welfare State. The emphasis on competitiveness (often described as "global" competitiveness) is one that finds echoes in cities – and in national policies for cities – across the globe.

Indeed, just as the model of urban policy emerging from the Keynesian Welfare State is deeply rooted in the experience of the United States, the UK and (to a lesser extent) the other countries of Western Europe, so the model of the entrepreneurial city can be seen to draw on the experience of cities that have come to represent the new globalized competitiveness – and particularly the cities of the Asia-Pacific. So, for example, the notion of enterprise zones which, as we have seen, took on an important ideological role in the United States and the United Kingdom in the 1980s was borrowed from their experience (Hall 1977) and finds a range of expressions in export processing zones and free ports across the globe, which are often free of local planning controls, health and safety regulations, and labor rights. The mobilization of forms of "enterprise zone" in the shape of special economic zones open to foreign investment and focused on export-oriented industrialization has underpinned dramatic economic growth and particularly urban growth (including the growth of new "megacities" such as the Pearl River Delta – see, e.g. Castells 2000, p. 407) in China through the 1980s and 1990s and into the twenty-first century. In a distorted echo of the role they were expected to play in the United Kingdom, the special economic zones were initially seen "as social and economic laboratories, in which foreign technological and managerial skills might be observed and adopted, albeit selectively" (Ye and Xu 1996, p. 232). The scale of these initiatives, however, and the care with which they were managed by the state, suggest a role that goes far beyond anything expected of the enterprise zones in Britain or the United States.

Hong Kong has been used to represent the archetype of the entrepreneurial city. Jessop and Sum (2000) suggest that it is possible to identify some cities as entrepreneurial actors in their own right or, at least to conclude that "urban blocs claiming to speak on behalf of cities … have become more explicitly entrepreneurial" (Jessop and Sum 2000, p. 2310). They specify three characteristics that might come together to define particular cities as "entrepreneurial": such cities develop innovative strategies to maintain (and develop) their economic competitiveness with others; the strategies developed in them are "real," overt and actively pursued (i.e. not merely to be inferred from economic success); those promoting such strategies are explicit in appealing to entrepreneurial discourses (Jessop and Sum 2000, p. 2289). Jessop and Sum summarize this in the notion of "glurbanization" – i.e. "entrepreneurial strategies that are concerned to secure the most advantageous insertion of a given city into the changing interscalar division of labor in the world economy" (Jessop and Sum 2000, p. 2294).

They explore this understanding of the entrepreneurial city through a case study of Hong Kong, describing the way in which the city has repositioned itself in the face of a series of fundamental economic and political shifts, including the move of manufacturing from the city to the urban settlements of south China and the active redefinition of Hong Kong as regional financial center and coordinator of production (Jessop and Sum 2000, pp. 2297–308). In the late 1990s there were active debates about whether Hong Kong should reposition itself as a "business/service/financial" hub around a "knowledge-information-based" regional economy or as a "high tech manufacturing center," built around the development of a stronger research and development base (Jessop and Sum 2000, pp. 2302–3). In other words different options were under active consideration for the entrepreneurial positioning of Hong Kong in a globalized world of competitive urban space. By the end of the 1990s, Jesop and Sum point to a series of initiatives that sought to build on opportunities created by the development of information technology (in developing a so-called "Cyberport") alongside a drive to reposition Hong Kong as Asia's "world city," as it takes on a leading role in an "emerging multi-centered city-region" that incorporates the Pearl River Delta as well as other Chinese regions (Jessop and Sum, p. 2308).

One implication of this view of the entrepreneurial city seems to be that cities have a significant degree of autonomy in determining the strategies they wish to pursue. And this is also consistent, for example, with the Singapore experience, where (national) state and city are combined. Singapore's commitment to improving its competitive position has been clearly expressed in a series of strategies explicitly directed towards positioning it strongly within global markets. Through the 1990s plans were prepared that were intended "to develop Singapore as an e-commerce hub for hi-tech companies, an educational center for international institutions, a regional medical center and a 'tourism' capital" (Chang 2000, p. 818). One of these initiatives was directed towards transforming the city into an "intelligent island" – based around a broadband network linking the population at work, at home, and in education. The aim was to link and integrate different parts of society in building an all-pervasive information technology culture, as well as linking a series of high-tech research and production sites (Richardson 1997 quoted in Allen 1999, pp. 190–1; Jessop and Sum 2000, p. 2309). A National Technology Plan mapped out a technology corridor within which a new Science Park was positioned. This Park can be seen as an example of "the national/urban drive towards excellence in research and technology, [and] the commercial interest of a particular government-linked property developer" as part of "a deliberate and state-driven attempt to attract the location of R&D activities by global corporations" (Phillips and Young 2003, pp. 708–9).

Like Hong Kong, with which it competes directly, Singapore has sought to define itself as a global city. And, as a result, suggests Allen (1999, p. 191), it "has officially set itself the task of becoming creative; creative in the manipulation of signs and symbols, creative in managing the rhythms and flows of information, creative in all the ways that are thought to matter in a changing global economy." As well as supporting a range of initiatives focused on particular economic sectors, Singapore has also sought to redefine itself as "Global City for the Arts" on the grounds that global cities are "centres of economic and sociocultural power" (Chang 2000, p. 819).

However, the emphasis on cities as the (relatively autonomous) central driving force of the new entrepreneurialism may be exaggerated. This is recognized by Jessop and Sum, who point out that entrepreneurialism can also be seen as a "state level response in so far as cities are coming to replace firms as national champions in international competition" (Jessop and Sum 2000, p. 2310). Governments increasingly launch and sponsor urban mega projects as part of a process that is aimed at redefining their own big cities as world cities, and this is, in turn, seen as a key element in shifting perceptions of the nations of which they are a part from third to first world status (Douglass 2000, p. 2322) or their transformation into "modern" nations (Olds 2001, p. 161). This is, perhaps, particularly clear in those cities that have played a central part in national development strategies, such as Seoul, Tokyo and Shanghai (Hill and Kim 2000; Saito 2003; Zhang 2003).

So, for example, although South Korea is sometimes described as a city-state – as the "Seoul Republic" (Hill and Kim 2000, p. 2178) – and is home to around half of South Korea's population (Douglass 2000, p. 2320), this is rather a different form of "city-state" from that of Singapore because of the extent to which the national remains a defining element of official rhetoric (expressed in a series of national plans of one sort or another) (see, e.g. Hong 1996). Tokyo is often included in lists of world or global cities, but – as Hill and Kim 2000 note – this may have the effect of understating the centrality of its role within Japan as a "national development state." In this context, "Tokyo is in effect a national champion" (Hill and Kim 2000, p. 2178).

The implication of this is that apparently entrepreneurial initiatives (such as a project to develop the Waterfront along familiar entrepreneurial lines) are deeply embedded within national as well as urban plans, bringing together representatives of different levels of government and national capital. Saito (2003) carefully charts the interaction between national, local and property development in the attempt to position Tokyo as global city, through the development of the Waterfront project, describing "the exercise of strategic national policy through carefully crafted institutional arrangements in which the public and private sectors maintained a delicately balanced relationship with consensus and conformity with the framework of the capitalist developmental state" (Saito 2003, p. 304).

The case of Shanghai reflects another distinctive experience. In many respects it seems to exhibit all the symptoms of the entrepreneurial city. It has experienced massive growth since the 1970s and all the architectural symbols of globalizing modernity are to be found there, from high rise buildings to new palaces of consumption, from new elites to marginalized populations in newly created slums, from the making of a new financial center to heritage-based gentrification. The language of promotional entrepreneurialism has been mobilized to reflect a range of different ambitions for the city as it has been reimagined first as the "Paris of the Orient" and more recently as "the Fortune City" (Zhang 2003, p. 1688).

Until the 1970s and early 1980s Shanghai's development was explicitly fostered as a focus of national economic policy, acting as a production-based "cash cow" for national and not just local development, a "locomotive" of growth (Zhang 2003, p. 1552; Wu 2003, pp. 1682–3). From the mid 1980s its role began to change, as China's development path shifted, with the growth of massive new manufacturing centers and the making of new urban centers, such as the metropolitan region linking Hong Kong with the Pearl River Delta. The city was defined as an "open coastal city" and ringed by a series of special (and specialist) economic and development zones and was increasingly allowed to retain a higher proportion of the income it generated (Newman and Thornley 2005, p. 238; Olds 2001, pp. 175–6). Since 1992 Shanghai has continued to play a central role in national strategy, being identified in national policy as the "dragon head," driving the growth of the Yangtse River Delta region (Wu 2003, p. 1684).

It has increasingly been reimagined in national policy as a Chinese world city, capable of providing a counterweight to Hong Kong in the South. In this context, a regulatory regime was constructed to make it possible for local agencies "to entice the controllers of global flows of capital, technology and images to focus on the city ... with the aim of turning Shanghai, once again, 'into a financial and trading centre of the Asian and Pacific region'" (Olds 2001, p. 178). The Pudong area to the west of the city was identified as the largest special economic zone in China, as a "unified project of national importance" (Olds 2001, p. 196), and – most significantly – as one which incorporated a commitment to the development of a major financial center, alongside the more familiar zones focused on high technology manufacturing and port-based activities (Newman and Thornley 2005, pp. 238–9; Olds 2001, pp. 194–5).

As in the case of Tokyo, however, the continued importance of the central state does not mean there is no scope for a city focused agency – the Shanghai Metropolitan Government (SMG) has a clear role in the process, even if its scope is limited. The opening up of the Chinese economy has been accompanied by decentralization of power to cities like Shanghai, which have been enabled to retain more of the revenues generated from development. So, for example, the SMG took the lead in developing the planning framework for Pudong and has also been involved in its financing. However the decentralization process has also gone below the city level, so that, for example, the Pudong New Area Administration, while formally subordinate to the SMG effectively has responsibility for taking the project further, working with four dedicated development corporations created for different zones within Pudong, each of which has its own autonomy and access to private as well as public funding (see, e.g. Olds 2001, p. 195).

Zhang concludes that the metropolitan government has been effective in developing infrastructure and in acting as a form of broker between the growing market economy and "a powerful central state," but much less effective in selective intervention, that is, those which might be deemed most significant in the context of entrepreneurialism (Zhang 2003, p. 1568). While interurban competitiveness is an increasingly important driving force in China, to the extent that a "more entrepreneurial local state" has been created, "in the sense that the 'state' itself is a market player and can even use market instruments to achieve hidden political agendas," it has also been argued that, because the local state lacks "financial discipline and public accountability, [it] goes beyond its budgetary constraints and social responsibilities to recklessly mobilize market resources for urban infrastructure development and its own political objectives" (Xu and Yeh 2005, p. 284). For this reason, some of those committed to the entrepreneurial repositioning of the city (reflecting a wider vision of neo-liberal globalization) have argued that it is only if the city (and country) open themselves up more fully to global markets (and specifically to foreign direct investment) and introduce "policy measures that induce competitiveness," particularly in the service sector, that the city will be able to set itself on the "pathway" to becoming a world city (Yusuf and Wu 2002, p. 1234).

The extent to which the city itself can be described as "entrepreneurial" in the sense identified by Jessop and Sum (2000) remains questionable. Instead it has been strongly argued that while many of the features of "territorially based entrepreneurialism" or " bureaucratic entrepreneurialism" (Olds 2001, p. 191) are to be found in the city, this is more appropriately understood "as a state project in the post-socialist transition" (Wu 2003, p. 1673). It this context, therefore, it continues to be a powerful example of "a state-led world city" rather than an "entrepreneurial city" (Newman and Thornley 2005, pp. 237–46).

The definition of the "entrepreneurial city" introduced by Jessop and Sum is helpful in highlighting features that might be associated with the emergence of a new scalar or geographical social, political and economic settlement. However, because it is a model (or "ideal type") located within and derived from the wider model of the Schumpeterian Competition State, there is also a danger that its mobilization in the analysis of "entrepreneurialism" in practice may either lead to an exaggeration of the significance of some aspects of the process or to a dismissal of the extent to which particular experiences meet the template (see, e.g., Wu 2003). So, in particular, the emphasis in the definition (drawing on Schumpeter by analogy) on the extent to which cities labeled "entrepreneurial" must also be innovative effectively consigns most of those which might otherwise attract the epithet to the limbo of imitators. As Phillips and Yeung (2003) note in their discussion of Singapore's Science Park, even the initiatives that are explicitly intended to foster economic innovation may not do so. They point to the "Lack of significant R&D activities' in the Park" (Phillips and Yeung 2003, p. 722) (see Massey et al. 1992, for a powerful review of the gap between the "high tech fantasies" associated with science parks and the more mundane reality). What is most striking about the new urban competitiveness is the limited menu from which the urban promoters (and potential entrepreneurs) draw their policy tools, as each (global) boosterist fashion succeeds the last (from mega projects to high tech corridors; design led growth to waterfront development; from creativity to creative industries).

Strategies of Urban Competitiveness

The underlying logics of urban policy in an era of urban entrepreneurialism and global competitiveness are complex and uncertain. From one perspective the recognition of competition between cities, based along the fault lines of economic restructuring for increased economic efficiency could be argued simply to herald the end of urban policy as a distinctive area of policy. What is needed, if this argument were to be followed through, is an absence of policy or, rather, an active commitment to ensuring that the main obstacles to renewal and restructuring are removed (in the US case, a basic acceptance that the old industries and the cities associated with them are largely on the way out, so what is needed is to find ways of allowing the new to develop, wherever that may be, and whatever the urban form that is likely to be associated with it). This essentially seems to me to be the position argued by Peterson (1985), albeit with the recognition that support may be needed to carry the weakest for a transitional period, but even this should be handled on the same basis throughout the country, with no particular favoring of urban locations. It is consistent, too with the underlying principles set out during the Reagan and Thatcher periods, and was explicitly expressed in publications prepared in the dying years of the Carter administration (see, e.g. President's Commission 1980a,b).

In practice, however, this interpretation – however logical – is not the one that has come to dominate urban policy, since there has been a parallel stress on urban self help, which in effect reinforced the drive to urban competitiveness at local level. Alongside the broader shifts in the official languages of public policy towards an emphasis on economic opportunity, underpinned by a powerful theoretical social vision that placed the success of business and the power of the market at its center, there was also a shift in the ways that cities and the local governments that ran them began to be interpreted, and understood their own roles. As discussed in Chapter 1, some theorists – such as Molotch (1976), Logan and Molotch (1987) and Cox and Mair (1988, 1989, 1991) – identified the growth and development agenda as defining the nature of urban politics, and in practice therefore the approaches that underpinned urban policy (using terms such as "growth machine" and "growth coalition" to characterize the process) (similar understandings are implicit within urban regime theory – see, e.g. Stoker (1995); Stone (1989, 1993)).

The power of these approaches in helping us to understand the nature of urban policy is undeniable, and they capture some of the key changes that have been underway over the last two decades and more. In a European context, Mayer notes that increased social polarization within and between cities has been accompanied by, "an increasing mobilization of local politics in support of economic development." The local state, she argues, now "organizes and co-ordinates private capital accumulation by including other relevant actors," while withdrawing "from its collective consumption functions," as they are supplemented by a range of not-for-profit and private agencies (Mayer 1992, p. 256). However, there is a danger within these approaches of identifying an inexorable logic that may ignore some key aspects of urban politics and imply that some universal set of processes has been identified, so that it becomes difficult to understand the potential for change in policy focus (e.g. from "social reproduction" to economic growth as a paradigm and – potentially – back again) (see, e.g. Edwards 1997; Cochrane 1999; Ward and Jonas 2004). They tend to present the shift to a "growth agenda" as an inevitable one or, indeed, not even as a shift at all – to the extent that other forms of policy are simply not discussed.

They may also understate the potential of urban entrepreneurialism or, at any rate, urban bargaining in a global or international marketplace. In his discussion of Shanghai, as we have seen, Olds (2001) identifies some of the ways in which the national and local state has taken advantage of the new positioning of the city to generate new forms of development. In a rather different context, Savitch and Kantor (2002) review the experience of ten European and North American cities (including Paris, Glasgow, Milan, Detroit and Toronto) to suggest that there is more scope for effective negotiation about growth and development than is sometimes imagined (particularly in the United States) (Savitch and Kantor 2002, pp. 283–5). They acknowledge that some cities have little choice in the bargaining process and have to accept (indeed look for) whatever development is available. In such circumstances what is needed are national policies of redistribution or support. However, they also argue that those cities which start with more resources than others have to be prepared to mobilize them effectively and not just accept what is presented as market logic. So, for example, Savitch and Kantor (2002, p. 349) present Paris and Toronto as particular examples of good practice, because they were both able and ready to turn away development that was unattractive, at the same time as ensuring that positive development did take place (see also Molotch and Vicari 1988). From such a perspective, therefore, it becomes possible once more to recognize the extent to which urban policy – even in this most economized form – can be understood as social policy, since the choices being made are (or have the potential to be) between more or less socially beneficial outcomes and not just more or less efficiency or competitiveness.

Chapter 7

Taking the Cultural Turn

If the origins of urban entrepreneurialism are to be found in an emphasis on the building of competitive economies and industries, underpinned by the drive to recapture declining areas for profitable uses, its contemporary form has taken on a powerful "cultural" inflection. Since cities continue to be cultural centers and culture (in its many different forms) is a vital element in shaping competitiveness, it is perhaps not surprising that cultural policy as "the *conscious and deliberate manipulation* of culture" (Kearns and Philo 1993, p. 3) has taken on an increasingly central role in attempts to promote the economic potential and social value of cities. It appears to offer cities a far more positive role than the one that might be summarized in a process of competitive bidding for "footloose" industry.

In part the emergence of culture as a key tool in the armory of place promotion reflects its wider significance within the changing economic landscape of contemporary capitalism, reflected, for example, in the increased importance of the cultural industries and the key role of cities (as nodes in global systems as well as places with specific local characteristics) in sustaining them (Scott 2000). It is also reflected in the promotion of "destination" experiences (from theme parks to shopping malls) as the boundaries between shopping, learning, and the experience of culture have become increasingly blurred (see, e.g. Bianchini 2004; Zukin 2004). And the role of cultural networks in shaping the economic base and economic possibilities of cities is also widely acknowledged (see, e.g. from rather different perspectives; Landry and Bianchini 1995; Scott 2001; Florida 2002). Landry and Bianchini have argued that "Future competition between nations, cities and enterprise looks set to be based less on natural resources, location or past reputation and more on the ability to develop attractive images and symbols and project these effectively" and, they say, it is the "generation of knowledge through creativity and innovation" that provides the basis for successful economic development (Landry and Bianchini 1995, p. 12).

Cultural policy as translated into urban policy incorporates a series of interrelated but quite distinctive features. The first is focused on infrastructural investment intended to support processes of cultural production (expressed, e.g. in programs for the development of cultural industry districts or cultural industry quarters, within which there is a cluster of subsidized office space, rehearsal space and studio space for the use of cultural industries, such as music making). In some cases this may go further to involve direct state involvement in the process of production, for example, through investment in and management of museums or theatres or tourist promotion. This may be associated with a second set of activities, involving investment in or support for large scale ("flagship") cultural projects, often expressed in the form of prestige (or iconic) buildings of one sort or another but also sometimes in the form of major festivals or prestige events (most powerfully expressed in the competition for global events such as the Olympics or European Capital of Culture) (see Kong 2000, p. 387).

The drive to urban megaprojects which are not directly associated with the cultural industries may nevertheless also have a cultural aspect because of the way in which they are often associated with the mobilization of architectural symbolism, so that the buildings themselves (or sometimes just the plans for them) become markers of cultural prestige (see, e.g. Olds' discussion of the Rogers' plans for a new CBD in Shanghai) (Olds 2001, pp. 207–29), as part of a broader strategy of "branding" whose purpose is to position particular cities better in the urban hierarchy, making them more attractive to investors and to in-migrants of what Harvey has identified as "the right sort" (see also Sklair 2005). This, in turn, can be seen to shade into a more extended concern to provide the necessary infrastructure within which the creative class of innovators can flourish, as part of the process of gentrification, by which particular areas of cities are remade as places of what has been called "pacification" or "domestication by cappuccino" (Zukin 1995, p. 28; Atkinson 2003). It is in this context that the role of cultural policy as a means of delivering economic and social regeneration in particular ("inner city") areas is often mobilized.

Developing the Cultural Industries

Despite their differences, some of the arguments for investment in cultural activities retain strong echoes of more traditional approaches to urban economic regeneration, since they redefine them as "cultural and creative industries," that is economic enterprises in their own right, whose success can be measured in the same ways as any other investment, as a potential growth sector capable of delivering employment in its own right.

Scott (2000) argues that that regional clustering – in city-regions – is particularly significant for cultural industries, that is those industries producing cultural goods (including design-based industries and those concerned with film, music, and multimedia production). Although he recognizes the importance of globalized networks Scott also identifies a "global but polycentric and multifaceted system of cultural production" (Scott 2000, p. 211), within which he highlights the importance of "clusters of interdependent activities whose mutual proximity to one another creates complex, dynamic flows of agglomeration economies" (Scott 2000, p. 25). There is, he says, a "tendency for the emerging global cultural economy to condense out on the landscape in the form of a scattered patchwork of urban and regional production systems constituting the basic nerve centers of contemporary aesthetic and semiotic production" (Scott 2000, p. 216). As a result, he emphasizes the need to build "a local institutional milieu that offers attractive developmental conditions by securing certain external economies, i.e. those that are apt to be missing or destroyed under conditions of pure market competition" (Scott 2000, p. 187). This suggests an approach to economic development that is rather different from those that seek to attract mobile investment through the use of financial incentives or the building of multipurpose and undifferentiated business units. Instead the emphasis is placed on finding ways of providing socialized support to underpin private initiative, for example through the support and maintenance of networks, the provision of specialist training, city marketing, the gathering of market information, or assistance with cooperation and partnership.

In many British cities understandings like these have been translated into initiatives aimed at the development of their own "cultural industries quarters," providing premises, facilities and an environment that they hope will encourage the development of those industries, which it is believed will be the growth industries of the future (apparently taking over in the language of local economic development from the previously ubiquitous science parks) (see, e.g. Evans 2003a). In the case of Sheffield, for example, the focus was on music – e.g. with the foundation of a municipal recording studio (Red Tape) and a series of related spaces reoccupying older industrial buildings. Brown et al. (2000) and (Dabinett 2004) chart the ambiguous outcomes of local investment in the development of cultural quarters in Sheffield and Manchester. Modest success has been recorded, but the scale remains small, underpinned by forms of cultural consumption in galleries and coffee bars and continued state funding. The largest investment in Sheffield (in the National Lottery funded National Centre for Popular Music) has been unsuccessful, finally taken over by one of the city's Universities as a Student Union building. Where there have been successes (e.g. in the fostering of a dance music recording label) instead of staying in the city they have moved to London, which remains the center of cultural production in the United Kingdom. Nevertheless the commitment to the development of such quarters remains and has spread through the professional and policy networks, and the rise of cultural strategies and strategies for developing the "creative city" are becoming ubiquitous (see, e.g. Dabinett 2004; Wood and Taylor 2004). The construction of a Multimedia Super Corridor in Malaysia, stretching out from the massive Petronas Towers in Kuala Lumpur (explicitly built to be the tallest in the region), as well as the development of a strategy to construct and promote Singapore as "an intelligent island" suggest that this is a global urban agenda, rather than one restricted to the cities of the West (Allen 1999; Krätke 2003; Teo 2003).

Even the institutions of high culture have been incorporated into this language of economics, employment creation and interurban competition. It is not hard to find policy documents which remind us that "The competition does not stand still, with prestige investments in regional centers within Europe (e.g. Bilbao Guggenheim) and within the UK (e.g. Tate Modern, new Imperial War Museum in Manchester) all commanding 'must see' status" (Scottish Executive 2002, p. 144). More positively, Wilks-Heeg and North (2004) list some of the claims that have been made for the economic impact of a range of cultural investments in Britain: the Tate Modern is said to be worth £100m to the local economy and to have generated about 3,000 jobs; while it has also been calculated that the Eden Project in Cornwall has generated £111m and supports nearly 5,500 jobs (Wilks-Heeg and North 2004, p. 306). Similarly Plaza (2000) suggests that the Guggenheim in Bilbao has generated a significant increase in the number of tourists visiting the city and thus generated income locally.

Such arguments also underpin the investment in convention centers across the cities of the United States and also increasingly across the world – many of which now seem to have their own International Convention Center (often alongside World Trade Centers).

Hong Kong's contribution (Asia World-Expo) is within walking distance of the airport, has a dedicated railway station and has 10 exhibition halls which together incorporate a space of 750,000 sq ft, as well as an auditorium which seats 13,500 people. Centers like these promise direct employment in the tourism-related and hospitality industries – for example, in hotels and restaurants (see Fainstein and Gladstone 1999 for a discussion of the regeneration effects of tourism). Along similar lines, proposals for a range of supercasinos in the cities of the United Kingdom are expected to lead to regeneration through economic activity, through direct employment generated, as well as the spending of those visiting them. In the United States, the attempt to attract and retain sports franchises of one sort or another combines a desire to access the employment generation aspects of such activities as well as the prestige apparently associated with them (see, e.g. Euchner 1999). Sports franchises may not exist (or be tradeable) in the same way in the United Kingdom as in the United States but in the United Kingdom, too, the importance of having a major football league team (preferably Premiership) team is widely recognized by the boosterists, as reflected in the arguments underpinning the process by which Wimbledon FC moved to Milton Keynes to be relabeled the Milton Keynes Dons. This is expressed quite explicitly in Milton Keynes Community Strategy, where it is argued that "a real city needs its own football league team" (Milton Keynes Local Strategic Partnership 2004). This leaves city governments to bargain from a position of weakness, whether directly offering subsidies of one sort or another or making concessions by granting planning permission for associated profitable land development.

The extent of the economic and regeneration impact of such activities has been questioned. So, for example, Evans (2003b) suggests that the success of the Tate Modern has been at the expense of the Tate Britain; Gomez and Gonzalez (2001) suggest that the economic impact of the Guggenheim Bilbao has been exaggerated; and Tranter and Keeffe (2004) argue that event tourism based around motor racing events in Canberra has had more negative than positive side effects; while Austrian and Rosentraub (2002) critically assess the economic impact of sports-related investment in US cities (see also Miller 2002). However, the potential impact remains a strong argument in the language of urban policy professionals as well as the emergent professionals of the cultural industries, who are identified by McGuigan as "those particular sections that are directly employed in practice of cultural mediation and consumer management" (McGuigan 1996, p. 39).

Higher education is another increasingly significant target of and player in urban policy. It is widely recognized that universities are important as direct employers as well as potential sources on the basis of which other forms of growth may take place. Universities are seen to have the potential to transform cities and the regions of which they are a part not only through their direct impact on the local economy but also in their potential to provide the basis for other forms of related – "knowledge-based" – employment and more generally to contribute to making up the cultural capital and "cosmopolitanism" of cities (Charles and Benneworth 2001, pp. 60–1). So, for example, the expansion of higher education in Britain has ensured that central parts of many of its major cities are now sustained by the spending of students. They are identified as the drivers behind what has been described as the "24" hour city and the private rented housing sector has been revived by the same process. At the same time, however, universities are expected to be the drivers (or at any rate catalysts) for the new economy, not only in terms of their own activities within research laboratories and related work, but also in their ability to launch spin-off developments in the form of science parks or to construct a wider culture within which high tech or knowledge-based or creative development will be encouraged to take place, whether in the shape of science parks (see, e.g. Massey et al. 1992) or in helping to make up a local culture that is attractive to the creative class (Florida 2002).

In the United Kingdom, Cambridge with its science park is the iconic example of success to which others aspire, and attempts have even been made by other cities to draw on that success – so, for example, the Oxford to Cambridge Arc (which is sponsored by a number of Regional Development Agencies) represents an attempt to identify a space stretching between the two poles of Oxford and Cambridge, within which it is hoped a more integrated knowledge economy can be constructed (O2C 2003). Along the same lines, in the economic strategy developed as part of the program for doubling Milton Keynes in size as part of the government's sustainable communities plan for the South-East of England, the need for a campus-based university is explicitly identified as one of the five pillars required to ensure that balanced and sustainable growth can be attained (MKELP 2004). In the context of regional policy, the United Kingdom's Department of Trade and Industry has explicitly identified a role for universities as "powerful drivers of change," as, "the seedbed for new industries, products and services and … the hub of business networks and industrial clusters of the knowledge economy" (DTI/DfEE 2001, para 3.13). Universities themselves (or at any rate some of them) have increasingly come to present themselves as drivers of economic change and particularly as contributing to the building of the promised knowledge economy, working together in regional partnerships to achieve this (see, e.g. Charles 2003; Charles and Benneworth 2001; Harloe and Perry 2004).

Tourism has played a particular role in the arguments for and development of a "cultural" focus for urban policy, both in its own right (i.e. as a significant generator of employment) and as a way of developing an attractive "brand" for the city. Tourism is a major industry for many urban areas – as Evans (2003b) notes, for example, New York and London each attract enough foreign tourists to place them in the top ten nations for overseas visitors. As a result, Fainstein and Judd argue that "Cities are sold just like any other consumer product" (Fainstein and Judd 1999b, p. 4) and Judd identifies the "promotion of culture and tourism as a principal component of the new economic development strategy" (Judd 1999, p.35). So, for example, alongside its definition of itself as the "Silicon Valley of the East" Penang has developed a strong tourist strategy, with promotion based around access to "nature," heritage tours, "agro tourism" (introducing tourists to village life), the cruise industry, as well as Sun and sea (Teo 2003, p. 555). The offer to tourists is one that promises "authenticity" although, as Teo suggests, this is more like a process of "imagineering."

It has been strongly argued that this process encourages what Bianchini (2004) calls "banalization" and uniformity. One extensive survey of tourist brochures and related pro-motional material produced in England and Wales concluded that they tended, "to focus on the past and be generally backward looking," as well as representing "places as culturally uniform." They did not "show diversity" but instead tended "to promote a similar, bland mix of facilities and attractions for every area" (Murray 2001, p. 9, quoted in Bianchini 2004). The conclusion has been drawn that "Packaging and promoting the city to tourists can destroy its soul. The city is commodified, its form and spirit remade to conform to market demand, not residents' dreams" (Holcomb 1999, p. 69).

In this context, the accusation has been made that cities become little more than theme parks (see, e.g. Sorkin 1992) and Zukin has suggested that far from being simply a fantasy world for tourists, Disneyworld has itself become a model of urban development suitable for adaptation and implementation in the "real" world, and not just in the form of the Seaside in Florida which was famously used as the location for the film *The Truman Show* (Zukin 1995, pp. 52–5. See also Chapter 5). Nor are such developments limited to the countries of the West, since tourism has become an increasingly important driver in many poorer and developing countries. In the case of Penang, for example, "locals feel increasingly peripheralized" (Teo 2003, p. 558) because its refashioning "into a modern cosmopolis with a good infrastructure and yet as rich heritage of culture and history set in a tropical clime has exaggerated these selected themes at the expense of the local lived cultures" (Teo 2003, p. 560) (for a discussion of the impact of tourism on the cities of South-East Asia, see Mullins 1999).

In the process of tourism promotion, the promoters attempt to build on existing ("locally rooted") traditions and understandings to reposition places along lines which fit with the limited range of images preferred by upmarket tourists and potential investors (Kearns and Philo 1993; Judd and Fainstein 1999). However, this also makes it difficult to accept that we are simply witnessing a process of homogenization, since not only does the marketing of places for tourism (as Fainstein and Judd 1999a note) rely on the identification of particular niches for different places (they are not simply selling themselves as the same, but as different and distinctive experiences), but it also relies on formal and informal negotiation with the local residents who come to represent it. The paradox remains that the search for competitive difference (uniqueness or "authenticity") may lead to the construction of similarity as the same symbols are mobilized in different places, while that process is itself consistently undermined by the same search.

Making Space for the Creative Class

The role of culture in urban development and competitiveness between cities has been given a significant boost by arguments that have placed "creativity" at the heart of the new economy – the economy that is expected to replace the old economy of Fordist mass production, as also the routinized economy of financial and other services. Cultural policy has become a commonplace in the toolbox of the urban policy professional since, as noted by Scottish Enterprise, in seeking to make places attractive to those working and investing in the knowledge industries, they "have to be distinctive either physically e.g. attractive waterfront business districts, or culturally e.g. diverse and creative cultural mix" (Scottish Enterprise 2004, p. 3).

These arguments were given a popular theoretical base, entering the mainstream of urban policy, with the publication of Florida's book on the rise of the "creative class," which others might identify as "knowledge workers" (Florida 2002). He claims to have identified a new (and growing) social class which he calls the "creative class" and argues that the rise of this class has fundamentally changed and will continue to change the ways in which we live our lives. It is, Florida says, "the dominant class in society" (Florida 2002, p. xiv), representing some 30 percent of the US workforce, and being made up of "people who add economic value through their creativity" (Florida 2002, p. 68). The new "class" is made up of knowledge workers of one sort or another, and its core is made up of those "whose economic function is to create new ideas, new technology and/or new creative content" although this core is also associated with a broader group of "creative professionals" whose work is characterized by their use of independent judgement (Florida 2002, p. 8).

This is a "class" defined by its economic role, but of fundamental importance to Florida's argument, it is also associated with its own social and cultural identity and characteristic consumption patterns. Florida constructs an image of the creative class which is overwhelmingly positive – these are the new elite whose members not only drive economic growth, but also help to construct (indeed demand the right to live in) liveable cities, characterized by a high quality of life and which "offer a variety of economic opportunities, a stimulating environment, and amenities for every possible lifestyle" (Florida 2002, p. 11). Florida argues against attempts to rebuild traditional communities and the notion of embedded "social capital" suggesting instead that new forms of social cohesion are required for the creative age. He maintains that members of the creative class are attracted by "more flexible, quasi-anonymous" communities where they can "plug in" relatively quickly and feel at ease; that is places of opportunity where people can be themselves and not be trapped in any singular constraining "identity" (Florida 2002, p. 220).

Florida's approach inverts the traditional mantra of local economic development, with its stress on the need to attract inward investment and develop industry to create jobs and grow population and economy. Instead he maintains that members of the creative class are moving to creative centers, which in turn become economic winners, because people want to live there. Florida identifies place rather than corporation as the key economic organizing principle and provides a shopping list for local policy makers in seeking to attract members of the creative class, which he summarizes in the notion of "quality of place." The key factors that make places attractive are, he says (Forida 2002, pp. 223–31):

- *Thick labor market*: that is the existence of many job opportunities (an economy that is not dominated by one or a few employers).
- *Lifestyle*: expressed as easy access to a wide range of recreational activities, including nightlife but also a range of other cultural opportunities, such as theatre, art galleries and outdoor sports.
- *Social interaction*: opportunities for easy informal interaction, for example in cafes and book shops.
- *Diversity*: diversity of age groups, ethnicity and sexual orientation as a sign of openness, as well as measure of "excitement" and "energy." Florida uses the existence of a gay community as a measure of diversity in his ranking of cities.
- *Authenticity and uniqueness*: in other words a place that is not dominated by the ubiquitous chains of cafes, restaurants or shops, but has "real buildings, real people, real history" (Florida 2002, p. 228). For Florida a local music scene would be another expression of this.
- *Identity*: place rather than employer as a signifier of status.

Florida seeks to identify the uneasy balance between the different aspects of city life that make particular cities attractive to the creative class. They provide opportunities for interaction, but also space in which to retreat for relaxation; they offer space to create the experience of urban life, rather than just to consume it; they mix older buildings with newer uses; they offer a "buzz" but also security – these are not threatening spaces (see also Lloyd's discussion of what he calls "neo-bohemia" which explores the intersection between traditional bohemian traditions in some older urban areas with the new economy, sponsoring redevelopment of former industrial areas) (Lloyd 2002). Florida develops a creativity index, with the help of which he ranks cities (with San Francisco at the top and Memphis at the bottom of metropolitan areas with populations over 1 m), implicitly offering the challenge to policy makers of finding ways of moving up the rankings. And, despite sceptical comments from those who question his empirical base as well as his policy nostrums (see, e.g. from very different perspectives Malanga 2004; Peck 2005), the extent to which Florida's conclusions have both been taken to confirm the validity of culturally-based initiatives and to underpin the launch of more is clear. He himself has been in high demand as advisor to local authorities throughout North America and his conclusions have more widely been used further to justify the use of "culture" as an economic development tool.

As Peck notes, Florida's approach very quickly found its enthusiastic supporters in some-times surprising places far beyond the United States precisely because it is so well suited to the "competitive landscape" in which what he calls "the fast-policy regime that has been constructed around cities" as each looks for the next "creative fix" (Peck 2005, p. 767). In the United Kingdom, it could even be argued that some aspects were already incor-porated within existing ideologies of local economic development (see, e.g. Landry 2000, which not only predates Florida but provides a toolkit for urban policy professionals seeking to develop cultural policy initiatives – initiatives intended to foster the growth of creative industries, to build the creativity of urban areas and to make cities attractive to what has come to be called the creative class). Florida himself has applied his approach to Europe (developing a specific Euro-creativity index) concluding that the Scandinavian countries, the Netherlands and Belgium are the ones with most evidence of creative potential, with Ireland as an "up and comer." The United Kingdom and Germany are deemed to be falling behind (Florida and Tinagli 2004). The enthusiasm for the development of indices and the rank-ing of cities has also found its local expression, for example in the form of the Boho index developed by Demos for a conference on *Boho Britain: Creativity, Diversity and the Remak-ing of our Cities* held in 2003 and sponsored not only by Demos (a think tank) but also the British Urban Regeneration Association (representing all the major public and private actors in urban development and urban regeneration) and the Royal Institute of Chartered Survey-ors. This index purported (using slightly different measures to those utilized by Florida) to identify the most bohemian of British cities and, therefore, their creative potential, as well, perhaps as their housing market potential. Manchester was identified among Britain's largest cities as the country's "answer to San Francisco" while Sunderland languished in 40th place (Demos 2003).

In some of its expressions the drive to "creativity" has the potential to challenge traditional understandings of urban policy which define the "inner city" as the problem – instead it comes to represent an opportunity that does not exist in new developments, in the suburbs or in the CBDs. So, for example, Landry (2000) sees the inner city as the ideal location within which "creativity" can flourish, in which it is possible to create opportunities for new ways of working not least because it has a history, but one which no longer determines the present, and because there are spaces which it is possible to occupy at relatively low cost. This means that, new creative networks can be built. It also suggests that it is not possible to build purpose built spaces for these activities, which undermines the scope for development outside the older urban areas. From this perspective, the old urban areas offer interstitial spaces which the "new" cannot provide, spaces ripe for gentrification and the making of cosmopolitan – or "bohemian" – promise (see, e.g. Lloyd 2002; Rofe 2004). Even in Shanghai, where the making of the new has dominated over the reclamation and reworking of the old, the district of Xintiandi has been remade, with the construction of new apartment buildings in the midst and on the edge of a reimagined and reshaped neighborhood made up of structures of the old city. Behind the old frontages are to be found upscale restaurants and shops, rather than the overcrowded housing of the past, whose residents have been relocated to the outskirts of the city. As the architect responsible comments, "This is not an authentic restoration … My aim was to respect the … special characteristics of the area but to create a living environment that would be commercially viable" (quoted in Cole 2005).

Place Marketing, Architecture, Brand and Spectacle

In the world of the globalized marketplace, cities have been discursively positioned in a wider competitive market, within which they are required to fight for investment and development, but in different ways – i.e. not just through competitive bidding to the lowest level, through offering more and more financial incentives. Harvey powerfully summarizes the position in noting that, "The active production of places with special qualities becomes an important stake in spatial competition between localities, cities, regions and nations. Corporatist forms of governance can flourish in such spaces, and themselves take on entrepreneurial roles in the production of favorable business climates and other special qualities. And it is in this context that we can better situate the striving … for cities to forge a distinctive image and to create an atmosphere of place and tradition that will act as a lure to both capital and people 'of the right sort'" (Harvey 1989a, p. 295).

The emphasis of place marketing is increasingly on redefining – or reimagining – each individual city in ways that fit with dominant perceptions of urban success (see, e.g. Kearns and Philo 1993; Gold and Ward 1994). In line with the overall managerialist agenda, there has been a growing influence of and borrowing from approaches first developed in business and management in the development of visions and strategies and the mobilization of forms of "branding." Urban initiatives of one sort or another have increasingly been tasked with developing alternative visions for the areas over which they are expected to have responsibility. The argument is that "a strong widely supported and understood 'vision' for the future is a pre-requisite for a successful city" (Scottish Executive 2002, p. 206). The nature of the visions helps to position places differently in the disjointed world of competitive welfarism.

So, for example, City Pride (launched in 1994) was an initiative which sought to bring together representatives of business and the public sector in some of England's bigger cities (including London, Birmingham, and Manchester) with the aim of fostering strategic policy planning as a means of positioning cities to compete more effectively in – what was increasingly understood to be – an increasingly competitive global environment. The Vision for Manchester, Salford, and Trafford promised that by 2005 (i.e. over a 10 year period, moving forward "into the twenty-first century") the area would be unchallenged as a "European Regional Capital," "and international City of outstanding commercial, cultural and creative potential," and "an area distinguished by the quality of life and sense of well-being enjoyed by its residents" (Manchester City Council 1994, p. 4). The wider community planning process has helped to ensure that such approaches have become almost ubiquitous, so that, for example, in the case of Milton Keynes we are told that "The community has a clear vision for the future of our great city" (Milton Keynes Local Strategic Partnership 2004, p. 4) and the city's economic vision is summed up in the ambition to transform Milton Keynes from "new town to international city" (MKELP 2004). As Deas indicates, "The argument [is] that only by thinking strategically, ambitiously and imaginatively, viewing each city in terms of its de facto city-region and creating a series of related initiatives and institutions, could competitiveness be sustained in the global context" (Deas 2005, p. 209).

The fashions of recent years have been clear: even the most landlocked cities have done their best to find some sort of waterfront and we have seen the emergence of some rather surprising places as cities of culture. Singapore has sought to redefine itself as "Renaissance city" or "global city for the arts" with the ambition of becoming an auction center, a regional center of theatre and a tourist center – "a fun city with creative people, artistic events and a culturally vibrant environment" (Chang 2000, p. 819). This strategy has been pursued not only "for economic reasons ... but also for sociocultural reasons (enrichment of Singaporeans and nation-building)" (Chang 2000, p. 819). The role of cities as cultural centers has now been widely recognized and strategies that seek to build on this recognition have been developed in a wide range of places from Bilbao to Barcelona, Berlin to Vienna, New York to Las Vegas, Glasgow to Huddersfield, Singapore to Sydney. Culture has come to be seen as an economic asset, not just something to be pursued for its own sake or to improve the quality of life of individuals (see Zukin 1995; Kong 2000; Garcia 2004).

At the end of the twentieth century, Berlin provided a particularly powerful example of the way in which the process of reimagination was used to reposition a city. It sought to reenter "normal" urban history, having been excluded from it as a divided city, at least since 1945. West Berlin was an island of capitalism in the sea of East German communism, while East Berlin was the capital of the German Democratic Republic cut off from Western Europe by the Cold War. A key element in the process of redefinition has been the use of symbolic imagery of city center redevelopment (particularly in the Potsdamer Platz), with its office blocks, cultural quarters and shopping experiences. Through the 1990s, there was a popular glorification of major building sites with a series of pamphlets guiding tourists around them (e.g. Schneider and Schubert 1997). The symbolism of redevelopment was clear, bringing in global imagery and global architects (the "Global Intelligence Corps" identified by Olds 2001, pp. 147–51) to highlight Berlin's role as a world city. But this global imagery existed alongside a conscious drive to maintain what was understood to be "Prussian" style with stone cladding and building up to the street line (Cochrane and Passmore 2001).

The Potsdamer Platz is now back at the center of Berlin, having been divided by the Wall as an area of dereliction until 1990. It was one of the historical centers, its busy streetlife a feature of interwar postcards in much the same way as Piccadilly Circus or Trafalgar Square in London. International architects (such as I.M.Pei, Richard Rogers and Helmut Jahn) were commissioned to design a series of prestige office buildings, constructing a vision which set out to define Berlin as a world city, with buildings like those of other world cities. The buildings incorporate large numbers of shops, hotels and offices, as well as residential space and what looks like a remarkable number of cinemas (including two big-screen IMAX cinemas). According to Dr Manfred Gentz, a member of the Daimler-Benz AG Board, the company "has harnessed its entrepreneurial energy and vision of the future to the task of replacing this jewel in the old and new capital – with its old lustre but a new refinement." It is "a symbol of starting out into a common European future" (Info Box 1996, p. 111).

In other words, the process of development itself became a means of defining Berlin as a place of the future. The popular pamphlets on Berlin's building sites proudly described the Potsdamer Platz as the biggest building site in Europe. A bright red exhibition center (the Info Box) placed on stilts at the center of the building sites on the Potsdamer Platz became a major tourist site, attracting 2 million visitors between its opening in October 1995 and January 1997. The visitors to the Info Box were explicitly expected to accept the imagination of architects, planners and developers for the reality of the city in the process of becoming something greater (Info Box 1996).

At the center of this process was a cultural repositioning of the city, reflected in a wider cultural policy. So, for example, the Sony Centre at the heart of the Potsdamer Platz development with its cafes, restaurants, cinemas and cinema museum, is central to its role as "destination" experience. The Potsdamer Platz itself has become the central location for Berlin's annual film festival. At the same time, even as the financial pressures on the city have become tighter and tighter, more museums have been opened while others have been relaunched, each reflecting a different understanding of Berlin's history and offering a different prospect for the future – from the German-Russian Museum to the Museum at Checkpoint Charlie; from the German Historical Museum to the Pergamon; from Libeskind's Jewish Museum to the Holocaust Memorial; from the Berlinische Galerie, with its focus on art from the Weimar years, to the Alte Nationalgalerie, with its focus on the nineteenth century; from Mies van der Rohe's Neue Nationalgalerie to the Hamburger Banhof for modern and contemporary art. Here the politics of culture are not only about making Berlin a new destination experience for tourists, but also about finding ways of redefining the city and – even – the nation of which it has so recently become capital (Cochrane 2006).

Garcia (2004) has identified a shift from straightforward city marketing to the process of "branding" as a result of which culture is now seen to flow from business aspirations, rather than exist in its own right to be marketed to others – in the language of the marketing professionals culture has to be seen instead "as part of a holistic destination brand" (Tibbot 2002; quoted in Garcia 2004, p. 316). As a result, suggests Evans (2003b, p. 420) in referring to their prestige cultural assets (buildings, museums, or areas), "Cultural strategists and civic leaders now use the language of real estate agents to describe their potential as 'flagships', 'chesspieces', 'nodes', paralleling the 'anchor store' in shopping malls and the 'must see' attractions on the tourist itinerary." In other words, they seek to locate them within the broader "brand" of the city and, indeed, to define the city through them. Evans also highlights the potential of "brand decay" – pointing to the risk that a single identification may not be sustainable – and the need for a more pluralist image. So, for example the use of Charles Rennie Mackintosh as a symbol of Glasgow as a city of culture has already lost its edge, he suggests, and he identifies similar dangers for Barcelona if it presents itself as Gaudi city and for Bilbao as little more than the home of the Guggenheim museum designed by Frank Gehry (see also, e.g. Gomez and Gonzalez 2001).

Benjamin long ago suggested that world exhibitions were "places of pilgrimage to the commodity fetish," schools "in which the masses, forcibly excluded from consumption, are imbued with the exchange value of commodities to the point of identifying with it" and given "access to a phantasmagoria which a person enters in order to be distracted" (Benjamin 1999, pp. 17–18). Today, it might be suggested that such destination experiences perform a similar role, even if now the masses are fully incorporated into consumption. In an echo of Benjamin's comments, Harvey describes the way in which "the display of the commodity" has become "a central part of the spectacle, as crowds flock to gaze at them and at each other in intimate and secure spaces like Baltimore's Harbor Place, Boston's Feneuil Hall, and a host of enclosed shopping malls … all over America," and he might have added all over the United Kingdom, too (Harvey 1989c, p 271).

These are "destination" experiences, as well as shopping centers, in the sense that they offer a complete experience, which goes beyond the desire to visit a particular shop, visit a particular restaurant or take advantage of an internal ski slope or other leisure experience. They are what Stevenson (2003) describes as "festival market places." In such places she suggests, "The manufactured environment is simultaneously an object of intrinsic sensory pleasure, and, as the setting for a range of leisure activities, acts as the facilitator of the experience of pleasure" (Stevenson 2003, p. 101).

The "city as spectacle" might be expected to provide a means of unifying the different aspects of urban policy in the context of attempts to manage the disorderly city. On the one hand, it promises the arrival of "safe" developments (for shopping or office workers) in privately policed prestige developments, while on the other it offers the vision of a revived city with which it is possible even for the excluded to identify, whether it is a "city of culture" or is mobilizing support for a bid to attract the Olympics (see, e.g. Cochrane et al. 2002; Mooney 2004). Nevertheless, Harvey is sceptical about the extent to which the popular mobilization of "spectacle" through the construction of fabulous environments of one sort or another can be sustained. He argues that, "The mobilization of the spectacle has its unifying effects, but it is a fragile and uncertain tool for unification, and to the degree that it forces the consumer to become a 'consumer of illusions' contains its own specific alienations" (Harvey 1989c, p. 273). The divisions it generates or reinforces create their own additional pressures. On the one hand large scale redevelopment, sponsored by urban development corporations and other agencies, serves to renew and redefine some areas of the city, bringing them back into productive use (see, e.g. Byrne 1997), while others – the peripheral estates and other areas of social housing – become sinks for the poor and the delinquent, places to be managed and to be presented as terrible warnings to the middle classes and the respectable (disciplined and ordered) poor.

In this context, Stevenson suggests that a broader notion of cultural planning may provide a way forward and contrasts the process of creating festival marketplaces as "Americaniza-tion" with "cultural planning" and the "creative city – as 'Europeanization'" (Stevenson 2003, pp. 104 ff.). The extent to which such a clear distinction can be made between actually existing developments in the United States and Europe may be questionable, but the argument is that a more creative approach is possible, which seeks to integrate new developments with the context within which they find themselves, taking advantage of what exists, rather than setting out to create palaces of spectacle in a wider urban desert.

Culture as Regeneration

It sometimes appears, however, as if the power of imagination, plus property development and architectural style, is assumed to be enough to transform what used to be accepted as the stubborn realities of urban-industrial decline. Initiatives have included waterfront developments in Baltimore, London's Docklands and Barcelona, canalside developments in Birmingham and also, increasingly, cultural developments based around iconic buildings of one sort or another (e.g. Gehry's Guggenheim in Bilbao and the Baltic Gallery in Newcastle/Gateshead). Cultural policy has been mobilized as a key element in the development of broad based policies for urban regeneration throughout Europe (see, e.g. Bianchini and Parkinson 1993; Wilks-Heeg and North 2004), but not only in Europe.

It is decaying urban sites that have been transformed into the "festival marketplaces" identified by Stevenson (2003, p. 100). She lists some of the better known examples: the process was pioneered in Boston, before being taken up in Baltimore's Harbor Place, New York's South St. Seaport, London's Docklands, Sydney's Darling Harbour and San Francisco's Pier 39 (Stevenson 2003, p. 101). Such projects clearly have little directly in common with the "traditional" notions of inner city policy even in their incarnation as regeneration (see, e.g. Loftman and Nevin 1996, 2003). There has been a shift in emphasis away from dereliction, decline and decay, towards one which stresses the potential for spectacle of urban areas, what Edwards (1997, p. 826) has described as a "new urban glamour policy." In Britain, the use of National Lottery money has helped to reinforce this trend by providing a source of funds for major capital investments, without offering continued revenue support which has also meant it has been difficult to sustain them (see, e.g. Griffiths 1998).

The rise of urban cultural entrepreneurialism can be seen in the intense global interurban competition for high profile events and feature developments, such as the Olympics or the European City (now Capital) of Culture, but this is just one reflection of the way in which mega cultural events have been used (successfully or unsuccessfully) as drivers of regeneration. This tradition seems to have begun with the Barcelona Olympics in 1992, which appeared to provide evidence of the way in which such global events could be mobilized to deliver significant local benefits. In one respect, they provided a means for levering investment from central government, so that investment went on urban improvements rather than sports facilities, but they also went further to provide the basis for very effective place marketing (Gold and Gold 2005, p. 207). The focus of the Olympics brought physical transformation, beautification and cultural festivals and helped to reposition Spain in the post-Franco era as no longer just being sea and sand for low end tourism (Gold and Gold 2005, pp. 206–12). At the same time instead of being an industrial center on the edge of Spain, Barcelona was able to present itself as an attractive destination and center of Catalonia, a region emerging in its own right from the national prison of Franco's Spain (for a wider discussion of the new Barcelona, see McNeill 1999).

A similar strategy was adopted in Sydney 2000, where the Olympics were used to promote regeneration (e.g. Homebush Bay and Rozelle Bay) while at the same time being used to reposition Australia as a "new" nation and one that was multicultural and sophisticated, not trapped in the monocultural stereotypes of surfer, beer, and barbecue (Gold and Gold 2005, pp. 252–9; McManus 2004). Beijing's success in attracting the Olympics for 2008, owes more to the repositioning of China as a "modern" nation, than to any regeneration strategy, but London's bid for the 2012 Olympics was similarly driven by a stress on multiculturalism – London as the embodiment of the globe – alongside a commitment to using the Olympics as a means of bringing new investment to the regeneration of the East End of London (as part of the wider program of development in the Thames Gateway). Although there remains some scepticism about the positive legacy of the Olympics in terms of facilities left behind, this bringing together of image–making with investment remains the holy grail of urban cultural policy. The involvement of cities in bids is seen as a means of levering in funds (from public and private sources) and of raising the profile of the cities involved in the global urban hierarchy (even where the bids themselves are unsuccessful – see, e.g. Cochrane et al. 1996).

The development of prestige projects is an ever present element of contemporary local regeneration strategies, alongside the discovery of the "creative class" and the drive to support the new creative industries. Prestige projects have been criticized as castles in a surrounding urban desert – not connected, but parachuted in from above. The connection of high profile developments to their surrounding environment has increasingly been questioned. There certainly is some justification for this, as the projects appeal to an external audience as much as and often more than a local one. Just the names of the "star" architects being mobilized in the different cities is, perhaps enough to illustrate this – Gehry, Foster, Pei, Libeskind, Koohlhaas seem ubiquitous, with Gehry's trademark style, apparently being given a local expression representing sails in Bilbao, but representing an undulating musical form in Seattle, and Libeskind's shiny metal deconstruction representing a broken Star of David in Berlin and the crystalline peaks of the Rockies in Denver.

In several cases the long term viability of projects has been marginal and several have proved impossible to sustain. It has been argued that however successful the Guggenheim in Bilbao has been in the short-term, its links into the local economy are insufficiently strong and its continued ability to attract tourists may depend on the extent to which other localities develop counter attractions (the global Guggenheim "brand" may ultimately not be strong enough to carry the weight expected of it and the "uniqueness" of Gehry's design may itself be overtaken by the next architectural marvel, in much the same way as Richard Rogers' Pompidou center in Paris has been overshadowed by the new) (see, e.g. McNeill 2000; Gomez and Gonzalez 2001; Evans 2003b, pp. 432–3).

However, the potential of the projects as a focus for more active involvement by a wider range of urban interests has also been identified in some cases. So, for example, in the case of Vienna's Museumsquartier, de Frantz (2005) charts the ways in which the project was recaptured by local populations because of the diverse cultural meanings associated with it – relating the new developments to local understandings and not just setting them within global cultural discourses. In the case of Glasgow, the initiatives associated with the European City of Culture were subjected to severe critique because of the way in which they seemed to marginalize and redefine the city's history and the experience of its residents. However, the expectation that the identification of Glasgow as European City of Culture and the gentrification of areas such as the Merchant City was part of a process by which the local population would be manipulated and repositioned within a global ideology alien to Glasgow's popular traditions, has not been fulfilled – the debates themselves highlight the continuing tensions and the ways in which the new initiatives have themselves been captured and redefined by those on whom it was assumed they would work (see, e.g. Boyle and Hughes 1991; Mooney 2004). Berlin has faced dramatic pressures in its attempts to redefine itself as "global" city, national capital or ordinary place: the tensions and debates around its new architecture as well as its politics of memory and museums are well recorded (see, e.g. Cochrane and Passmore 2001; Krätke 2001; Huyssen 2003; Till 2005). Culture remains a highly contested area, even in the face of these attempts to reposition places in global hierarchies and to fit in with global discourses, whether of the exotic and decadent or the "glamorous" and sophisticated.

Some Ambiguities of Culture

The dominant mode of intervention in many inner cities that are targeted for renewal and regeneration, may now be to find ways of "gentrifying" them or (if we restrict the use of the term to the particular process by which middle class people move into, improve and increase the "value" of working class housing in older urban areas) bringing them back into more productive uses, for consumption, tourism, high end accommodation, and even the new economy. So, for example, according to Evans and Foord (2003, p. 172), even the design led "urban renaissance" promised by Rogers (1999), has the objective of connecting "potentially threatening areas to the core city by effectively colonizing them" (Evans and Foord 2003, p. 172). The process of cultural planning may offer a means of doing this which is not directly oppressive or even manipulative, while nevertheless achieving forms of incorporation – and even a positive acceptance of change – through processes of what Allen (2003) describes as seduction. In other words, as Evans and Foord (2003) suggest, urban cultural policy, however much it is represented through prestige projects or cultural festivals, is also about reshaping and reimagining local populations and communities and the ways in which they work. It is here that opportunities may exist to tap into the metropolitan, multicultural "richness" identified by Worpole and Greenhalgh (1999).

The dominant understanding of urban cultural policy as an asset to be mobilized in the process of urban competition, and as a defining characteristic of effective urban entrepreneurialism, may be misleading or incomplete in some important respects. Chatterton and Unsworth (2004) suggest that there is still a continuing tension between the view of culture as aesthetic development and its mobilization as a resource in the process of generating economic development, which sometimes finds its expression in the development of local cultural strategies. Equally important, may be the extent to which culture has to be understood as something that is shared by communities and is "an essential element of everyday life and identity" (Evans and Foord 2003, p. 167). There is a continuing tension between approaches to culture which see it as something to be mobilized for promotion or marketing and those which are aimed at supporting, improving or reflecting communities and their shared (or contested) understandings (Dowling 1997). In some respects this has been recognized within urban cultural policy, for example, through the sponsorship of neighborhood-based or ethnic community-based festivals of one sort or another, alongside the more globally oriented festival events.

In some cases initiatives of this sort are consistent with the wider ambitions of urban policy, since "culture is seen as a new resource that, if correctly mobilized, could maximize the potential of local areas and neighborhoods as well as whole cities" (Evans and Foord 2003, p. 167), and there are many examples of "urban branding" at the neighborhood (or community) level. Smaller areas may be repackaged in ways that make it possible to "sell" them, too, building on the US model with its emphasis on urban villages (from Little Italy to Chinatown) even where the local population may no longer fit the label quite so well. So, for example, food has been used as a means of identifying particular areas in several British cities – Bangla town in East London, the Balti triangle in Birmingham, and Curry town in Bradford. Bianchini argues that this form of recognizing (and using) diversity is narrow and ultimately inflexible. It sets up a series of monocultural experiences in the city, effectively offering a caricature of each, which ensures that the "brand" is unlikely to be sustainable. Instead he argues for a wider approach (which he calls "intercultural urban design") capable of recognizing the fine grained differences that coexist within cities, supporting and sponsoring festivals that energize and involve residents across cultures and not just within them (Bianchini 2004, pp. 220ff). The rise of "culture" as a core aspect of urban policy not only brings with if the prospect of reshaping cities according to some globalized and relatively homogeneous vision of their marketability and suitability as place of residence for the "creative class", but may also open up the possibility of challenge and question – allowing scope for the development and presentation of alternative ways of understanding how best to live in cities.

Chapter 8

Neo-liberalism and the Globalization of Urban Policy

It has been strongly argued that we are living in an era of global (and globalized) neo-liberalism, and that this has both given urban policy an increased salience and has helped to redefine the nature of urban policy itself. In some contexts, neo-liberalism may be used as little more than a multi-purpose insult, sprayed in the direction of those (from World Bank to most national political leaders and spokespeople for multinational companies) who are blamed for all of the world's ills, but it has also been explored more rigorously to provide a powerful framework within which the nature of economic and political change and restructuring can be analyzed. The broad argument has been summarized by Jones and Ward (2002) who suggest that the "seemingly unconnected process of state restructuring and policy formation" should be seen as "outcomes of the same process of ideologically infused political decision-making that *cannot* be separated from the inherent contradictions of capital accumulation" (Jones and Ward 2002, p. 474). Smith (2002) sets out the break between neo-liberalism and the political/economic formation it replaces particularly starkly. He argues that, in contrast to the Keynesian welfare state, the neo-liberal state is agent of, rather than regulator of the market – focused on capitalist production (or "social production") rather than social reproduction.

Defining neo-liberalism is not straightforward, however, and there are tensions between the different ways in which has been mobilized theoretically. Some stress that it is an ideological concept, taken up by particular classes or elites to justify the strategies they have chosen to adopt (Harvey 2000, 2005); sometimes it is presented as if it had the potential to become the foundation of a new regulatory settlement (Jones and Ward 2002); some suggest that it represents a fundamental shift from the politics of social reproduction to those of capitalist production (Smith 2002); while others argue that social reproduction remains an important issue (even if imagined differently) (Gough 2002); for some its hegemonic power is the starting point of analysis to the extent that there is little space for any alternative politics (Jones and Ward 2002); others explore the extent to which a balance between different potential strategies is always being negotiated and renegotiated albeit in the context of a broad neo-liberal agenda (Gough 2002; Jessop 2002b; Larner 2003); some suggest we have moved the "rolling back" of the state to the "rolling out" of neo-liberalism through purposeful state intervention (Peck and Tickell 2002); others seem to be saying that the new urban policy is little different from the approach adopted by the princes of the Renaissance (Moulaert et al. 2001); at times neo-liberalism appears to be the driving force for political change, but elsewhere it is simply used as a term to capture all aspects of contemporary policy, without the need to analyze the forces that underlie its construction in any depth.

At the core of these debates, however, is a shared understanding that this is a global and globalizing process, one that means it is no longer possible simply to focus on a series of more or less autonomous national policy regimes. Jessop approaches neo-liberalism as a "new economic project" (or a series of state projects) that attempts to reimagine market liberalism in response to economic globalization, the interrelated state crises of the last decades of the twentieth century (of the "Keynesian welfare national state," the East Asian development state and the Soviet state system), and the rise of movements of resistance that have themselves emerged in response to these changes (Jessop 2002b, p. 452). Smith, too, emphasizes the importance of globalization, which he defines in terms of global processes of production – that is production organized across national boundaries (Smith 2002, p. 433). Jessop usefully identifies a number of key features of neo-liberalism, which include: economic liberalization within and across borders; privatization of state owned or provided services, as well as the use of market style approaches in the public sector; rolling back of traditional forms of state intervention, coupled with the espousal of new forms intended to foster economic innovation and competitiveness; the spread of partnership approaches to governance involving representatives of business (Jessop 2002b, p. 454). Gough (2002, pp. 411–12) further identifies the sponsorship of competition between places as an example of market approaches in practice and points to the encouragement of "possessive individualism" (which includes the creation of semiprivatized public space, and the intensified policing of private property).

Harvey sets out the role of neo-liberalism as ideology, underpinning what he sees as "a political project to re-establish the conditions for capital accumulation and to restore the power of economic elites"(Harvey 2005, p. 19), while Peck and Tickell identify it as a "new religion" (Peck and Tickell 2002, p. 381). Similarly Gough suggests that, "A majority feeling emerged among the elite that something radical had to be done to defuse this threat" (Gough 2002, p. 410). Harvey highlights the extent to which the ideology of neo-liberalism is a form of utopianism – that is a belief that the "perfect" market will produce "perfect" outcomes (Harvey 2000, pp. 175–9) – and he highlights the "inherent destructiveness of free-market utopianism" (Harvey 2000, p. 177), exploring the inherent contradictions of the model both in theory and in practice (see also Bourdieu 1998 on neo-liberalism as a "utopia of unlimited exploitation").

It is for this reason that Harvey concludes that the "utopian theory" of neo-liberalism has principally been used as justification for the broader political program that he has identified, rather than itself being the driver of change (Harvey 2005, p. 19). In particular, he notes the extent to which the state is needed to maintain the context within which the market operates (e.g. including policing and even the use of populist nationalism to maintain legitimacy) even while this may undermine the free operation of markets. Drawing on Polanyi, he argues that, "If free markets . . . undermine state powers, then they destroy the conditions of their own functioning. Conversely, if state power is vital to the functioning of markets, then the preservation of that power requires the perversion of freely functioning markets" (Harvey 2000, p. 181). A similar point is made by Gough (2002), who emphasizes the internal contradictions that beset neo-liberalism as he interprets it. As he defines neo-liberalism it embodies the understanding that: "Private property is to be freed from collective rights and obliga-tions, in particular from state interference, though the state is required all the more strongly to protect property from infringement by others" (Gough 2002, p. 405). He strongly argues that attempts to deny the extent to which capital is "socialized" (i.e. not simply a product of individual choice and individual decision making) themselves cause problems for its efficient operation. A failure to engage with the imperatives of social reproduction also undermines capitalist production – the politics of social reproduction are not just of interest to the social democrats and the working class (Gough 2002, p. 408). For him, because of the "immanence of socialization, the present day political-economy of cities involves a complex interplay of neo-liberal interventions, longstanding forms of socialization and new or revived forms of coordination" (Gough 2002, p. 413).

Gough provides a series of examples of the ways in which what Brenner and Theodore (2002b) call "actually existing neo-liberalism" responds to the demands of socialization, even while apparently espousing a more consistent form of market-based neo-liberalism. Even the involvement of business organizations in urban politics, while reflecting a belief in the dom-inance of business that is consistent with neo-liberalism, he says, implies a more collective (rather than individualized) understanding, and the existence and promotion of sectoral clus-ters similarly undermines the purity of neo-liberal rhetoric (Gough 2002, pp. 413–16). But Gough also notes the significance of attempts to mobilize the "community" (or "communi-ties") as a means of sustaining social reproduction and social control, "mobilization of the community from above," he argues, operates not only to "reduce the cost overheads of the poor but to reproduce the poor as effective labor power." He stresses the ways in which "top-down community socialization has fostered conservative social relations and has headed off challenges to the forms of power that create poverty" (Gough 2002, p. 418), and provides the examples of quasi-wage employment (in third sector organizations) as a means of socializing workers into low wage labor as well as noting the extent to which many of the initiatives are oriented towards the disciplining of young people. He argues that this form of state sponsored community-based socialization has actually helped to sustain some of the wider ambitions of neo-liberalism. In other words, according to Gough, although at an ideological level, the moralism associated with community based initiatives contradicts some of the key tenets of neo-liberalism. "Socialisation through community has . . . been able to further the class aims of neo-liberalism by constituting the poor as a real reserve army and by instilling self-discipline and self-reliance" (Gough 2002, p. 418).

The urban policy that flows from these understandings of neo-liberalism (whatever the tensions between them) has two related aspects. One is concerned with ways of expressing "free-market utopianism" in the form of the built environment. Harvey offers the specific example of what he calls the "commercialized utopianism" of the urban development corpo-rations sponsored by Margaret Thatcher in the 1980s (promising the delivery of a new society through state sponsored property development). He describes the selling of places (such as Baltimore) as a form of "utopian presentation," producing "commercialized and degenerate utopian forms all round us" (Harvey 2000, p. 181) (see also Chapter 7). Similarly, Swyngedouw et al. (2002) view large scale Urban Development Projects as "the material expression of a devel-opmental logic that views megaprojects and place-marketing as a means for generating future growth and for waging a competitive struggle to attract investment capital" (Swyngedouw et al. 2002, p. 543; see also Rodriguez et al. 2003).

The second is focused on ways of managing the growing inequality between and within cities– as rich areas grow richer, and poor ones poorer (Harvey 2000, p. 178). So, one key task of urban policy is to find effective ways of managing the consequences of uneven development, for example, through the disciplinary "revanchism" identified by Smith (1996b). The fundamental shift identified by Smith (2002) is from a policy process driven by the concerns of social reproduction towards one reflecting the impulses of capitalist production. The "so-called urban crisis of the late 1960s and 1970s," he argues, "was widely interpreted as a crisis of social reproduction, having to do with the dysfunctionality of racism, class exploitation, and patriarchy and the contradictions between an urban form elicited according to the criteria of accumulation and one that had to be justified in terms of the efficiency of social reproduction" (Smith 2002, p. 432). By contrast contemporary urban policy focuses on ways of fostering and enabling processes of capitalist production and managing the associated social divisions, rather than seeking to reduce them. He suggests that the repositioning of cities as "platforms of global production," instead of being located within regions that themselves are part of national systems of production, also implies that the national economy is "delinked from and independent of its cities," which means that nation states no longer have any particular interest in supporting cities (or their residents) through social policy (Smith 2002, p. 434).

Smith links two apparently unconnected processes, which reflect the different ways in which neo-liberalism may be expressed in different contexts. So, he focuses on the emergence of a new urbanism in the countries of the South and East: "We are," he says, "seeing a broad redefinition of the urban scale – in effect a new urbanism – that refocuses the criteria of scale construction, in this case towards processes of production and towards the extraordinary urban growth in Asia, Latin America, and Africa" (Smith 2002, p. 430). Asia, Latin America, parts of Africa are, he contends, "leading incubators in the global economy, progenitors of a new urban form, process and identity" (Smith 2002, p. 436). Davis (2004) views these processes more pessimistically, arguing that the working out of neo-liberalism (often expressed through the structural adjustment policies of the International Monetary Fund) has helped to create what he describes as a "Planet of Slums." He quotes a report on slums prepared by UN-Habitat, which suggests that "instead of becoming a focus for growth and prosperity, the cities have become a dumping ground for a surplus population working in unskilled, unprotected and low wage informal service industries and trade" (UN-Habitat 2003, p. 46).

The withdrawal of the state in the countries of the West from involvement with issues of social reproduction does not, of course, in itself mean that they lose their political salience, but within this paradigm, their meaning certainly shifts and the role of the state is trans-formed. Smith argues that there is strong evidence of "heightened state activism in terms of social control . . . the emergence of more authoritarian state forms and practices" (Smith 2002, p. 437). One aspect of this may find its expression in active forms of policing (some themselves explored by Smith 1996b), and Smith argues that the process of gentrification (particularly in the cities of Europe and North America) can also have apparently "softer" expressions which have equally powerful (equally "hard") effects in practice. So, he suggests that large scale multifaceted urban regeneration plans have effectively displace large numbers of work-ing class residents (on a scale still greater than the urban renewal and slum clearance of the 1960s). As he puts it, "gentrification portends a displacement of working-class residents from urban centers" (Smith 2002, p. 440) but also increasingly finds expression in "more modest, neighborhood development" (Smith 2002, p. 442). Gentrification – itself a complex alliance between state backed "regeneration" and investment by financiers and property companies, many of whom have global interests – he suggests, "has evolved into a vehicle for transforming whole areas into new landscape complexes that pioneers a comprehensive class-inflected urban remake" integrating housing with shopping, restaurants, cultural facilities open space and so on (Smith 2002, p. 443). It has itself come to define core aspects of competition between cities, as they seek to define themselves as successes, while attracting investment from outside: "the construction of new gentrification complexes in central cities across the world," confirms Smith (2002, p. 443), "has become an increasingly unassailable capital accumulation strategy for competing urban economies."

Gentrification can be seen as a process by which middle class groups gradually colonize the inner cities, mobilizing their resources (and those of the banks and building societies) to do so and to benefit from the subsequent rise in property values (a sort of privatized version of Howard's economic model for the garden cities). But Smith is quite clear of the role of "gentrification" as a tool of urban policy. He stresses its key role within discourses and practices of urban regeneration, and notes the extent to which this has become a global language, or certainly one that stretches across the more prosperous countries of the world. "Gentrification as a global urban strategy," he argues, "is a consummate expression of neo-liberal urbanism. It mobilizes individual property claims via a market lubricated by state donations and often buried as regeneration" (Smith 2002, p. 446).

Jones and Ward (2002) focus specifically on British urban policy. They suggest that under neo-liberalism, cities take on a "crisis-management role" and that urban policy is given the responsibility for managing the "contradictions of previous state led interventions" (as part of the process of managing the "crisis of crisis management" identified by Offe 1984) (Jones and Ward 2002, p. 475). In other words, they maintain that the state is acting not so much in response to economic crisis, "but to *crises in the rationality and legitimacy of the state and its intervention*" (Jones and Ward 2002, p. 480). Blair's New Labour government has chanted the mantra of "joined up" government as a solution to many of the problems of the cities and the policies directed towards solving them, and Gough (2002), too, confirms that the "problem" identified is a real one. However, he emphasizes the hopelessness of trying to resolve it by the means proposed. Government failure and the complexity and inconsistency of policy initiatives do not, he argues, occur accidentally. On the contrary they are consequences of the broader neo-liberal drive to the fragmentation of government (and governance) within particular policy fields, as well as between them (Gough 2002, pp. 419–20).

In other words, according to Jones and Ward (2002) it is not surprising that urban policy tends to look like a mess of fragmented and overlapping initiatives, some of which seem to contradict each other, while some simply repeat old mistakes. Urban policy has been tasked with trying to deal with the unintended consequences of previous intervention, reflecting the "exhaustion of policy repertoires [sic] under neo-liberalism," and as a result has been "made to shoulder the responsibility for a *devolved rationality crisis*" (Jones and Ward 2002, p. 481). They argue that urban entrepreneurialism is best seen as a "scalar crisis displacement political strategy" (in other words the political failure of national and international strategies for the management of the impact of economic crises has, in part been met, by shifting the political emphasis to the greater or lower success of individual cities in the process of territorial competition) (Jones and Ward 2002, p. 481).

They identify three main principles that underpin the "new" urban policy. First, they suggest that we are seeing a shift in the geographies of state regulation (or what they identify as "sites for crisis containment") to the urban (Jones and Ward 2002, p. 482). They argue that a "significant effort," is being made, "by the state to construct and regulate crisis at the urban scale" (Jones and Ward 2002, p. 485). They chart "a process of centrally orchestrated localism" of functions through the 1980s and 1990s, whose purpose was to bypass the existing structures of local government and the bureau-professions associated with them (Newman 2001). New institutional forms (such as business agencies and partnerships) have been sponsored to deliver neo-liberalism locally alongside new regional structures. Second, they point to a move towards the use of "competition" as a form of policy making, so that resources are distributed on the basis of competitive bidding rounds. "A cornerstone of neo-liberalism," they say, "has been the state's internalizing and subsequent creation in institutional form of interurban competition" – examples include City Challenge and SRB Challenge funds (Jones and Ward 2002, p. 484). Third, they stress the extent to which the problem itself is redefined as one of coordination (or, rather, a lack of coordination), so that it becomes one, "not just of economic decline but rather one of failed management" (i.e., a crisis of crisis management, an issue which is discussed more fully in Chapter 3) (Jones and Ward 2002, p. 482).

From the perspective of Jones and Ward, this emphasizes the extent to which such initiatives are principally concerned to "regulate the *previous* years of state intervention" (Jones and Ward 2002, p. 486). In Britain the logical extension of these initiatives and the emergent urban forms regulation is embodied in the central government sponsored creation of local strategic partnerships and community planning partnerships, which are expected to take the lead in the development of overarching Community Strategies, which now have to be produced in each local authority area. Jones and Ward describe this as a move towards "a recentralizing of the right to manage rationality crises with the state apparatus" (Jones and Ward 2002, p. 488).

The Discontents of Neo-liberalism

In some respects, approaching urban policy through the prism of neo-liberalism is helpful, particularly because it enables and encourages us to move beyond the detail of particular cases to identify not only broader patterns of change but also more fundamental drivers of change. However, there is always a danger that such an overarching approach may simply be taken for granted as encapsulating the nature of contemporary politics so that everything that actually takes place is taken to exemplify neo-liberalism, in an almost circular fashion. Instead of opening up a discussion of the ways in which new institutional arrangements and new policy spaces are being constructed, this may make it more difficult to understand the nature of the process. Seeking to isolate a political philosophy (albeit one that promises to deliver the "best shell" for capitalism) as somehow providing the underlying driving force of policy change across the world is (as Harvey 2005 acknowledges) ultimately likely to be a fruitless task. And redefining it as a fundamental (inexorable) structural or regulatory shift is equally unpersuasive. The decision to identify a new regulatory fix as "neo-liberal" has the advantage of being able to draw on the philosophical principles and political ideologies of neo-liberalism to help explain it, but it also means that it may be increasingly difficult to hold the two together, when the processes of regulatory (or political) settlement seem to draw on other ideological parents.

As we have seen, many of the features of urban policy in practice fit uneasily with some of the expectations associated with stronger – liberal – expressions of "neo-liberalism," and redefining "neo-liberalism" to include these features seems rather perverse. However, Peck and Tickell mobilize the term creatively, to emphasize the extent to which neo-liberalism is a political project and point to the ways in which it has changed over time – it is, they point out "neither monolithic in form nor universal in effect" (Peck and Tickell 2002, p. 384). This allows them to periodize the process of neo-liberalization and to stress that what is happening is indeed a process rather than a completed project. So, they argue, the agenda of neo-liberalism has moved from the destruction of old "Keynesian-welfarist and social collectivist institutions" to the building of "neo-liberalized state forms, modes of governance, and regulatory relations" (Peck and Tickell 2002, p. 384).

The benefit of such an interpretation for the analysis of urban policy is that it provides a means of exploring its contribution to that process, and, in particular, to the building of what might be defined as "neo-liberalized" regulatory state forms. Drawing on Hardt and Negri (2000), Peck and Tickell (2002, p. 400) point to the pervasiveness of "diffused power" and it could be argued that the way in which urban policy has developed and sent its tentacles through wide sections of society and structures of government is a powerful example of this. While still operating within a framework that focuses on "neo-liberalism" this approach makes it possible to explore how neo-liberalism is being actively constructed in practice, rather than simply assuming that it exists. Brenner and Theodore (2002b) also emphasize the importance of recognizing that there are differences between "actually existing neo-liberalisms" because they are path dependent, arising out of the particular national contexts within which they find themselves.

Jessop, too, while finding the notion of neo-liberalism a helpful one, is reluctant to accept that there has been a shift to a unified global neo-liberal regime, and also questions the extent to which there are any fully-formed neo-liberal regimes in any particular countries. Instead he prefers to use the two ideal types of the "Keynesian welfare national state" and the "Schumpeterian workfare postnational regime" or "Schumpeterian competition state" to explore the contemporary shifts in state regimes. The latter is characterized by a policy emphasis towards economic innovation and competitiveness, rather than state planning; a move away from (unproductive) welfare towards the expectation that individual welfare is best achieved through paid employment; a decline in the significance of national forms of government and an increased role for local, regional and supranational levels; and the emergence of new forms of partnership and network organization (Jessop 2002b, pp. 460–9. See also Jessop 2002a, Chapters 2 and 3).

As a result Jessop is at pains to point out that a range of strategies may be adopted which enable particular state regimes to position themselves more or less effectively in response to it. He identifies four ideal type possibilities – neo-liberalism, neostatism, neo-corporatism and neo-communitarianism – and recognizes that in practice responses are likely to borrow from each, even if neo-liberalism remains the dominant form. He also suggests that different approaches may be adopted at different state scales (Jessop 2002b, pp. 461–4). "Thus," he notes, "even where both the national and international levels are dominated by attempts to promote a neo-liberal regime shift, the urban level may be characterized more by neocorporatism, neostatism, and neocommunitarianism" (Jessop 2002b, p. 464).

Jessop goes further to question the extent to which liberalism is suited to contemporary capitalism (echoing the arguments of Gough 2002), which is characterized by a higher degree of coordination than earlier (nineteenth century) forms of competitive capitalism. As a result he stresses the need to identify the centers of institutional gravity around which particular settlements (or "actually existing neo-liberalisms") may emerge (Jessop 2002b, p. 457). "Actually existing neo-liberalism," he suggests, "also tends to promote 'community' (or a plurality of self-organizing communities) as a flanking, compensatory mechanism for the inadequacies of the market mechanism" (Jessop 2002b, pp. 454–5). In this model, the urban has a central role in the development and implementation of economic and social policy, and is an important site across which various partnerships and other forms of governance play.

By emphasizing the centrality of economic competitiveness and the shift away from welfare, the analytical emphasis of the neo-liberal paradigm may – as Ward and Jonas 2004 suggest – make it more difficult to recognize the continued significance of political engagement ("conflict, divisions, struggles, and strategies") around collective provision. The interaction between collective provision and economic development, they suggest, tends to be forgotten or marginalized in approaches that see neo-liberalism as defining the direction of policy change and political action, because of the extent to which they privilege issues of "production" (Ward and Jonas 2004, p. 2127). State spending on social and economic infrastructure may be increasingly instrumental, explicitly oriented (as in the case of the sustainable communities program discussed in Chapter 6) towards supporting growth and sustaining the labor market, but it still nevertheless provides a space within which political mobilization of different sorts can take place.

Too narrow an interpretation of neo-liberalism is also misleading, insofar as it makes it difficult to recognize the mix of political sources that comes together in shaping the new urban policy. It is necessary to recognize, as Barnett puts it, that the "ongoing changes in the terms of public policy debate involve a combination of different factors that add up to a much more populist reorientation in policy, politics and culture" (Barnett 2004, p. 10. See also Clarke 2004). Some of these seem to owe rather more to traditional conservative approaches to public policy than to "liberalism" of any sort – as we have seen, for example, in Chapter 5, they stress moral imperatives, they seek to involve members of the community in policing themselves. Back in the days of Thatcher, there was a similar debate between those who wished to identify her as little more than a born-again nineteenth century liberal and those who sought more complex explanations for the hegemonic power of Thatcherism. Hall (1988) developed the notion of authoritarian populism to capture this, and one aspect of the new urban policy is precisely the attempt to construct a "popular" vision of the future. Swyngedouw et al. seem to capture something similar in suggesting that the "New Economic Policy is the policy platform of" what they call "conservative liberalism." "Contrary to what its ideology sustains," they argue, "conservative liberalism is not against state intervention; rather it seeks to reorient state intervention away from monopoly market regulation, towards supporting economic growth and competitiveness" (Swyngedouw et al. 2002; Rodriguez et al. 2003, p. 33). This particular formulation might be seen as little more than a variant of neo-liberalism, but the existence of a "conservative" strand to the new urban policy is hard to ignore.

While acknowledging the force of arguments for the existence of "rolled out" neo-liberalism, Raco highlights the "hybridity of approaches and rationalities" that are being mobilized in the British government's sustainable communities plan, in particular noting the investment in social reproduction as well as an engagement with "the demands made by a variety of social groups" (Raco 2005b, pp. 325 and 343). In other words, Raco suggests that the process of urban policy in practice is rather more complex, contested and open than even the notion of a "rolled out" neo-liberalism might imply. Larner puts this forcefully in arguing that "in these accounts of neo-liberalism, for all their geographical and scalar diversity, little attention is paid to the different variants of neo-liberalism, to the hybrid nature of contemporary policies and programmes, or to the multiple and contradictory aspects of neo-liberal spaces, techniques, and subjects" (Larner 2003, p. 509). From this perspective it is the process of making up the new arrangements that matters most, rather than the particular characterization, so that "neo-liberalism" becomes rather more contingent, something that is always in the process of construction and reinvention rather than a universally applicable template.

The Rise of Global Urban Policy: Delivering Economic Growth

If the language and politics of neo-liberalism help to frame and shape localized responses to global processes, it is also important to consider some of the ways in which a global urban policy has been actively promoted by global agencies and through global networks. The World Bank has played an important part in this process, explicitly developing an urban policy of its own, with a particular emphasis on the importance of social capital and its development. The Bank has set itself clear corporate goals of reducing poverty, promoting market based growth, building durable institutions, and protecting the environment (World Bank Infrastructure Group Urban Development 2000, p. 40). For the World Bank the emphasis of urban policy is on the role that cities can play in enabling wider development. From this perspective (in contrast to the dominant discourses which were traditionally expressed in national urban policies) cities are not problems in themselves – on the contrary their success is seen as a vital underpinning for wider social and economic development of "poor" countries. Cities are only "problems" when they do not perform this propulsive role, and the expectation is that as long as obstacles are removed and the potential is understood, they will be able to do so. Here the issue is not how to deal with the decline of the inner cities but rather relates to the creation of megacities (see also Castells 2000) and the growth of "shanty towns" as well as the major imbalance in the distribution of national income between urban and rural areas – the challenge is to find ways of ensuring that the income generated in urban areas also finds its way to other parts of the country. The connections between this approach and the "new conventional wisdom" discussed in Chapter 6 will be clear enough, but it is nevertheless perhaps worth emphasizing that this goes further: not only is the competitiveness of cities identified as the main driver but it is precisely in those parts of the cities that were previously identified as standing in the way of development that hope is said to lie.

These understandings already underpinned the urban policy agenda developed by the Bank for the 1990s, and which presented a "policy framework for improving the contribution of cities to economic growth" (World Bank 1991, Chapter 2). Here it is argued that it is essential to "take a broader view of urban issues" moving beyond issues relating to housing and residential infrastructure, and instead what is emphasized is "the productivity of the urban economy and the need to alleviate the constraints on productivity" by enhancing the productivity of the urban poor by increasing the demand for labor. In addition the importance of paying more attention to the deterioration of urban environment and to develop a more robust research and evidence base is stressed (World Bank 1991, p. 4). Urban poverty is to be overcome through growth and it is made clear that there is no trade off between strategies to promote economic and those aimed at reducing poverty. While economic growth is not sufficient to deliver poverty reduction, it is certainly deemed to be necessary and the implicit assumption is that the two are fundamentally interlinked. To achieve a significant reduction in poverty it is necessary (according to this argument) to increase productivity at the individual, household, firm and urban levels (World Bank 1991, pp. 44–5).

The framework for development is, of course, fundamentally assumed to be given by the norms of a global (capitalist) economy. As Mayer suggests, the World Bank argues for "the need for market-supporting policies and for interventions in civil society to compensate market deficits," and she also draws attention to the World Bank web-site on social capital which largely reproduces Putnam's arguments and "presents rather romanticized views of family and civil society" (Mayer 2003, p. 115). Corruption and clientilism are identified as evils and emphasis is placed on good governance and to the value of partnership with or contracting out to agencies in the private sector or civil society. Emphasis is placed on the need to "focus on citywide policy reform, institutional development and high priority investments" (World Bank 1991, p. 4) and the rigidity of regulatory regimes as limiting the productive potential of households and firms in cities is highlighted (World Bank 1991, p. 38).

The rhetoric of the World Bank has changed over the years, even as some of the core arguments have remained the same. A more recent World Bank urban strategy places even greater emphasis on cities as drivers of national growth, and the purpose of the strategy is identified as being to ensure "that countries extract the most benefit from urbanization" (World Bank Infrastructure Group Urban Development 2000, p. 6), harnessing it "to promote more equitable growth of incomes in the nation as a whole" (World Bank Infrastructure Group Urban Development 2000, p. 37) (see particularly Annex A). A positive commitment to urban growth is seen as a necessary element in a development strategy even if it is in itself not enough to guarantee wider development. It must be seen as part of a national development strategy, and this, it is argued, also highlights the need for national urban strategies, both to correct possible market failure as well as to overcome the possibility of government failure (The World Bank Infrastructure Group Urban Development 2000, p. 63). Although "efficient" urban development will help reduce poverty, at present cities work in ways which are seen to reproduce it (the slums in Indian cities and *favelas* of Rio de Janeiro are presented as examples of places where urban policy undermines growth). Ways of dealing with urban poverty have to be found since it is also held to be bad for economic growth and stability.

In the early twenty-first century the World Bank's President was talking of the importance of "Empowering the people of the slums" but this was an expression of the same drive to develop the basic infrastructures of governance and overcome the problem of corruption (Wolfensohn 2001, p. 46). If anything, however, the stress on the urban was powerfully reinforced since, "We are moving now . . . from nation-state lending, to provincial and state lending, to urban lending" (Wolfensohn 2001, pp. 46, 47). "City-regions," he emphasized, "can be and are the engines of growth. They are the places for opportunity" (Wolfensohn 2001, p. 47). The broad model is one that moves away from the provision of "handouts" or even provision of services to the poor to one that seeks to draw the poor into the process of growth – Wolfensohn positively describes the comprehensive approach developed in Johannesburg, suggesting that "They are seeking to enfranchise the people" (Wolfensohn 2001, p. 47).

The strategy is very clearly presented as driven by a vision of "sustainable cities" (The World Bank Infrastructure Group Urban Development 2000, pp. 46–52), which is summarized under four headings – livability, competitiveness, good governance and management and bankability. Livability focuses on improving the quality of life of the poor and (although the term is not used directly) seeking to reduce their social exclusion by improving their access to "the resources of society" which in turn is expected to strengthen cities' contribution to economic development. It includes concerns relating to the urban environment, health and transport. Competitiveness – as we have seen – is a familiar mantra of contemporary urban policy and in this context it is argued that the drive to increased competitiveness through the development of "diversified growth strategies" will help to underpin urban employment and investment growth – even if it is also recognized that the national macroeconomic context is fundamental in shaping what is possible for individual cities. In this model the city is understood as "an enabling environment within which firms and individuals are competitive" (The World Bank Infrastructure Group Urban Development 2000, p. 48).

Good governance and management are increasingly presented as fundamental prerequisites for successful and sustainable urban development, and are seen as a means of challenging forms of corruption, which undermine development strategies. UN-Habitat (described by the UN as its "human settlements programme") launched a global campaign on urban governance in 1999 to support this agenda, offering a range of policy tools to achieve this goal. The World Bank is committed to "capacity building" for effective metropolitan management. Finally, bankability – or financial sustainability – relates to the ability of cities (and city governments in particular) to generate sufficient revenue to support the infrastructural needs of economic growth, as well as "financial soundness" and – where possible – creditworthiness (which gives access to capital markets). The achievement of bankability is particularly difficult for the cities of the developing world, when so much of the economy is informal or may be described as a "shadow economy" (The World Bank Infrastructure Group Urban Development 2000).

As part of the strategy for achieving these ambitions, the Cities Alliance was formed in 1999, bringing together the World Bank and the UN Center for Human Settlements (UN-Habitat) in a "multidonor partnership," with an emphasis on supporting the development of city development strategies and "scaled up programs for the poor." This global coalition of cities and their development partners is intended "to support the process through which city dwellers themselves can participate in defining their vision for their city, and to commit to nationwide and citywide programs of slum regeneration that will help the urban poor to get their share of the economic promise of cities" (Wolfensohn 2001, p. 47). The purpose of the Alliance is to develop strategies on the basis of which priorities can be identified and therefore to show how outside assistance would help to foster development (The World Bank Infrastructure Group Urban Development 2000, p. 64). The city development strategies fostered under the aegis of the Cities Alliance are aimed at bringing together "broad coalitions of stakeholders" and identifing possibilities for economic development and what is needed to take them forward.

Capacity building has been the focus of a series of initiatives, supported, for example through direct co-operation between cities or through the IULA (International Union of Local Authorities). An action plan for developing "slum upgrading" was launched by the Cities Alliance in 1999 and endorsed at the UN Millennium Summit in 2000. The strategy of "slum upgrading" represents a significant break with approaches that favor the renewal and removal of slums, to replace them with ready made modernity. According to UN-Habitat, "Upgrading has significant advantages; it is not only an affordable alternative to clearance and relocation, but it also minimizes the disturbance to the social and economic life of the community" (UN-Habitat 2003, p. 127). The new approaches identify "wellsprings of entrepreneurial energy" within the slums while recognizing that, "their brutal physical conditions limit residents' ability to realize welfare improvements from their own efforts alone" (Cities Alliance 1999, p. 2). "Slums," we are told, "can be divided into two broad categories: slums of hope; and slums of despair" (UN-Habitat 2003, p. 9; see also Lloyd 1979 for a more developed discussion of what might constitute "slums of hope"). In other words what was previously described as dysfunctional, part of the problem, rather than the solution, is redefined as part of the solution – indeed a fundamental aspect of the solution – even if it is acknowledged that the extent to which "participatory slum improvement" has been realized in practice remains limited (UN-Habitat 2003, p. 132). Davis (2004) is more dismissive, arguing that the informal workers of the slums are more concerned with finding ways of daily survival than generating entrepreneurial activities – the "real trend" he suggests "is the reproduction of absolute poverty" (Davis 2004, p. 26).

The drive to a global urban policy with an emphasis on building economic competitiveness is not restricted to the World Bank or, indeed, to the cities of the "developing" world. The OECD approaches urban policy through a similar lens, which has been given expression in a series of publications relating to particular cities, under the broad heading of "urban renaissance." Reports have been prepared for Belfast (OECD 2000), Canberra (OECD 2002) Glasgow (OECD 2003b), and Berlin (OECD 2003a). They start from an underlying principle that "A place based approach is needed to improve endogenous development and enhance competitiveness" (OECD 2003b, p. 127). It is said to be a "well-established fact that cities are locomotives for national economic growth" (OECD 2003b, p. 128) and each report starts from the assumption that the city under consideration is "at a turning point." More important perhaps, each also sets out a program stressing the importance of competitiveness with the aim of building an entrepreneurial city, characterized by environmental sustainability. Each highlights the role of the private sector and particularly the need for public-private partnerships. Each stresses the importance of social cohesion as an element required to underpin growth, not least because (it is argued) there is otherwise a danger of failing to take advantage of the contribution that excluded or marginalized populations can make to growth, particularly in the development of the "new" economy. So, in the case of Berlin, emphasis is placed on "activating under-utilised markets," creating new jobs and integrating marginalized communities, particularly the Turkish community. Subsidy based solutions are explicitly excluded.

The OECD's distaste for the public sector is well expressed in the discussion of the relative strengths of capital cities in the Berlin report (OECD 2003a). While capital cities may have some strengths, it is argued, (because they have good telecommunications infrastructure, good airports and transport infrastructure, above average levels of education among the workforce and are relatively cushioned from political and economic upheaval) they also exhibit fundamental flaws. According to the OECD the main problems are that "generous" government salary packages and terms and conditions make it difficult for others – particularly "startups" – to compete as workers; that able young people are attracted by the "cachet" of government employment, because of its high status; and that "in capital cities the mentality of the population is often that of the bureaucrat, rather than that of the entrepreneur" (OECD 2003a, p. 157).

The new global commonsense was brought together in a report prepared for a Global Conference on the Urban Future held in Berlin, Germany, July 4–6, 2000 (Hall and Pfeiffer 2000). The conclusions spelled out in the report echo the "new conventional wisdom" identified by Buck et al. (2005) and discussed in Chapter 6. The conference (URBAN 21) was convened under the aegis of the Global Initiative for Sustainable Development sponsored by Brazil, Germany, Singapore and South Africa. The four partner countries held regional conferences in their respective regions in preparation for the Global Conference. At the core of the report are the claims not only that the population of the world is becoming increasingly urbanized, but also that, for the first time urban residents increasingly "form part of a single networked globe" (Hall and Pfeiffer 2000, p. 5). The familiar claim that cities are "engines of economic growth" is repeated (Hall and Pfeiffer 2000, p. 51). A clear checklist of the (seven) essential elements of a sustainable city is set out in the report: a sustainable urban economy (defined through access to "work and wealth"); a sustainable urban society (expressed as "social cohesion and social solidarity"); sustainable urban shelter (i.e. "decent affordable housing for all"); a sustainable urban environment (reflected in the existence of "stable ecosystems"); sustainable urban access (achieved through "resource conserving mobility"); sustainable urban life (the making of "liveable cities"); and sustainable urban decision-making (defined as "empowering the city") (Hall and Pfeiffer 2000, pp. 16–34).

These elements or "dimensions," are presented as universal attributes or defining characteristics of the sustainable city, but the report also distinguishes between three types of cities: "the city coping with informal hypergrowth"; "the city coping with dynamism"; and "the weakening mature city coping with ageing" (Hall and Pfeiffer 2000, pp. 143–53). According to Hall and Pfeiffer, the first of these is characteristic of the emergent megacities of the developing world, the second set incorporates the successful cities of the new knowledge based economy, while the third is the familiar declining industrial city, finding it difficult to respond to the end of Fordism. Two potential scenarios are identified for each of these types of city, the first of which offers the "business as usual trend," while the second suggests how it might be possible with "sensitive" government intervention to "bend the trend" (Hall and Pfeiffer 2000, pp. 143–60).

Jessop (2002b) argues that the validity of the global neo-liberal agenda is simply taken for granted in the report. As a result, he suggests, while its authors argue that the social economy and the community need to be developed in the "hypergrowth cities of the developing world," utilizing the methods of neo-communitarianism, the purpose of doing this is to provide a stable infrastructure on the basis of which the wider agenda of neo-liberalism may be sustained. Meanwhile it is assumed that the "mature but declining cities of the Atlantic Fordist regions" should simply be opened up to unmediated forms of neo-liberalism. The final declaration of the Conference recommends that "cities and other levels of government should adopt effective urban policies and planning processes, which integrate the social, economic, environmental and spatial aspects of development" (Berlin Declaration 2000).

In this context, the tentative and uncertain emergence of a European urban policy highlights some of the possibilities and difficulties associated with the construction of urban policy across national boundaries. This urban policy has been expressed in a series of strategy documents produced by the European Commission, such as "Towards an Urban Agenda" (CEC 1997) and the "Framework for Action" for sustainable urban development (CEC 1998). They emphasize the need to support economic prosperity and generate employment in urban areas, but also to promote equal opportunities and social cohesion through improving the urban environment and (in an echo of the priorities of the World Bank) contributing to good urban governance. According to one of these reports, urban areas are Europe's "primary source of wealth creation and the center of its social and cultural development" (CEC 1997, p. 3), while elsewhere they are described as, "The dynamos of the European economy, enabling the EU to maintain a strong position in the global economy and community, while at the same time offering the scope to create employment, solve environmental problems and provide all citizens with a high quality of life" (CEC 1998, p. 3; see also Newman and Thornley 2005, p. 126).

However, this optimism is balanced by the recognition that "there are rising problems relating to rapid economic adjustments, unemployment, environmental conditions and traffic congestion but also poverty, poor housing, crime and drug abuse" (CEC 1997, p. 3). In other words, while cities are explicitly seen as "the motors of growth in an increasingly global economy," at the same time it is noted that "many of the worst problems facing society today are concentrated in urban areas" (European Commission 2003, p. 6) and the existence of the latter, it is said, can reduce the capacity of cities (and hence the European Union as a whole) to achieve the former. As a result, "only those cities which are capable of delivering top quality services and which have good infrastructural endowments can profit from the autonomy to attract activities which have a viable future and great added value" (CEC 1998, p. 8). Here, too, therefore urban policy must be given an explicit economic cast, which is consistent with the more explicit neo-liberal formulations discussed above – even social policy intervention is justified as delivering economic, that is competitive, benefits (see, e.g. Atkinson 2001, pp. 392ff.).

The core policy arguments within these documents emphasize the need to give an urban spin to the existing policies and initiatives (particularly the structural funds) of the EU, since the EU has no specific competence either for urban policy or spatial planning (see, e.g. CEC 1997, pp. 14–16 and CEC 1998, where the argument is more fully developed). In practice the distribution and management of structural funds, such as the ERDF (European Regional Development Fund), has provided funding for urban areas – it has been estimated that in the late 1990s they drew on nearly 40 percent of program allocations in Objective 1 areas and closer to 80 percent in Objective 2 areas (CEC 1997, p. 9), but now the argument is that such a bias should be more explicitly supported. The fundamental aim is to "promote a polycentric, balanced European urban system" (CEC 1998, p. 2), as a means of meeting "the challenge of globalization and economic restructuring: strengthening economic prosperity and employment in urban areas and working towards a balanced urban system" (CEC 1998, Annex, p. 1). The key challenges may be summarized as to find ways of reinforcing the competitiveness of cities; of challenging social exclusion and building community capacity; and achieving physical and environmental regeneration (European Commission 2003, pp. 6 and 26). The task is defined as the achievement of integration within cities (as well as a balanced development of cities across the European space), and stress is placed on "mix and diversity," ensuring that the city works "as a lively meeting place for all activities at all times of day," both providing a living space "living space" and helping to construct a collective identity (CEC 1997, p. 7).

There is one explicitly targeted program for urban areas funded through the ERDF as part of EU Cohesion Policy, but URBAN is a relatively small program (taking up 1 percent of the total funds available through the ERDF). It has a regeneration focus at urban and neighborhood level. In the second round of the program, the criteria for selection are familiar – average unemployment and crime are more than twice the average for EU urban areas and the proportion of immigrants is also more than twice the average for EU urban areas (presumably the proportion of immigrants is accepted as part of the problem definition because it may undermine "cohesion") (CEC 2002, pp. 11 and 14).

The tools being used are familiar enough, too, albeit with an environmental twist. There is an emphasis on physical and environmental regeneration, the renovation of buildings and the creation of green spaces; education and training (e.g. in entrepreneurship, but also other tradeable skills) for socially excluded groups; the creation of jobs – with specific reference to employment in environmental sectors, culture and creative industries, and service activities; the development of environmentally friendly public transport systems as well as the sponsorship of more sustainable uses and ways of generating energy; the more effective use of information technologies. The intention is to generate "innovative" models for economic social and economic regeneration of urban areas, particularly smaller urban areas and declining neighborhoods in bigger cities. URBAN projects are also supposed to foster new ways of participative involvement by communities, as well as partnerships between agencies from public, voluntary and private sectors (including different levels of government as well as the European Commission). The recognition that the EU cannot take a lead role in the direct delivery of urban policy across the member states is reflected in the emphasis placed on finding ways of sharing best practice of regeneration and sustainable development across Europe's cities (CEC 2002; European Commission 2003). Partnership and the sharing of good practice are described as "the URBAN method" (European Commission 2003, p. 16).

Other explicitly urban policy initiatives reinforce the emphasis on learning between cities and on competitiveness as a means by which this may be achieved. So, for example, through its sponsorship of an Urban Audit of 258 cities and towns, the EC seeks to encourage city authorities to compare themselves against others on a range of factors and, where appropriate, to rank themselves against similar cities, encouraging learning between them and possibly competition between them. This is also reflected in the process of identifying cities to act as European City of Culture (ECOC) (launched in 1985 and now retitled European Capital of Culture), which reinforces the notion of polycentricity by encouraging a range of cities to compete for the title. In other words, as Evans suggests, it becomes a means of giving the European project a cultural dimension, by adding "fuel to culture city competition, whilst at the same time celebrating an official version of the European urban renaissance" (Evans 2003b, p. 426). The award of the title to Glasgow in 1986 (for the year 1990) may have been the first case in which ECOC was to be used as "a catalyst to accelerate urban regeneration" but it has not been the last (Garcia 2004, p. 319).

Nevertheless, it is impossible to identify a fully developed urban policy and, insofar as there is a policy focus on cities, it tends to be located within the wider framework given by Europe-wide strategies for spatial development, which themselves remain "informal" (e.g. Williams 1999) because planning is not an EC competence, and in the drive towards greater social cohesion and economic competitiveness. The main emphasis of the spatial planning approach, expressed in the European Spatial Development Perspective agreed by ministers of member states in 1999 (Committee on Spatial Development 1999) stresses both the existence of and the normative ambition to sustain a polycentric, balanced, and cohesive Europe. As a result there is no attempt to identify particular cities as priorities for development but there is an explicit bias against concentration in "world cities" or other major nodes. Davoudi (2003, pp. 988ff.) argues forcefully that the notion of polycentricity has been captured by the EU as a normative ambition, rather than an analytic tool (i.e. a way of thinking about and analyzing development). In this context, she suggests, it is a convenient way of masking the tensions between the dominant approach of the European Commission (with its emphasis on competitiveness) which leads to differentiation between cities and the wish to achieve social cohesion and balanced development (i.e. development that ensures no areas are disadvantaged by development). She questions the realism of such an understanding of development, pointing to the ways in which it is underpinned by the emergence of new, as well as the reinforcing of existing, divisions between cities and within them.

The role of the European Union and its institutions may be greater in setting a wider context for national urban policies than in any direct involvement, because of their explicit linking of economic growth and competitiveness with issues of "social exclusion" (with its origins in French social policy) (see, e.g. Harloe 2001, p. 892). The redefinition of poverty as social exclusion and the argument that social exclusion itself undermines economic competitiveness makes it possible for the Commission to involve itself in this area of social policy, since it otherwise has no competence for direct involvement in social policy. Similarly, the emphasis of the Commission on partnership initiatives at local and regional levels (since it has no agencies capable of direct involvement) has reinforced the spread of partnership approaches within urban policy (see, e.g. Geddes 2000 for a discussion of EU-based social exclusion policies and the rise of local partnerships).

Looking for a Global Urban Policy

There is powerful evidence that urban policy has become a global phenomenon, rather than merely an aggregation of nationally distinctive urban policies, but it is less clear how this globalization finds its "localized" expression. It is certainly the case that some aspects of policy are shared and that there is an active learning process between different national policy communities. Peck highlights the importance of transatlantic policy transfer, suggesting that it has speeded up in recent years, in part because of the increased role of Think Tanks in spreading the gospel of neo-liberalism of which the United States has been seen as the paradigmatic model, despite the continuing significant differences between the economic, social and policy environments in the countries that are expected to be the objects of the transfer (Peck 2003, p. 228. See also Peck 2002). Private networks may be as important as public ones in this context. So, for example, the spread of new methods of surveillance such as CCTV and the electronic tagging of offenders in the United Kingdom were borrowed from the United States and seems to be a powerful example of the "speedy transfer" identified by Peck (Nellis 2000). However, Nellis goes further to suggest that the process may be rather more of a global phenomenon based on lobbying and "selling" by global commercial interests (Nellis 2000). There is a strong and growing global industry of crime control, which exists alongside and interpenetrates the state institutions which order its products.

The United States often seems to operate as a policy laboratory for policy makers in the United Kingdom, for whom the US is seen to prefigure the United Kingdom's own future. Yet the borrowings are generally reinterpreted for reuse in the United Kingdom, sometimes losing their force and almost always fitting uneasily with the United Kingdom's different institutional and social context. In other words it is apparent that the learning process is by no means a straightforward one, both because the "lessons" learned are filtered through the understandings of those doing the learning and because the contexts to which the borrowed policies are applied tend to differ significantly (and subtly) from those in which they were first developed.

It is also certainly the case that there is a broadly shared global economic policy context, whether reflected in the discourses of neo-liberalism or in the (apparently more neutral) language of competitiveness. Peck and Tickell summarize the global commonsense of what they see as neo-liberal competitiveness in a series of bullet points, which include: "a 'growth first' approach to urban development"; a "naturalization" of the market as the model for decision-making and distribution; a commitment to "lean government, privatization, and deregulation"; an external focus oriented towards the identification of potential competitors, rather than the welfare of residents; a limited range of policy tools clustered around forms of boosterism and property development; disciplinary intervention into cities and areas of cities that are defined as "failing"; and the targeting of the disorderly and the urban poor through forms of authoritarian governance (Peck and Tickell 2002, pp. 394–5). And this language has been reinforced by that of a number of international agencies seeking to develop their own urban policies or strategies for competitiveness. The message for the cities of the West and North is relatively simple – unless cities position themselves more effectively to be more competitive, they will inevitably decline, to be superseded by leaner and hungrier replacements (in India or China). And the message for the (mega) cities of the Third World is equally clear, and distinctive, albeit still within an overarching framework of competitiveness. There stress is placed on the need to build the social infrastructure capable of taking advantage of the creativity and informal networks that are currently in danger of being lost in the urban slums.

What is more questionable, however, is the extent to which these broad understandings and pressures have been able to construct a global template for urban policy. The continued vitality of urban policy and the extent to which it is reshaped and reinterpreted in practice both at national and local (even community) levels suggests that the process is more complex than such an understanding implies. Ward and Jonas argue both that redistributional (or welfare) policies are always "rooted in particular 'national' contexts and that they cut across and reinforce the already uneven development of neo-liberalism" (Ward and Jonas 2004, p. 2133). As Larner summarizes the position: "Although neo-liberalism may have a clear intellectual genesis, it arrives in different places in different ways, articulates with other political projects, takes multiple material forms and can give rise to unexpected outcomes" (Larner 2003, p. 511). And the extent to which transnational agencies, such as the World Bank and the European Union, are capable of (or even committed to) capturing and homogenizing or making consistent these differences also remains doubtful.

Chapter 9

Reshaping Welfare, Reimagining Urban Policy

There are no straightforward answers to be drawn from the various attempts to theorise urban policy that were considered in Chapter 1. None of them individually succeeds in capturing the complexity and uncertainty, negotiations and settlements, overlaps and tensions associated with the emergence and development of urban policy, or the understandings of the "urban" that underpin it. Yet each of them contributes something worthwhile to the analysis of the ways in which urban policy has been constituted in practice. Urban policy has been built up from a series of not always complementary projects and initiatives, in response to a range of problem definitions. Practitioners, professionals, and activists have ended up redefining themselves (and the "urban" of which they are parts) to meet the priorities of the various state sponsored initiatives. They have become enmeshed in and helped to reproduce powerful policy discourses. If they want to attract resources they have to behave in ways that fit the current problem definition. But by their actions, they have also helped to shape that definition.

We live in an urbanized society, which makes it difficult to specify the boundaries between urban and other social policies. As a result, perhaps, urban social policy can best be understood as an overlapping patchwork without any clear or consistent overall unified agenda. Meanings somehow have to be extracted from this complexity. Instead of starting from some perfect "scientific" definition, it may be helpful to explore the ways in which urban policy or urban policies emerge and change in practice through an active process of social construction (Clarke and Cochrane 1998).

It is possible to identify a repertoire of urban polices that may be drawn on and utilized in different ways at different times, helping to generate fluid understandings of what makes places urban. The "progress" of urban policy has been crablike, moving first in one direction then in another, since it is a changing mix of initiatives reflecting a changeable set of priorities and policy fashions, many of which owe little to the changing needs of urban areas and their residents. But shifts in approach within this ever changing policy field can also have dramatic effects on urban residents: they may find themselves defined as pathological or victims of a dependency culture; criminals or victims of crime; as congenitally incapable of being entrepreneurial. Communities may be understood as dysfunctional monocultures; as the equally dysfunctional sites of the war of each against all; or as vibrant and open yet socially cohesive social spaces through which shared moral responsibility can be generated to underpin urban prosperity. Cities may be defined as economic failures (which may mean that moving out is the solution); as the homes of unskilled labor, and the unemployable or workshy (from lone parents through the long-term sick to young working class – or black – men); as the main foundation on which economic growth can be built and social well-being achieved; or as the home of *flâneurs* and cafe society (which is not much fun if you are on the outside while the cultural elite has its fun); and so on. In other words, urban policy is not an innocent form of intervention, but itself helps to shape and define its object of intervention. Urban policy is both socially produced and helps to naturalize the urban problem, whose existence and form can be taken for granted. Dominant understandings of urban policy both reflect and influence the ways in which people experience urban living; urban policies help to define the urban "problem" or even the urban "crisis." They are not just responses to those problems but help to constitute them.

A broader direction of change can, however, be identified, which reflects and has helped to shape the restructuring of welfare states – with urban policy playing a key role in the making of new (post-Keynes, post-Beveridge, postwelfare) settlements (see, e.g. Hay 1996; Hughes and Lewis 1998), as well as helping to redefine social policy through the prism of global competitiveness and economic success.

From the start urban policy has been about redefinitions and different understandings. It has played a central place in the complex process of negotiation and renegotiation that has helped to reshape contemporary welfare – the postwelfare state. The Keynesian Welfare State itself has to be understood as a contradictory (and inherently unsustainable) structure, perhaps best understood as a "settlement" or series of settlements (see, e.g. Hughes and Lewis 1998), and the rise of urban policy can be seen both as part of the process of unsettling the old settlements and beginning to develop some of the principles that might define a new one. Its origins are to be found in a recognition of the failure of the Keynesian Welfare State to solve the problem of poverty, and of social divisions, as well as a belief that the costs of welfare were undermining the profitability of the private sector. The emergence of a recognizable field of urban policy in the 1960s was part of a wider move away from some of the grander promises of the Keynesian Welfare State. It reflected a shift in emphasis away from large scale comprehensive development and redevelopment, whether expressed in the building of large scale planned new towns or in policies of slum clearance, towards more piecemeal approaches based around different understandings of urban life.

In many respects, therefore, the emergence of urban policy was a response to failure both in the United States and the United Kingdom, even if, as Harold Wilson made clear, the new Urban Programme was still to be understood as an answer to violence and racism which sought to reassert "our faith that social grievances require social solutions – by positive social action by the state" (Wilson 1971, quoted in Edwards and Batley 1978, p. 63). In positive terms it could be understood as a response to the recognition that the postwar boom and the welfare states built around it had not solved all the problems of urban poverty. In its early years its development might even be seen as a last ditch attempt to rescue the welfare state from some of the challenges it faced, from below (in the form of urban social movements) and above (through the growing challenge of what came to be called the new right).

As one of the earliest symptoms of the growing disillusionment with the more universalist messages of the welfare states constructed in the two decades after the mid 1930s in the advanced industrial countries of the "West," the emergence of urban policy prefigured later debates around the need to "empower" communities and to move away from "dependence" on state benefits. Urban policies allowed the development of more targeted approaches (area-based means tests) and both responded to the weakening of, and helped further to undermine, dominant social policy models of universal citizenship, in which the universal citizen was perceived to be white, male, able-bodied and in full-time employment. The urban policy arena became one of constant experimentation, in which no sooner was one approach tried than another was pursued. Urban policy was constantly reinterpreted and used to reflect wider shifts of policy focus and popular political understandings. If it was difficult to shift the direction being taken by the welfare state as a whole because of its scale, it was much easier to shift that of urban policy.

If urban policy emerged in the context of the Keynesian Welfare State, with its national focus, it has been transformed by the impact of, and has helped to shape the politics of (neo-liberal) globalization. The new emphasis on urban competitiveness, whether expressed through the development of mega projects, cultural initiatives, place marketing, or the provision of social and economic infrastructure, has been part of the process of redefining "welfare" in terms that stress the importance of economic success for cities and access to employment for urban residents. These have been reflected in the emergence of forms of globalized and global urban policy as cities (and sometimes the nations of which they are a part) seek to position themselves in accordance with the new policy environment and global agencies seek to influence that environment.

The British Case

The British experience offers a particular case which helps both to illustrate the broader directions of change and to highlight the complex processes of negotiation as well as the tensions and ambiguities which underlie them.

Early initiatives were focused on problems of "race," while the rest of the welfare state remained resolutely "color blind." Soon, however, the focus shifted towards ways of encouraging community self-help, an early expression of attempts to move the poor away from "dependency" on the state and to save money by doing so. The redefinition of Britain's problems in terms of economic regeneration later found a clear expression in an urban policy shift focused on partnership, the reclamation of derelict land and the provision of small factory units. Later still, the excited bandwagon of urban entrepreneurialism and place marketing helped to reinforce and underpin the broader shift towards an enterprise state. Throughout it all – of course – the one consistency has been the apparently endless bleating for better coordination, increasingly couched in the language of managerialism.

Urban policy developed on the margins of mainstream social policy. This allowed it to carry a series of messages, which have often fitted uneasily with the concerns of that mainstream. So, for example, even in the late 1960s, urban regeneration, community work, and locally-based provision were presented as alternatives to traditional forms of welfare and to traditional forms of planning and urban renewal. Notions of multiple deprivation drove understandings that stressed both the possibility of targeted provision and of self-help. The emphasis on "individual, family and community malfunctioning" was clear, alongside the almost religious fervor associated with the ambition to regenerate communities and encourage individual self-improvement (Higgins et al. 1983, p. 7, pp. 14–19). These were not initiatives led by the professions of the welfare state, but – on the contrary – actively questioned their ways of working.

Even the economic and property development led initiatives of the 1980s could be seen to open up new possibilities and new understandings of welfare (Imrie and Thomas 1999). They questioned the dominant division between economic and social welfare policy (suggesting that without economic development there could be little social welfare) as well as directly challenging the roles of long-standing public sector professions. Perhaps most important, they encouraged and sponsored the incorporation of private sector agencies of one sort or another into the public policy process. Since 1945 there had been a clear division between the politics of economic policy and the politics of social welfare, but the development of urban regeneration as a distinctive policy field since the late 1970s was predicated on overcoming or transcending this division. The implicit division of labor between Keynes in economic policy and Beveridge in social policy was undermined by the attempt to develop the area-based "holistic" (and often economic development led) policies identified by Robson et al. (1994) and the DETR (1998).

The rise and reshaping of urban policy in the 1980s fitted well with the rise of a form of managerialist neo-liberalism (see Clarke and Newman 1997), because it allowed a move beyond an approach to social welfare, which was defined in terms of service provision or social transfer payments. Embedded within the developing British urban policy were crucial elements of what might be seen as a new, postwelfare state, political agenda. The underpinning rhetoric was clear: social welfare depends on economic (competitive) success; community self-help is better than dependence; public-private partnership is the way forward; social inequality is a necessary corollary of economic vitality, and is likely to be concentrated in some areas which need to be managed (or require more targeted assistance); market approaches and the use of not-for-profit agencies are necessarily better than state involvement. The new urban policy promises economic success to urban elites, while also setting out to manage the poor more effectively.

In some important respects, urban regeneration was reclaimed as a legitimate aspect of social policy under the Blair government. It moved in from the margins to take a much more central place (Ginsburg 1999). But this reflects the way in which understandings of social policy have shifted in recent years, with the move away from social welfare (or social reproduction) as the focus of attention towards an emphasis on the ways in which investment in social infrastructure may be needed to support economic success, at the same time as economic competitiveness is an essential prerequisite for individual well-being.

In the United Kingdom, this probably found its clearest initial expression in the Social Exclusion Unit's report on "Bringing Britain Together" and its explicit claim for urban regeneration as a legitimate focus for social policy attention. According to the report, the Unit was given the task of finding "integrated and sustainable approaches to the problems of the worst housing estates, including crime, drugs, unemployment, community breakdown, and bad schools etc." (Social Exclusion Unit 1998, Foreword). The report places a strong emphasis on finding ways of dealing with the problems faced by those living in these neighborhoods, in ways that are reminiscent of the approaches adopted in the 1960s and early 1970s. But it also more clearly and deliberately highlights the ways in which mainstream programs might be redirected to achieve change, instead of allowing the issue to remain on the margins of their attention. It seeks to identify "outcome" goals (lower long term unemployment and worklessness, lower crime levels, improved health, better qualifications) rather than "output" measures, such as "numbers of people helped into jobs and number of homes built" (Social Exclusion Unit 1998, para 6.6).

In some important respects, of course, these features could simply be seen as building on the changes of the 1980s following on from the neo-liberal agenda of Thatcherism (which was itself, of course a rather more complex phenomenon). The new urban regeneration agenda, whether in its expression as neighborhood renewal or as urban renaissance, is part of a wider move beyond or away from welfare statism, and the expectation of universal service provision. But it would be a mistake to see the new approaches to urban regeneration as nothing more than warmed over Thatcherism. The broader rhetoric of the "Third Way" (Giddens 1998) may be unconvincing, but – as Healey 2004 suggests – there certainly are significant shifts taking place here.

Most important, it is possible to identify a repositioning, which is emphasizing the significance of social exclusion as an obstacle to the economic success of cities and indeed to the economic success of the United Kingdom. Instead of believing that growth will solve problems, the understanding (however mistaken) is that the existence of deprivation may itself get in the way of growth. In this context a key management role for those involved in urban regeneration is to reduce social exclusion (admittedly rather narrowly defined), not for its own sake, but as an essential component of wider regeneration. The new approaches pick up on many of the forms of the 1980s, but seek to reimagine them in ways that begin to change their meanings – so partnership working is redefined as joined up thinking; competition seeks to create "beacons" rather than being simply a market surrogate, with only the "best" succeeding; the big schemes are being redefined as part of a process of design-led planning. All of these elements are consistent with the broader "modernization" agenda, that seems to have become the political common sense of neo-liberalism in its "actually existing" in Britain.

Escaping the Straitjacket?

The argument in this book has been that urban policy has to be understood as part of an active process of political and economic redefinition which is increasingly playing itself out across a range of scales, but focused on cities. Rather than looking for any single key which is capable of unlocking the complexity of this process, it is important to recognize that the making of urban policy is an active political process within which a wide range of (sometimes apparently contradictory) understandings are mobilized. Clearly, this does not mean, as Hall (1988, p. 156) stresses, that the economic (or material) context is irrelevant. Indeed, the direction and nature of contemporary urban development and economic change are of fundamental importance in shaping what is possible. But what the story of urban policy highlights is a process of building hegemony – that is one which involves the construction of "popular" legitimacy, and not one that can simply be imposed by a set of powerful elites.

In the particular case of the United Kingdom, this can best be seen in the whole series of initiatives focused on "community" in one way or another in the form of neighborhood renewal, the various new deals, the emphasis on capacity building, the active community initiatives launched through the Home Office and the rise of crime and community safety partnerships. These represent attempts to engage with and to build new forms of legitimacy and responsibility. The underlying principle can perhaps be summarized in the words of Tony Blair who argues that, "Strong communities depend on shared values and a recognition of the rights and duties of citizenship" (quoted in Hill 2000, p. 102). But, however strongly he asserts this principle, it remains one that is fragile and cannot simply be imposed. As Clarke suggests: "The work of constructing a neo-liberal hegemony is intensive, deploys different strategies, and encounters blockages, resistances and refusals. It has to engage other political-cultural projects – attempting to subordinate, accommodate, incorporate or displace them" (Clarke 2004, p. 102). He goes on to stress, that if "we draw attention to the grinding and uneven struggle to make the world conform . . . questions of conflict, contestation and the 'unfinished' become rather more significant" (Clarke 2004, p. 102). He sees "neo-liberalism" itself as something that "seeks to articulate multiple national populars" (Clarke 2004, p. 93), but also recognizes mobilization of other ideologies and "imaginings" (community-based conservatism as well as neo-liberal individualism).

If the dominant theoretical understandings of urban policy often seem to be rather bleak – whether because the unmanageable has to be managed, because there is no escape from the competitiveness agenda or because the urban has been captured by the agenda of neo-liberalism – an alternative (and much more positive) vision emerges from the work of writers (such as Amin et al. 2000; Sandercock 2000; Amin and Thrift 2002; Healey 2002, 2004; Massey 2004) who focus on what they see as the potential of cities to provide a platform for social and political engagement. Cities are understood as the products of flows and interconnections across space that link them into wider networks of economic and political relationships, which in their turn ensures that cities are defined by the coming together and juxtaposition of the social forces (people and cultures) connected into these networks in different ways. They are, as Massey argues, "the intersections of multiple narratives" or multiple space-times (Massey 1999), since places can effectively be seen as "a momentary coexistence of trajectories and relations; a configuration of multiplicities of histories all in the process of being made" (Massey 2000, p. 229; see also Massey 2004).

Cities bring different people together, requiring them to live together, even as they provide ways of reinforcing and developing new forms of segregation and division. Cities, argue Amin and Graham, are "places which bring together and superimpose diverse connections and disconnections" (Amin and Graham 1999, p. 9). Urban spaces become sites across which conflicts take place but also within which accommodations are negotiated, with particular places taking on symbolic meanings, which crystallize (for a time at least) the outcomes of those negotiations, sometimes as borders, sometimes as protected or open spaces. They are, as Sandercock (2000) puts it, the places where "strangers become neighbors." The challenge, therefore, as Healey suggests, is to resolve the collective "puzzle over how to manage our co-existence in shared spaces" (Healey 1997, p. 3).

The argument is set out particularly clearly by Amin and Thrift 2002. See also Amin et al. 2000, for whom cities provide the ingredients on the basis of which a civilized society can be constructed. They argue that modern cities remain "the cradle of invention and creativity" (Amin and Thrift 2002, p. 159). Cities, they suggest, are, "sites of everyday participation, intermingling with others and daily confrontation between the private and the public, between the citizen and institutionalized power" (Amin and Thrift 2002, p. 131). They neatly summarize what they see as the possibilities inherent in the modern city, which is "so full of unexpected interactions and so continuously in movement that all kinds of small and large spatialities continue to provide resources for political invention as they generate new improvisations and force new forms of ingenuity" (Amin and Thrift 2002, p. 157). It is the scale and intensity of such interactions and juxtapositions that make cities the places where such possibilities exist, and which make them less likely to exist in smaller towns and villages (see also Massey et al. 1999). Amin and Thrift seek to identify ways in which urban citizens connect through a series of overlapping formal and informal networks (of leisure, work, friendship, commerce, interest community, and so on).

This is understood as an urbanism of hope, rather than despair, which they see as drawing on Lefebvre's call for a move beyond the demand for citizens to have a *"right to the city"* towards, "a transformed and renewed *right to urban life*" (Lefebvre 1996, p. 138). Amin and Thrift challenge those who interpret the urban experience as a battlefield in which different groups seek to protect themselves from others behind real or socially constructed walls, finding ways of inscribing power relations on the geography of the city. In a sense while their arguments highlight the continuing tension at the core of "cityness" – between the search for security, the struggle for order and the celebration of difference, the emphasis on opportunity – they unashamedly celebrate the latter, arguing that the institutions of the city have the potential to provide "the opportunity for citizens to become something else and for mutuality to be strengthened" (Amin and Thrift 2002, p. 143).

Finding ways of taking advantage of this opportunity, however, is by no means straight-forward. Amin and Thrift maintain that the full potential of cities will not be realized unless an active process of education and involvement is pursued. As they put it "the problem of inculcating citizenship remains," because "in order to encourage citizenship as an everyday practice, people need to experience negotiating diversity and difference" (Amin and Thrift 2002, p. 151). They celebrate the "conversational anarchy" of places promoting friendship and shared experience (e.g. pubs, public libraries, community centers) and call for state funding for "social houses," which are capable of combining "political education and sociability" (Amin and Thrift 2002, p. 149). They set out a series of proposals for activities that would (they believe) assist with this process (including the provision of an incentive for everybody to work on a "voluntary" basis with the public services or in a voluntary organization in early adulthood).

Healey takes a similar approach to Amin and Thrift in defining the challenge as being "about the formation and expression of multiple identities, and about how to combine a concern for providing home environments which sustain human flourishing in diverse ways with an openness to the opportunities of the many networks and webs of relations which traverse the space of the city ... It is about the social qualities and values of the different nodes and networks, the places and flows of urban life" (Healey 2004, p. 160). But she is rather more explicit in seeing New Labour's urban policy initiatives as an "attempt to link the urban policy field and policy for land use and development, and re-cast the focus of urban policy from a concentration on 'problem areas' to a focus on the qualities of cities and their communities" (Healey 2004, p. 159). In sharp contrast to those who see those initiatives as part of the working out of a neo-liberal agenda, she suggests that, however "hesitant and fragmented ... they represent the "reawakening of a 'social democratic' agenda after two decades of 'neo-liberalism'" (Healey 2004, p. 159). She suggests that there is potential within the development of urban policy for initiatives that present opportunities to urban residents, rather than restricting them.

However, this does not mean that existing policies are presented as expressions of these opportunities. Even Healey, the most explicitly supportive of the New Labour initiatives, highlights the "contradictory emphases" within them (Healey 2004, p. 161) noting, in particular, the tension between those aspects of the "agenda aimed to release resources for economic activity" (i.e. the competitiveness agenda) and "objectives aimed to improve the quality of life experience and human flourishing for diverse people in diverse places," to which she believes emphasis ought to be shifted (Healey 2004, p. 162. See also her critique of the urban white paper, pp. 164–6) (for a more explicitly positive analysis of the new urban policy, see Hill 2000). Healey argues that the "social" needs to be articulated with more depth to give it a stronger voice in the struggle over defining a "balance" between the economic, environmental, and social dimensions of "well-being" and "sustainable development" (Healey 2004, p. 169).

In some respects, of course, and despite the celebration of the city, the policy conclusions draw by Amin and Thrift are not too far away from those of the communitarians with their stress on the remoralization of communities and individuals within them, even if the nature of the learning might be different. And the emphasis placed on the value of voluntary working (particularly for working class youth) also has echoes of the policy language of social exclusion and its belief in work as the way of escaping demoralization. Paradoxically, too, these arguments and those of Healey imply the construction of yet another form of "professionalization," albeit perhaps one closer to the brokerage role identified by Larner and Craig (2005). The reluctance to consider structural issues of power and inequality (because of the stress on openness and the potential to use a range of formal and informal networks to access power) runs the risk of minimizing the significance of the active processes of marginalization and disciplining that affect many of those living in cities. Even if, as Allen (2003) reminds us, individuals and organizations do not just possess (more or less power), but need to find ways of mobilizing it effectively (which means that is not always those we think of as the "powerful" who win in the battles over urban space), it is nevertheless also clear that some are so positioned that it is more likely that they will be able to do so effectively. As Fainstein puts it, there is a danger that such an approach "neglects fundamental questions of inequality in power opportunities and resources" (Fainstein 2001, p. 888). Simply promoting "sociability" will not resolve this, particularly as those living in the elite "bubbles" identified by Atkinson and Flint (2004) (see Chapter 5) are unlikely to participate.

Looking for a Way Out

As we have seen, there is a fundamental tension between different ways of understanding urban policy and its potential. On the one hand it may be analyzed as the working out of some wider political and economic logic, as one of the key sites across which the crisis of the Western welfare states plays itself out or the cities of the poor look for survival strategies in response to global neo-liberalism. And there is no doubt of the power of such visions. Urban policy has been at the center of the major changes that have taken place in redefining the meaning of social policy and the relationship between society and state over the last twenty-five years and more.

A second interpretation points to the extent to which cities offer the space within which new ways of living may be constructed and, in some versions at least, social justice fought for or aspired to. Cities become understood as the places where worlds of difference come together and positive interaction becomes possible. Again, there is no denying the power of such visions. Urban policy represents one of the ways in which the various players on the urban scene may become active in creating the spaces within which their self-activity may be realized. It may also be the arena within which negotiation over resources can take place.

And yet, if the logic of either approach is taken too far, each becomes unsustainable. The danger of the former is that it leaves us trapped in a world fundamentally determined by the working out of more or less inexorable processes of neo-liberalism. The options we seem to be left with are heroic and ultimately fruitless resistance or a fundamental recasting of the world economic and political system on a global basis. While the latter may be attractive, the steps from here to there are difficult to chart and even more difficult to take, which leaves us with the option of a weary fatalism, able to chronicle what is wrong in ever sharper detail, but for ever trapped in the present.

By contrast, the danger of the latter is that it leaves us equally politically disabled because it presents us with a utopia of the here and now in which because we will it, or because there are committed professionals to help with it, it becomes possible to positively negotiate our ways though the city. Agonism (that is a readiness to engage in discussion and negotiation) rather than antagonism becomes the basis for interaction because it ought to, without it always being clear how the "ought" can be transformed into political mobilization, or by whom. The danger is that the divisions of race, gender, class, and power, simply become defined away into networks of negotiation within which we all have to learn how to mobilize power – in a more sophisticated form of capacity building. This is, in a sense, no less "fatalistic," because it leaves those negotiating from a position of weakness (or just learning the ropes) relying on the generosity of those with whom they are negotiating. The *"right to urban life"* remains an abstract statement rather than a phrase capable of leading to transformation along the lines set out by Lefebvre.

A consideration of the ways in which urban policy has developed since its emergence as a distinctive policy field in the 1960s helps to indicate what is possible. This is not a policy area in which outcomes are given, in which a single agenda is being or can be forced through. It relies on continuing the construction of different visions for the city, which also turn out to be different visions for the wider society. In that sense, Harvey's call for a return to reimagined forms of utopian thinking – "spatio-temporal utopianism" – strikes an important chord (Harvey 2000). This is a policy area which, however practical it claims to be, is also always engaged in presenting different forms of utopia – from the utopia of the cohesive community to the utopia of entrepreneurial competitiveness; from the utopia of safety and security to the utopia of creativity and the urban "buzz"; from the utopia of suburbia to the utopia of the sidewalk; from the utopia of self-managed social integration to the utopia of holistic management and so on.

It is this which opens up a space within which debates about alternative futures can be launched or engaged in, even if at any one time that space appears to be dominated by the latest policy fashion apparently delivered from on high. The various utopias under discussion are not fixed, but fluid – indeed never presented as if they were utopias, always as if they were simply the practical proposals of practical men and women. And of course, they are always being constructed, and are never complete. It is often easier for professionals and activists simply to accept the visions, even if they are not persuaded by them, since that makes it possible to take advantage of the initiatives that flow from them, bending and interpreting them so that resources can be mobilized to fit the needs of local communities or disadvantaged groups. And of course, it is often easier for academics to criticize them without offering any alternative. The challenge is to find ways of taking the broader claims seriously while looking for ways of positively imagining alternatives.

In some respects there may be a danger of taking an overly fatalistic view of the changes that have taken place in recent years, in particular by identifying the move to an economic focus as necessarily reducing the scope for popular movements to influence or determine outcomes. In Chapter 6, for example, it was noted that a quite distinctive alternative approach to local economic policy had been developed in at least some British local authorities and the Greater London Council may even have been the first such authority to develop its own Cultural Strategy (Bianchini 1987). Others have also argued that professionals, as well as citizens and community groups, do not necessarily find themselves trapped within the agenda set by others, or set by some broader governmental logic. So, for example, Mollenkopf (1983) has argued that it is possible for public actors to take the initiative in ways that give previously excluded interests a stake and potentially, even to reshape the "contours" of private sector interests, a position close to those of the new urban left of the early 1980s in the United Kingdom.

More modestly Hill and Nowak (2002) argue strongly that the key task of urban policy in the "distressed cities" of the United States is not to look for ways of helping the poor, but rather to look for ways of transforming their central areas, to make them economically viable once again. In other words, they explicitly support the agenda of the urban entrepreneurs by giving it a "progressive" spin (see also Savitch and Kantor 2002 for a discussion of the differential bargaining potential of cities). While Fainstein rejects the easy assumption (of the "new conventional wisdom") that urban economic success cannot be delivered without social cohesion, she nevertheless also believes that the two can live alongside each other. In part she sees achieving this as being the role of the national state, which sets the policy parameters "in assuring the economic well-being of individuals and the mitigation of competitiveness" as well as dealing with "issues of just distribution" (Fainstein 2001, p. 888). "A persuasive vision of the just city," she argues, "needs to incorporate an entrepreneurial state that not only provides welfare but also generates increased wealth; moreover, it needs to project as future embodying a middle-class society rather than one only empowering the poor and disenfranchised" (Fainstein 2000, p. 468).

The development of urban policy has been fundamentally shaped by processes of contestation and negotiation. Running like a thread through all the various urban experiments and urban initiatives that have been discussed in this book has been the need to find means of incorporating citizens and communities into the strategies and more modest initiatives being pursued, and where possible to find ways of taking advantage of their strengths and commitment. And, of course, on a regular basis those being managed have sought to take advantage of the double sided nature of the relationship to pursue their own agendas, and those of the constituencies of which they are a part or which they represent. The very fact that the sites of interaction have varied so much across the years is a measure of vibrancy of urban politics, even if sometimes it may have felt quite different from below. Of course, Fainstein (1995, 2000) is right to remind us that these negotiations are taking place in the context of major inequalities of wealth and power, and Peck and Tickell (2002) to point to the constraints on the space for politics. And sometimes, too, they are experienced as fundamental (and unequal) conflicts rather than negotiations (Mitchell 2003; Smith 1996a). But, what matters in this context is that they ensure that the social and political settlements represented in the city remain uneasy and incomplete.

In a sense, "actually existing urban policy" is always an attempt to manage the unmanageable. In some ways this is reflected in the contemporary preference for the term "governance" (often in preference not only to "government" but also the "state") to capture the complexity and uncertainties of managing the urban. But the notion of "governance" itself offers hope to the new managers, who are persuaded that a different approach will enable them to manage by incremental negotiation and the decentralization of responsibilities to others (all – of course – ultimately accountable to them through some complex process of review). While opening up to "new managers" or "new professionals" may make it easier to incorporate them, it also (as Clarke 2004 suggests) places them in a rather more uneasy position where their mixed loyalties cannot be guaranteed.

The notion of "community" is – as we have seen, particularly in Chapter 4 – a much abused and battered concept, capable of being utilized to justify almost any strategy. It has been called a "slippery" concept and indeed it is. But the slipperiness is not a one way process. In other words, it can be used to identify areas and groups suitable for particular forms of management – or to be "empowered" to manage themselves in what is always a subordinate position. But it can also be claimed and mobilized by others who seek to challenge the position in which they find themselves and it can give legitimacy to those seeking to negotiate with the complex governance structures (or the state) which confronts them. Kling and Fisher are surely right to argue that "people will continually find ways to construct new movement forms and to assert control of their lives" even if doing so is not always straightforward (Fisher and Kling 1993a, p. 324). As Larner and Craig (2005) indicate, the processes by which activists seek to influence policy are often difficult, since those involved have to work in political spaces that are sometimes very narrow (and can be made narrower still by the decision of the state). But these are nevertheless often spaces within which action can take place and existing arrangements challenged.

The challenge remains, of course, how to bring together the small scale acts of contestation and more positive negotiation in ways that can bring more extensive change – mechanisms that might make it possible to enable a fuller vision of social justice to be achieved than the conditional and stunted form promised through the pursuit of the social exclusion or "respect" agendas. This is where the bigger debates – the debates around the visions – may offer hope. Not surprisingly, however, so far community representatives have proved reluctant to buy into the ten year strategies they have been presented with, when they have more immediate concerns troubling them. And the consultative mechanisms (such as local strategic partnerships) charged with developing some of them remain rather distant and seem irrelevant. Nevertheless, making the link between the continued detailed practices of urban political engagement and the wider ambitions of (and visions that underpin) urban policy is the challenge we face.

Benjamin suggests that city "streets are the dwelling place of the collective," which is, "an eternally wakeful, eternally agitated being that – in the space between the building fronts – lives experiences, understands, and invents as much as individuals do within the privacy of their own four walls" (Benjamin 1999, p. 879). It is this which continues to make urban policy such an important field of political engagement. The urban remains a site across which mobilization of all sorts is possible and not always with what might be thought of as progressive or pluralist ends. If it is perhaps most obviously the arena within which resistances of various sorts can be generated, but it is also the space where it is possible to come together in broad formal and informal collectivities in ways that suggest that there may also be different and more positive ways of living together.

References

Aldridge, N. (2005) *Communities in Control: Creating Better Public Services.* London: Association of Chief Executives of Voluntary Organisations/Social Market Foundation.

Alinsky, S. (1971) *Rules for Radicals.* New York: Vintage.

Alinsky, S. (1989) *Reveille for Radicals.* New York: Vintage.

Allen, J. (1999) Cities of power and influence: settled formations, in Allen, J., Massey, D., and Pryke, M. (eds.), *Unsettling Cities. Movement/Settlement.* London: Sage.

Allen, J. (2003) *Lost Geographies of Power.* Oxford: Blackwell.

Allen, J. and Massey, D. (eds.) (1988) *The Economy in Question.* London: Sage.

Allen, J., Massey, D. and Cochrane, A. (1998) *Rethinking the Region.* London: Routledge.

Amin, A. (2003) Unruly strangers? The 2001 urban riots in Britain. *International Journal of Urban and Regional Research*, 27, 2: 460–3.

Amin, A. (2004) Regions unbound: towards a new politics of space. *Geografiska Annaler B*, 86, 1: 33–44.

Amin, A. and Graham, S. (1999) Cities of connection and disconnection, in Allen, J., Massey, D., and Pryke, M. (eds.), *Unsettling Cities.* London: Routledge.

Amin, A., and Thrift, N. (eds.) (1994) *Globalization, Institutions, and Regional Development in Europe.* Oxford: Oxford University Press.

Amin, A. and Thrift, N. (2002) *Cities. Reimagining the Urban.* Cambridge: Polity.

Amin, A., Cameron, A., and Hudson, R. (1998) *Welfare to Work or Welfare as Work? Combating Social Exclusion in the UK.* Durham: Department of Geography, University of Durham.

Amin, A., Massey, D., and Thrift, N. (2000) *Cities for the Many, Not the Few.* Bristol: Policy Press.

Amnesty International (2005) "They come in shooting": policing socially excluded communities, http://web.amnesty.org/library/print/ENGAMR 190252005.

Anderson, B. (1983) *Imagined Communities: Reflections on the Origins and Spread of Nationalism.* London: Verso.

Anderson, J. (1990) The "new right", Enterprise Zones and Urban Development Corporations. *International Journal of Urban and Regional Research*, 14, 3: 468–89.

Arthurson, K. (2002) Creating inclusive communities through balancing social mix: a critical relationship or tenuous link? *Urban Policy and Research*, 20, 3: 245–61.

Atkinson, Rob. (1995) Post-war urban policy in Britain: changing perceptions and problems. *Policy Studies*, 16, 4: 6–17.

Atkinson, Rob. (1999) Discourses of partnership and empowerment in contemporary British urban regeneration. *Urban Studies*, 36, 1: 249–70.

Atkinson, Rob (2001) The emerging "urban agenda" and the European Spatial Development Perspective: towards an EU urban policy. *European Planning Studies*, 9, 3: 385–406.

Atkinson, Rob and Cope, S. (1997) Community participation and urban regeneration in Britain, in Hoggett P. (ed.), *Contested Communities. Experiences, Struggles, Policies*. Bristol: Policy Press.

Atkinson, Rob and Moon, G. (1994) *Urban Policy in Britain. The City, the State and the Market*. Basingstoke and London: Macmillan.

Atkinson, Rowland (2003) Domestication by cappuccino or a revenge on urban space? Control and empowerment in the management of public spaces. *Urban Studies*, 40, 9: 1829–43.

Atkinson, Rowland and Blandy, S. (2005) Introduction: international perspectives on the new enclavism and the rise of gated communities. *Housing Studies*, 20, 2: 177–86.

Atkinson, Rowland and Flint, J. (2004) Fortress UK? Gated communities, the spatial revlt of the elites and time-space trajectories of segregation. *Housing Studies*, 19, 6: 875–92.

Atkinson, Rowland, Blandy, S., Flint, J., and Lister, D. (2004) *Gated Communities in England*. London: Office of the Deputy Prime Minister.

Audit Commission (1991) *The Urban Regeneration Experience: Observations from Local Value for Money Audits*. London: HMSO.

Austrian, Z. and Rosentraub, M. (2002) Cities, sports, and economic change: a retrospective assessment. *Journal of Urban Affairs*, 24, 5: 549–564.

Back, L. and Keith, M. (2004) Impurity and the emancipatory city: young people, community safety and racial danger, in Lees L. (ed.), *The Emancipatory City? Paradones and Possibilities*. London: Sage.

Bacon, R. and Eltis, W. (1976) *Britain's Economic Problem: Too Few Producers*. London: Macmillan.

Baeten, G. (2001) Cliches of urban doom: the dystopian politics of metaphors for the unequal city – a view from Brussles. *International Journal of Urban and Regional Research*, 25, 1: 54–69.

Ball, M. and Maginn, P. (2005) Urban change and conflict: evaluating the role of partnerships in urban regeneration in the UK. *Housing Studies*, 20, 1: 9–28.

Banfield, E. (1970) *The Unheavenly City*. Boston: Little, Brown and Company.

Banfield, E. (1974) *The Unheavenly City Revisited*. Boston: Little, Brown and Company.

Barnekov, T., Boyle, R., and Rich, D. (1989) *Privatism and Urban Policy in Britain and the United States*. Oxford: Oxford University Press.

Barnett, C. (2004) The consolations of "neoliberalism." *Geoforum*, 36: 7–12.

Bauman, Z. (2000) *Liquid Modernity*. Cambridge: Polity.

Beck, U. (1992) *Risk Society. Towards a New Modernity*. London: Sage.

Begg, I. (ed.) (2002) *Urban Competitiveness. Policies for Dynamic Cities*. Bristol: Policy Press.

Belina, B. and Helm, G. (2003) Zero tolerance for the industrial past and other threats: policing and urban entrepreneurialism in Britain and Germany. *Urban Studies*, 40, 9: 1845–67.

Benington, J. (1976) *Local Government Becomes Big Business*. London: Community Development Project Information and Intelligence Unit.

Benjamin, W. (1999) *The Arcades Project*. Cambridge, MA: Belknap Press of Harvard University Press.

Berlin Declaration (2000) *Berlin Declaration on the Urban Future*. July 6, 2000, www.wiego.org/papers/Declaration-final.doc

Berry, B. (1985) Islands of renewal in seas of decay, in Peterson, P. (ed.), *The New Urban Reality*. Washington DC: Brookings Institute.

Bianchini, F. (1987) GLC R.I.P. Cultural policies in London 1981–1986. *New Formations*, 1: 103–17.

Bianchini, F. (2004) The cultural impacts of globalization and the future of urban cultural policies, in Johnstone, C. and Whitehead, M. (eds.), *New Horizons in British Urban Policy. Perspectives on New Labour's Urban Renaissance*. Aldershot: Ashgate.

Bianchini, F. and Parkinson, M. (eds.) (1993) *Cultural Policy and Urban Regeneration. The West European Experience*. Manchester: Manchester University Press.

Blackman, T. (1995) *Urban Policy in Practice*. London: Routledge.

Blair, Thomas (1974) *The International Urban Crisis*. St. Albans: Paladin.

Blair, Tony (1997) Speech at Aylesbury Estate, June 2, 1997. Available on Social Exclusion Unit Website. http://www.socialexclusion.gov.uk/news.asp?id=400

Blair, Tony (1998) *The Third Way: New Politics for the New Century*. London: The Fabian Society.

Blunkett, D. and Green, G. (1983) *Building from the Bottom. The Sheffield Experience*. Fabian Tract 491. London: The Fabian Society.

Boddy, M. (2002) Linking competitiveness and cohesion, in Begg, I. (ed.).

Boddy, M. and Fudge, C. (eds.) (1984) *Local Socialism? Labour Councils and New Left Alternatives*. Basingstoke: Macmillan.

Boddy, M. and Parkinson, M. (eds.) (2004) *City Matters. Competitiveness, Cohesion and Urban Governance*. Bristol: Policy Press.

Bohl, C. (2002) *Place-Making: Developing Town Centers, Main Streets and Urban Villages*. Washington, DC: Urban Land Institute.

Booth, C. (1902) *Life and Labour of the People in London*. London: Macmillan.

Bourdieu, P. (1986) Forms of capital, in Richardson, J. (ed.), *Handbook of Theory and Research for the Sociology of Education*. New York: Greenwood Press.

Bourdieu, P. (1998) *Acts of Resistance: Against the New Myths of Our Time*. Cambridge: Polity.

Boyle, M. and Hughes, G. (1991) The politics of the representation of "the real": discourses from the left on Glasgow's role as European City of Culture, 1990. *Area*, 23, 3: 217–28.

Branson, N. (1979) *Poplarism 1919–1925. George Lansbury and the Councillors' Revolt*. London: Lawrence and Wishart.

Brenner, N. and Theodore, N. (2002a) *Spaces of Neoliberalism: Urban Restructuring in North America and Western Europe*. Oxford: Blackwell.

Brenner, N. and Theodore, N. (2002b) The urbanization of neoliberalism: theoretical debates. Cities and geographies of "actually existing neoliberalism." *Antipode*, 34, 3: 349–79.

Brindley, T., Rydin, Y., and Stoker, G. (1988) *Rethinking Planning: The Politics of Urban Change in the Thatcher Years*. London: Routledge.

Brown, A., O'Connor, J., and Cohen, S. (2000) Local music policies within a global music industry: cultural quarters in Manchester and Sheffield. *Geoforum*, 31, 4: 437–51.

Brownill, S. and Darke, J. (1998) *"Rich Mix": Inclusive Strategies for Regeneration*. Bristol: Policy Press.

Buck, N. (2005) Social cohesion in cities, in Buck, N., Gordon, I., Harding, A. and Turok, I. (eds.), *Changing Cities. Rethinking Urban Competitiveness, Cohesion and Governance*. Basingstoke: Palgrave Macmillan.

Buck, N., Gordon, I., Harding, A., and Turok, I. (eds.) (2005) *Changing Cities. Rethinking Urban Competitiveness, Cohesion and Governance*. Basingstoke: Palgrave Macmillan.

Burns, D., Hambleton, R., and Hoggett, P. (1994) *The Politics of Decentralisation. Revitalising Local Democracy*. Basingstoke: Macmillan.

Burton, P. (1997) Urban policy and the myth of progress. *Policy and Politics*, 25, 4: 421–37.

Burton, P., Goodlad, R., Croft, J., Abbott, J., Hastings, A., Macdonald, G., and Slater, T. (2004) *What works in Community Involvement in Area-Based Initiatives? A Systematic Review of the Literature*. Home Office On-line Report 53/04. London: Home Office.

Byrne, D. (1997) National social policy in the United Kingdom, in Pacione, M. (ed.), *Britain's Cities. Geographies of Division in Urban Britain*. London: Routledge.

Byrne, D. (1999) *Social Exclusion*. Buckingham: Open University Press.

Campbell, B. (1993) *Goliath. Britain's Dangerous Places*. London: Methuen.

Cantle, T. (2001) *Community Cohesion: A Report of the Independent Review Team* (Chaired by Ted Cantle). London: Home Office.

Castells, M. (1977) *The Urban Question*. London: Edward Arnold.

Castells, M. (1978) *City, Class and Power*. London: Macmillan.

Castells, M. (1983) *The City and the Grass-Roots. A Cross-Cultural Theory of Urban Social Movements*. London: Edward Arnold.

Castells, M. (1998) *End of Millennium. Volume III of The Information Age. Economy, Society and Culture*. Oxford: Blackwell.

Castells, M. (2000) *The Rise of the Network Society. Volume I of The Information Age. Economy, Society and Culture*. Second edition. Oxford: Blackwell.

CEC (1997) *Towards an Urban Agenda in the European Union*. Communication from the Commission, COM(97) 197 final, May 6, 1997. Brussels: Commission of the European Communities.

CEC (1998) *Sustainable Urban Development in the European Union: A Framework for Action*. Communication from the Commission COM(98) 605 final, October 28, 1998. Brussels: Commission of the European Communities.

CEC (2002) *The Programming of the Structural Funds 2000–2006: An Initial Assessment of the Urban Initiative*. Communication from the Commission COM (2002) 308 final, June 14, 2002. Brussels: Commission of the European Communities.

Chanan, G. (2003) *Searching for Solid Foundations. Community Involvement and Urban Policy*. London: Office of the Deputy Prime Minister.

Chang, T. (2000) Renaissance revisited: Singapore as a "global city for the arts." *International Journal of Urban and Regional Research*, 24, 4: 818–31.

Charles, D. (2003) Universities and territorial development: reshaping the regional role of UK universities. *Local Economy*, 18, 1: 7–20.

Charles, D. and Benneworth, P. (2001) *The Regional Mission: The Regional Contribution of Higher Education*. National Report. London: Universities UK.

Charlesworth, J. and Cochrane, A. (1994) Tales of the suburbs: the local politics of growth in the South-East of England. *Urban Studies*, 31, 10: 1723–38.

Chatterton, P. and Unsworth, R. (2004) Making spaces for culture(s) in Boomtown. Some alternative future for development, ownership and participation in Leeds city centre. *Local Economy*, 19, 4: 361–79.

Checkland, S. (1976) *The Upas Tree. Glasgow 1875–1975. A Study in Growth and Contraction*. Glasgow: Glasgow University Press.

Cities Alliance (1999) *Cities without Slums. Action Plan for Moving Slum Upgrading to Scale*. Washington DC: The World Bank/UNCS (Habitat).

Clapson, M. (2003) *Suburban Century. Social Change and Urban Growth in England and the USA*. Oxford: Berg.

Clarke, J. (2002) Reinventing community? Governing in contested spaces. Paper presented at Conference on *Spacing Social Work – on the Territorialization of the Social*, Bielefeld, November 14–16.

Clarke, J. (2004) *Changing Welfare Changing States. New Directions in Social Policy*. London: Sage.

Clarke, J. and Cochrane, A. (1998) The social construction of social problems, in Saraga, E. (ed.), *Embodying the Social: Constructions of Difference*. London: Routledge.

Clarke, J. and Newman, J. (1997) *The Managerial State. Power, Politics and Ideology in the Remaking of Social Welfare*. London: Sage.

Clarke, J., Gewirtz, S., and McLaughlin, E. (eds.) (2000) *New Managerialism, New Welfare*. London: Sage.

Clarke, M. and Stewart, J. (1991) *Choices for Local Government from the 1990s and Beyond*. London: Longman.

Coates, K. and Silburn, R. (1970) *Poverty: The Forgotten Englishman*. Harmondsworth: Penguin.

Cochrane, A. (1986a) Community politics and democracy, in Held, D. and Pollitt, C. (eds.), *New Forms of Democracy*. London: Sage.

Cochrane, A. (1986b) Local employment initiatives: towards a new municipal socialism? in Lawless, P. and Raban, C. (eds.), *The Contemporary British City*. London: Harper and Row.

Cochrane, A. (1988) In and against the market? The development of socialist local economic strategies, 1981–1986. *Policy and Politics*, 16, 3: 159–68.

Cochrane, A. (1999) Redefining urban politics for the 21st century, in Jonas, A. and Wilson, D. (eds.), *The Urban Growth Machine. Critical Perspectives Two Decades Later*. Albany, NY: State University of New York Press.

Cochrane, A. (2000) New Labour, new urban policy, in Dean, H., Sykes, R., and Woods, R. (eds.), *Social Policy Review 12*, Newcastle: Social Policy Association.

Cochrane, A. (2006) Making up meanings in a capital city: power, memory and monuments in Berlin. *European Urban and Regional Studies*, 13, 1: 21–40.

Cochrane, A. and Clarke, A. (1990) Local enterprise boards: the short history of a radical initiative. *Public Administration*, 68, 3: 315–36.

Cochrane, A. and Passmore, A. (2001) Building a national capital in an age of globalization: the case of Berlin. *Area*, 33, 4: 341–52.

Cochrane, A., Peck, J., and Tickell, A. (1996) Manchester plays games. The local politics of globalization. *Urban Studies*, 33, 8: 1317–34.

Cochrane, A., Peck, J., and Tickell, A. (2002) Olympic dreams: visions of partnership, in Peck, J. and Ward, K. (eds.), *City of Revolution. Restructuring Manchester*. Manchester: Manchester University Press.

Cockburn, C. (1977) *The Local State. Management of Cities and People*. London: Pluto.

Cole, T. (2005) Proud of a new "heaven on earth." *Financial Times* December 17/18, W 13.

Coleman, R. (2003) Images from a neoliberal city: the state, surveillance and social control. *Critical Criminology*, 12, 1: 21–42.

Coleman, R. (2004) Watching the degenerate: street camera surveillance and urban regeneration. *Local Economy*, 19, 3: 199–211.

Colenutt, B. (1999) New deal or no deal for people based regeneration? in Imrie, R. and Thomas, H. (eds.), *British Urban Policy and the Urban Development Corporations*, 2nd edition. London: Paul Chapman.

Collins, C. (1997) The dialogics of "community": language and identity in a housing scheme in the West of Scotland, in Hoggett, P. (ed.), *Contested Communities. Experiences, Struggles, Policies*. Bristol: Policy Press.

Commission on Social Justice (1994) *Social Justice. Strategies for National Renewal*. London: Vintage.

Committee on Spatial Development (1999) *ESDP. European Spatial Development Perspective. Towards Balanced and Sustainable Development of the European Union*. Luxembourg: Office for the Official Publications of the European Communities.

Community Development Project (1977a) *The Costs of Industrial Change*. London: CDP Inter-Project Editorial Team.

Community Development Project (1977b) *Gilding the Ghetto. The State and the Poverty Experiments*. London: CDP Inter-Project Editorial Team.

Connell, J. and Kubisch, A. (1998) Applying a theory of change approach to the evaluation of comprehensive community initiatives: progress, prospects, and problems, in Fulbright-Anderson K., Kubisch A., and Connell J. (eds.), *New Approaches to Evaluating Community Initiatives. Volume 2 Theory, Measurement, and Analysis*. Washington DC: The Aspen Institute.

Cooke, P. (1989) (ed.), *Localities. The Changing Face of Urban Britain*. London: Unwin Hyman.

Cowley, J. (1977) The politics of community organising, in Cowley, J., Kay, A., Mayo, M., and Thompson, M. (eds.), *Community or Class Struggle?* London: Stage 1.

Cox, K. (1998) Spaces of dependence, spaces of engagement and the politics of scale, or: looking for local politics. *Political Geography*, 17, 1: 1–23.

Cox, K. (2001) Territoriality, politics and the "urban." *Political Geography*, 20: 745–62.

Cox, K. and Mair, A. (1988) Locality and community in the politics of local economic development. *Annals of the Association of American Geographers*, 72, 2: 307–25.

Cox, K. and Mair, A. (1989) Urban growth machines and the politics of local economic development. *International Journal of Urban and Regional Research*, 13, 1: 137–46.

Cox, K. and Mair, A. (1991) From localised social structures to localities as agents. *Environment and Planning A*, 23, 2: 155–308.

Cuthill, M. (2003) The Contribution of human and social capital to building community well-being: a research agenda relating to citizen participation in local government in Australia. *Urban Policy and Research*, 21, 4: 373–91.

Dabinett, G. (2004) Creative Sheffield: creating value and changing values? *Local Economy* 19, 4: 361–79.

Davies, H., Nutley, S., and Smith, P. (eds.) (2002) *What Works? Evidence-Based Policy and Practice in Public Services*. Bristol: Policy Press.

Davies, J. (2004) Conjuncture or disjuncture? An institutionalist analysis of local regeneration partnerships in the UK. *International Journal of Urban and Regional Research*, 28, 3: 570–85.

Davis, M. (1990) *City of Quartz. Excavating the Future in Los Angeles*. London: Verso.

Davis, M. (1998) *Ecology of Fear. Los Angeles and the Imagination of Disaster*. New York: Metropolitan (the first hb publication).

Davis, M. (2002) *Dead Cities*. New York: New Press.

Davis, M. (2004) Planet of slums. Urban involution and the informal proletariat. *New Left Review*, 26: 5–34.

Davoudi, S. (2003) Polycentricity in European spatial planning: from an analytical tool to a normative agenda. *European Planning Studies*, 11, 8: 979–99.

Deas, I. (2005) Synchronization, salesmanship and service delivery: governance and urban competitiveness, in Buck, N., Gordon, I., Harding, A., and Turok, I. (eds.), *Changing Cities. Rethinking Urban Competitiveness, Cohesion and Governance*. Basingstoke: Palgrave Macmillan.

Deas, I., Robson, B., Wong, C., and Bradford, M. (2003) Measuring neighbourhood deprivation: a critique of the Index of Multiple Deprivation. *Environment and Planning C: Government and Policy*, 21: 883–903.

Demos (2003) *Boho Britain Creativity Index*. London: Demos. http://www.demos.co.uk/uploadstore/docs/BOHO_creativity_index.doc

DETR (1997) *Involving Communities*. London: Department of the Environment Transport and the Regions.

DETR (1998) *Modern Local Government. In Touch with the People*. London: HMSO.

DETR (2000) *Our Towns and Cities: The Future. Delivering an Urban Renaissance*. London: Department of the Environment, Transport and the Regions.

DETR (2001a) *Local Strategic Partnerships. Government Guidance Summary*. London: Department of the Environment, Transport and the Regions.

DETR (2001b) *A Review of the Evidence Base for Regeneration Policy and Practice*. London: Department of the Environment, Transport and the Regions.

Diamond, J. (2001) Managing change or coping with conflict? – Mapping the experience of a local regeneration partnership. *Local Economy*, 16, 4: 272–85.

Diamond, J. (2004) Local regeneration initiatives and capacity building: whose "capacity" and "building" for what? *Community Development Journal*, 39, 2: 177–89.

Diamond, J. and Liddle, J. (2005) *Management of Regeneration: Choices, Challenges and Dilemmas*. London: Routledge.

Dikec, M. (2006) Two decades of French urban policy: from social development of neighbourhoods to the republican penal state, *Antipode*, 38, 1: 59–81.

DoE (Department of the Environment) (1987) *An Evaluation of the Enterprise Zone Experiment*, Department of the Environment. London: HMSO.

DoE (1994) *Single Regeneration Budget Challenge Fund*, Guidance Note 1, London: Department of the Environment.

Dolowitz, D., Hulme, R., Nellis, M., and O'Neill, F. (2000) *Policy Transfer and British Social Policy. Learning from the USA?* Buckingham: Open University Press.

Donnison, D. and Middleton, A. (eds.) (1987) *Regenerating the Inner City. Glasgow's Experience.* London: Routledge and Kegan Paul.

Douglas, M. (1966) *Purity and Danger: An Analysis of the Concepts of Pollution and Taboo*. London: Routledge.

Douglass, M. (2000) Mega-urban regions and world city formation: globalisation, the economic crisis and urban policy issues in Pacific Asia. *Urban Studies*, 37, 12: 2315–35.

Dowling, R. (1997) Planning for culture in urban Australia. *Australian Geographical Studies*, 35, 1: 23–31.

Driver, F. (1993) *Power and Pauperism: the Workhouse System, 1834–1884*. Cambridge: Cambridge University Press.

DTA (2002) *Fabulous Beast: Stories of Community Enterprise from the Development Trust Association*. London: Development Trusts Association.

DTA (2005) *About the DTA*. Development Trusts Association. http:www.dta.org.uk

DTI/DfEE (Department of Trade and Industry/Department for Education and Employment) (2001) *Opportunity for All in a World of Change: A White Paper on Enterprise, Skills and Innovation*. London: Her Majesty's Stationery Office.

DTLR (Department of Transport, Local Government and the Regions) (2001) *Strong Local Leadership: Quality Public Services*. London: HMSO.

Duncan, S. and Goodwin, M. (1988) *The Local State and Uneven Development*. Cambridge: Polity.

Dunleavy, P. and Hood, C. (1994) From old public administration to new public management. *Public Money and Management*, 14, 3: 9–16.

Dutton, J. (2000) *New American Urbanism. Re-Forming the Suburban Metropolis*. Milan: Skira.

The Editors of Fortune (1958) *The Exploding Metropolis. A Study of the Assault on Urbanism and How Our Cities Can Resist It*. Garden City, NY: Doubleday.

Edwards, J. (1995) Social policy and the city. *Urban Studies*, 32, 4–5, 695–712.

Edwards, J. (1997) Urban policy: the victory of form over substance? *Urban Studies*, 5–5, 825–43.

Edwards, J. and Batley, R. (1978) *The Politics of Positive Discrimination. An Evaluation of the Urban Programme 1967–77*. London: Tavistock.

Eisenschitz, A. and Gough, J. (1993) *The Politics of Local Economic Policy. The Problems and Possibilities of Local Initiative*. Basingstoke: Macmillan.

Eisenschitz, A. and Gough, J. (1996) The contradictions of neo-Keynesian local economic strategy. *Review of International Political Economy*, 3, 3: 434–58.

Etzioni, A. (1995) *The Sprit of Community*. London: Fontana.

Euchner, C. (1999) Tourism and sports. The serious competition for play, in Judd, D. and Fainstein, S. (ed.), *The Tourist City*. New Haven: Yale University Press.

Euchner, C. and McGovern, S. (2003) *Urban Policy Reconsidered. Dialogues on the Problems and Prospects of American Cities*. New York: Routledge.

European Commission (2003) *Partnership with the Cities: The URBAN Community Initiative*. Luxembourg: Office for the Official Publications of the European Communities.

Evans, G. (2003a) Cultural industries quarters – from pre-industrial to post-industrial production, in Bell, D. and Jane, M. (eds.) *City of Quarters: Urban Villages in the Contemporary City*. Aldershot: Ashgate.

Evans, G. (2003b) Hard branding the cultural city – from Prado to Prada. *International Journal of Urban and Regional Research*, 27, 2: 417–40.

Evans, G. and Foord, J. (2003) Shaping the cultural landscape: local regeneration effects, in Miles, M. and Hall, T. (ed.), *Urban Futures. Critical Commentaries on Shaping the City*. London: Routledge.

Evans, K. (1997) "It's all right 'round here if you're a local' ": community in the inner city, in Hoggett, P. (ed.), *Contested Communities. Experiences, Struggles, Polices*. Bristol: Policy Press.

Everingham, C. (2003) *Social Justice and the Politics of Community*. Aldershot: Ashgate.

Fainstein, S. (1995) Urban redevelopment and public policy in London and New York, in Healey, P., Cameron, S., Davoudi, S., Graham, S., and Madani-Pour, A. (eds.), *Managing Cities: The New Urban Context*. Chichester: Wiley.

Fainstein, S. (2000) New directions in planning theory. *Urban Affairs Review*, 35, 4: 451–78.

Fainstein, S. (2001) Competitiveness, cohesion and governance: their implications for social justice. *International Journal of Urban and Regional Research*, 25, 4: 884–8.

Fainstein, N. and Fainstein, S. (1982) Restoration and struggle: urban policy and social forces, in Fainstein, N. and Fainstein, S. (eds.), *Urban Policy under Capitalism, Urban Affairs Annual Review*, Vol. 22. Beverly Hills, CA: Sage.

Fainstein, N. and Fainstein, S. (1996) Urban regimes and black citizens: the economic and social impacts of black political incorporation in US cities. *International Journal of Urban and Regional Research*, 20, 1: 22–37.

Fainstein, S. and Gladstone, D. (1999) Evaluating urban tourism, in Judd, D. and Fainstein, S. (ed.), *The Tourist City*. New Haven: Yale University Press.

Fainstein, S. and Hirst, C. (1995) Urban social movements, in Judge, D., Stoker, G. and Wolman, H. (eds.), *Theories of Urban Politics*. London: Sage.

Fainstein, S. and Judd, D. (1999a) Cities as places to play, in Judd, D. and Fainstein, S. (eds.), *The Tourist City*. New Haven: Yale University Press.

Fainstein, S. and Judd, D. (1999b) Global forces, local strategies and urban tourism, in Judd, D. and Fainstein, S. (eds.), *The Tourist City*. New Haven: Yale University Press.

Fairclough, N. (2000) *New Labour, New Language*. London: Routledge.

Faith in the City (1985) *A Call for Action by Church and Nation. A Report of the Archbishop of Canterbury's Commission on Urban Priority Areas*. London: Church House Publishing.

Fisher, R. and Kling, J. (1993a) Conclusion: prospects and strategies for mobilization in the era of global cities, in Fisher, R. and Kling, J. (eds.), *Mobilizing the Community. Local Politics in the Era of the Global City*. Newbury Park, CA: Sage.

Fisher, R. and Kling, J. (eds.) (1993b) *Mobilizing the Community. Local Politics in the Era of the Global City*. Newbury Park, CA: Sage.

Fitzpatrick, T. (2001) New agendas for social policy and criminology: globalization, urbanism and the emerging post-social security state. *Social Policy and Administration*, 35, 2: 212–29.

Florida, R. (2002) *The Rise of the Creative Class: and How It's Transforming Work, Leisure, Community and Everyday Life*. New York: Basic Books.

Florida, R. and Tinagli, I. (2004) *Europe in the Creative Age*. London: Demos.

Foote, J. (2001) Whose community? *Soundings*, 18: 33–41.

Ford Foundation (1998) *Seizing Opportunities. The Role of CDCs in Urban Economic Development*. New York: Ford Foundation.

Forrest, J. and Poulsen, M. (2003) Multiculturalism and the spatial assimilation of migrant groups: the Melbourne and Sydney experience, paper presented to "State of Australian Cities" National Conference, Parramatta, December 3–5.

Forrest, R. and Kearns, A. (1999) *Joined-up Places? Social Cohesion and Neighbourhood Regeneration*. York: Joseph Rowntreee Foundation.

Forrest, R. and Kearns, A. (2001) Social cohesion, social capital and the neighbourhood. *Urban Studies*, 38, 12: 2125–43.

Foucault, M. (2000) *Fearless Speech*. New York: Semiotext(e).

de Frantz, M. (2005) From cultural regeneration to discursive governance: constructing the flagship of the Museumsquartier Vienna as a plural symbol of change. *International Journal of Urban and Regional Research*, 29, 1: 50–66.

Friedman, L. (1977) The social and political context of the War on Poverty: an overview, in Haveman, R. (ed.), *A Decade of Federal Antipoverty Programs. Achievements, Failures and Lessons*. New York: Academic Press.

Fyfe, N. (1997) Crime, in Pacione, M. (ed.), *Britain's Cities. Geographies of Division in Urban Britain*. London: Routledge.

Fyfe, N. (2004) Zero tolerance, maximum surveillance? Deviancew, difference and crime control in the late modern city, in Lees, L, (ed.), *The Emancipatory City? Paradoxes and Possibilities*. London: Sage.

Gamble, A. (1985) *Britain in Decline: Economic Policy, Political Strategy and the British State*, 2nd edition. London: Macmillan.

Gans, H. (1962) *The Urban Villagers*. New York: The Free Press.

Gans, H, (1968) *People and Problems: Essay on Urban Problems and Solutions*. New York: Basic Books.

Garcia, B. (2004) Cultural policy and urban regeneration in Western European cities: lessons form experience, prospects for the future. *Local Economy*, 19, 4: 312–26.

Garland, D. (2001) *Culture of Control: Crime and Social Order in Contemporary Society*. Oxford: Oxford University Press.

Geddes, M. (1997) *Partnership against Poverty and Exclusion?* Bristol: Polity Press.

Geddes, M. (2000) Tackling social exclusion to the European Union? The limits to the mew orthodoxy of local partnership. *International Journal of Urban and Regional Research*, 24, 4: 782–800.

Giddens, A. (1998) *The Third Way. The Renewal of Social Democracy*. Cambridge: Polity.

Gilbert, M. (1999) Place, politics, and the production of urban space: a feminist critique of the growth machine thesis, in Jonas, A. and Wilson, D. (eds.), *The Urban Growth Machine. Critical Perspectives Two Decades Later*. Albany, NY: State University of New York Press.

Gilchrist, A. (2000) The well-connected community: networking to the "edge of chaos." *Community Development Journal*, 35, 3: 264–75.

Gilchrist, A. (2003) Community development in the UK – possibilities and paradoxes, *Community Development Journal*, 38, 1: 16–25.

Gilroy, P. (1987) *There ain't no Black in the Union Jack. The Cultural Politics of Race and Nation*. London: Hutchinson.

Ginsburg, N. (1999) Putting the social into urban regeneration policy. *Local Economy*, 14, 1: 55–71.

Gittell, R. and Vidal, A. (1998) *Community Organizing. Building Social Capital as a Development Strategy*. Thousand Oaks, CA: Sage.

GLC (1985) *The London Industrial Strategy*. London: Greater London Council.

GLC (1986a) *The London Financial Strategy*. London: Greater London Council.

GLC (1986b) *The London Labour Plan*. London: Greater London Council.

Glennerster, H. and Midgley, J. (eds.) (1991) *The Radical Right and the Welfare State. An International Assessment*. Hemel Hempstead: Harvester Wheatsheaf.

Glennerster, H., Lupton, R., Noden, P., and Power, A. (1999) *Poverty, Social Exclusionand Neighbourhood: Studying the Area Bases of Social Exclusion*. Case Paper 22. London: Centre for the Analysis of Social Exclusion, London School of Economics.

Goetz, E. (1996) The US war on drugs as urban policy. *International Journal of Urban and Regional Research*, 20, 3: 539–49.

Gold, J. and Gold, M. (2005) *Cities of Culture. Staging International Festivals and the Urban Agenda, 1851–2000*. Aldershot: Ashagte.

Gold, J. and Ward, S. (1994) Place Promotion. *The Use of Publicity and Marketing to Sell Towns and Regions*. Chichester: John Wiley.

Goldsmith, W. (2000) From the metropolis to globalization: the dialectics of race and urban form, in Marcuse, P. and Kempen, R. van (eds.), *Globalizing Cities. A new Spatial Order*. Oxford: Blackwell.

Gomez, M. and Gonzalez, S. (2001) A reply to Beatriz Plaza's "The Guggenheim-Bilbao Museum effect." *International Journal of Urban and Regional Research*, 25, 4: 888–900.

Gordon, I. and Buck, N. (2005) Introduction: cities in the new conventional wisdom, in Buck, N., Gordon, I., Harding, A. and Turok, I. (eds.), *Changing Cities. Rethinking Urban Competitiveness, Cohesion and Governance*. Basingstoke: Palgrave Macmillan.

Gough, J. (2002) Neoliberalism and socialisation in the contemporary city: opposites, complements and instabilities. *Antipode*, 34, 3: 405–26.

Graham, S. and Clarke, J. (1996) in Muncie, J. and McLaughlin, E. (eds.), *The Problem of Crime*. London: Sage.

Graham, S. and Marvin, S. (2001) *Splintering Urbanism: Networked Infrastructures, Technological Mobilities and the Urban Condition*. London: Routledge.

Greenberg, M. (1999) *Restoring America's Neighbourhoods: How Local People Make a Difference*. New Brunswick, NJ: Rutgers University Press.

Griffiths, R. (1998) The National Lottery and competitive cities, in Oatley, I. (ed.), *Cities, Economic Competition and Urban Policy*. London: Paul Chapman.

Gripaios, P. (2002) The failure of regeneration policy in Britain. *Regional Studies*, 36, 5: 568–77.

Gurr, T. and King, D. (1987) *The State and the City*. Basingstoke: Macmillan.

Gyford, J. (1985) *The Politics of Local Socialism*. London: George Allen and Unwin.

Hale, R. and Capaldi, A. (2004) *Who pays for Local Services? The Balance of Funding between Government and Councils*. London: Local Government Association.

Hall, P. (1977) Green fields and grey areas, in *Proceedings of the Royal Town Planning Institute Annual Conference*. London: Royal Town Planning Institute.

Hall, P. (1982) Enterprise zones: a justification. *International Journal of Urban and Regional Research*, 6, 3: 416–21.

Hall, P. and Pfeiffer, U. (2000) *Urban Future 21: A Global Agenda for Twenty-first Century Cities*. London: Spon.

Hall, S. (1988) *The Hard Road to Renewal. Thatcherism and the Crisis of the Left*. London: Verso.

Hall, S., Critcher, T., Jefferson, T., Clarke, J., and Roberts, B. (1978) *Policing the Crisis. Mugging, the State and Law and Order*. London: Macmillan.

Halsey, A. (1973) in *Times Educational Supplement*, February 9.

Hambleton, R. and Taylor, M. (1994) Transatlantic urban policy transfer. *Policy Studies*, 15, 2: 4–18.

Hammersley, M. (2005) Is the evidence-based practice movement doing more good than harm? Reflections on Iain Chalmers' case for research-based policy making and practice. *Evidence and Policy*, 1, 1: 85–100.

Haney, L. (2004) Introduction: Gender, welfare and states of punishment. *Social Politics*, 11, 3: 333–62.

Harding, A. (2005) Governance and socio-economic change in cities, in Buck, N., Gordon, I., Harding, A. and Turok, I. (eds.), *Changing Cities. Rethinking Urban Competitiveness, Cohesion and Governance*. Basingstoke: Palgrave Macmillan.

Harloe, M. (2001) Social justice and the city: the new "liberal" formulation. *International Journal of Urban and Regional Research*, 24, 1: 889–97.

Harloe, M. and Perry, B. (2004) Universities, localities and regional development: the emergence of the "mode 2" university? *International Journal of Urban and Regional Research*, 28, 1: 213–23.

Hardt, M. and Negri, A. (2000) *Empire*. Cambridge, MA: Harvard University Press.

Harrington, M. (1962) *The Other America. Poverty in the United States*. New York: Macmillan (Page references to 1963 edition, Baltimore: Penguin).

Harvey, D. (1989a) *The Condition of Postmodernity*. Oxford: Blackwell.

Harvey, D. (1989b) From managerialism to entrepreneurialism: the transformation in urban governance in late capitalism. *Geografiska Annaler*, 71B, 3–17.

Harvey, D. (1989c) *The Urban Experience*. Oxford: Blackwell.

Harvey, D. (2000) *Spaces of Hope*. Edinburgh: Edinburgh University Press.

Harvey, D. (2005) *A Brief History of Neoliberalism*. Oxford: Oxford University Press.

Haveman, R. (ed.) (1977) *A Decade of Federal Antipoverty Programs. Achievements, Failures and Lessons*. New York: Academic Press.

Hay, C. (1996) *Re-stating Social and Political Change*. Buckingham: Open University Press.

Haylett, C. (2003) Culture, class and urban policy: reconsidering equality. *Antipode*, 35, 1: 55–73.

Hayton, K. (1996) A Critical Examination of the Role of Community Business in Urban Regeneration. *Town Planning Review*, 67, 1: 1–20.

Healey, P. (1997) *Collaborative Planning. Shaping Places in Fragmented Societies*. Basingstoke: Macmillan.

Healey, P. (2002) On creating the "city" as a collective resource. *Urban Studies*, 39, 10: 1777–92.

Healey, P. (2004) Towards a "social democratic" policy agenda for cities, in Johnstone, C. and Whitehead, M. (eds.), *New Horizons in British Urban Policy. Perspectives on New Labour's Urban Renaissance*. Aldershot: Ashgate.

Higgins, J., Deakin, N., Edwards, J., and Wicks, M. (1983) *Government and Urban Poverty. Inside the Policy-Making Process*. Oxford: Blackwell.

Hill, D. (2000) *Urban Policy and Politics in Britain*. Basingstoke: Macmillan.

Hill, E. and Nowak, J. (2002) Policies to uncover the competitive advantages of America's distressed cities, in Begg, I. (ed.), *Urban Competitiveness. Policies for Dynamic Cities*. Bristol: Policy Press.

Hill, R. and Kim, J. (2000) Global cities and developmental states: New York, Tokyo and Seoul. *Urban Studies*, 37, 12: 2167–95.

HMSO (1977) *Policy for the Inner Cities*. London: Her Majesty's Stationery Office.

Hoatson, L. and Grace, M. Public Housing redevelopment: opportunity for community regeneration? *Urban Policy and Research*, 20, 4: 429–41.

Hoggett, P. (1997a) Contested communities, in Hoggett, P. (ed.), *Contested Communities. Experiences, Struggles, Policies*. Bristol: Policy Press.

Hoggett, P. (ed.) (1997b) *Contested Communities. Experiences, Struggles, Policies*. Bristol: Policy Press.

Holcomb, B. (1999) Marketing cities for tourism, in Judd, D. and Fainstein, S. (eds.), *The Tourist City*. New Haven: Yale University Press.

Home Office (1968) *Urban Programme Circular No. 1*. London: Home Office.

Home Office (1999) *Report of the Policy Action Team on Community Self-Help*. PAT Report No. 9. London: Active Community Unit, Home Office.

Home Office (2002) *Active Communities: Initial Findings from the 2001 Home Office Citizenship Survey*. London: Home Office.

Hong, S. W. (1996) Seoul: a global city in a nation of rapid growth, in Lo, F. and Yeung, Y. (eds.), *Emerging World Cities in Pacific Asia*. Tokyo: United Nations University Press.

Hood, C. (1991) A public management for all seasons? *Public Administration*, 69, 1: 3–19.

Hood, C. (1996) Beyond 'progressivism': a new 'global paradigm' in public management, *International Journal of Public Administration*, 19, 2: 151–177.

Howard, E. (1902/1965) *Garden Cities of Tomorrow*, edited by F. J. Osborn with a preface by Lewis Mumford. London: Faber and Faber.

Hughes, G. (1997) Policing late modernity. Changing strategies of crime management in contemporary Britain, in Jewson, N. and MacGregor, S. (eds.), *Transforming Cities. Contested Governance and New Spatial Divisions*. London: Routledge.

Hughes, G. and Lewis, G. (eds.) (1998) *Unsettling Welfare: the Reconstruction of Social Policy*. London: Routledge.

Hughes, G., McLaughlin, E. and Muncie, J. (eds.) (2002) *Crime Prevention and Community Safety. New Directions*. London: Sage.

Huyssen, A. (2003) *Present Pasts. Urban Palimpsests and the Politics of Memory*. Stanford, CA: Stanford University Press.

Imrie, R. and Raco, M. (2003a) Community and the changing nature of urban policy, in Imrie, R. and Raco, M. (eds.), *Urban Renaissance? New Labour, Community and Urban Policy*. Bristol: Policy Press.

Imrie, R. and Raco, M. (eds.) (2003b) *Urban Renaissance? New Labour, Community and Urban Policy*. Bristol: Policy Press.

Imrie, R. and Thomas, H. (eds.) (1999) *British Urban Policy and the Urban Development Corporations*, 2nd edition. London: Paul Chapman.

Indymedia (2003) The Duke and churns turn the screws on the working class, www.indymedia.orguk/en/regions/liverpool/20/03/12/282695.html

Info Box (1996) *Info Box. The Catalogue*. Berlin: Dirk Nishen.

Jacobs, J. (1958) Downtown is for people, in The Editors of Fortune. *The Exploding Metropolis. A Study of the Assault on Urbanism and How Our Cities Can Resist It*. Garden City, NY: Doubleday.

Jacobs, J. (1961) *The Death and Life of Great American Cities*. New York: Random House (Page references to 1964 edition, Harmondsworth: Penguin).

Jahn-Khan, M. (2003) The right to riot? *Community Development Journal*, 38, 1: 32–42.

Jessop, B. (1997) The entrepreneurial city. Re-imaging localities, redesigning economic governance, or restructuring capital? in Jewson, N. and MacGregor, S. (eds.), *Transforming Cities. Contested Governance and New Spatial Divisions*. London: Routledge.

Jessop, B. (2002a) *The Future of the Capitalist State*. Cambridge: Polity.

Jessop, B. (2002b) Liberalism, neoliberalism, and urban governance: a state-theoretical perspective. *Antipode*, 34, 3: 452–72.

Jessop, B. and Sum, N.-L. (2000) An entrepreneurial city in action: Hong Kong's emerging strategies in and for (inter)urban competition. *Urban Studies*, 37, 12: 2287–313.

Jewson, N. and MacGregor, S. (eds.) (1997) *Transforming Cities. Contested Governance and New Spatial Divisions*. London: Routledge.

Johnson, C. and Osborne, S. (2003) Local Strategic Partnerships, neighbourhood renewal, and the limits to co-governance. *Public Money and Management*, 23, 3: 147–54.

Johnson, L. (2003) SOS – sustaining our suburbs, paper presented to "State of Australian Cities" National Conference, Parramatta, December 3–5.

Johnstone, C. (2004) Crime, disorder and the urban renaissance, in Johnstone, C. and Whitehead, M. (eds.), *New Horizons in British Urban Policy. Perspectives on New Labour's Urban Renaissance*. Aldershot: Ashgate.

Johnstone, C. and Whitehead, M. (eds.) (2004) *New Horizons in British Urban Policy. Perspectives on New Labour's Urban Renaissance*. Aldershot: Ashgate.

Jones, M. and Ward, K. (1998) Grabbing grants? The role of coalitions in urban economic development. *Local Economy*, 1, 1: 28–38.

Jones, M. and Ward, K. (2002) Excavating the logic of British urban policy: neo-liberalism as the "crisis of crisis management." *Antipode*, 34, 3: 473–94.

Judd, D. (1999) Constructing the tourist bubble, in Judd, D. and Fainstein, S. (eds.), *The Tourist City*. New Haven: Yale University Press.

Judd, D. and Fainstein, S. (eds.) (1999) *The Tourist City*. New Haven: Yale University Press.

Judge, D., Stoker, G., and Wolman, H. (eds.) (1995) *Theories of Urban Politics*. London: Sage.

Katz, P. (1993) *The New Urbanism: Towards an Architecture of Community*. New York: McGraw Hill.

Kearns, A. (2003) Social capital, regeneration and urban policy, in Imrie, R. and Raco, M. (eds.), *Urban Renaissance? New Labour, Community and Urban Policy*. Bristol: Policy Press.

Kearns, A. and Parkinson, M. (2001) The significance of neighbourhood. *Urban Studies*, 38, 12: 2103–10.

Kearns, G. and Philo, C. (1993) *Selling Places. The City as Cultural Capital, Past and Present*. Oxford: Pergamon.

Keith, M. (2004) Knowing the city? 21st century urban policy and the introduction of local strategic partnerships, in Johnstone, C. and Whitehead, M. (eds.), *New Horizons in British Urban Policy. Perspectives on New Labour's Urban Renaissance*. Aldershot: Ashgate.

Keith, M. and Cross, M. (1993) Racism and the postmodern city, in Cross, M. and Keith, M. (eds.), *Racism, the City and the State*. London: Routledge.

Kelling, G. and Coles, M. (1996) *Fixing Broken Windows: Restoring Order and Reducing Crime in our Communities*. London: Martin Kessler Books.

King, M.L. (1963) I have a dream, http://www.americanrhetoric.com/speeches/Ihaveadream.htm

King, M.L. (1964) *Why We Can't Wait*. New York: Signet.

Kintrea, K. (1996) Whose partnership? Community interests in the regeneration of a Scottish housing scheme. *Housing Studies*, 11: 287–306.

Kong, L. (2000) Culture, economy, policy: trends and development. *Geoforum*, 31, 4: 385–90.

Kotz, M. (1977) Discussions, in Haveman, R. (ed.), *A Decade of Federal Antipoverty Programs. Achievements, Failures and Lessons*. New York: Academic Press.

Kramer, R. (1969) *Participation of the Poor: Comparative Case Studies in the War on Poverty*. Englewood Cliffs, NJ: Prentice Hall.

Krätke, S. (2001) Berlin: towards a global city? *Urban Studies*, 38, 10: 1777–99.

Krätke, S. (2003) Global media cities in a world-wide urban network. *European Planning Studies*, 11, 6: 605–28.

Kraus, N. (2003) Local policymaking and concentrated poverty: the case of Buffalo, New York. *Cities*, 21, 6: 481–90.

Kundnani, A. (20901) From Oldham to Bradford: the violence of the violated. *Race and Class*, 43, 2: 105–31.

Lambeth Inner Area Study (1977) *Inner London: Policies for Dispersal and Balance, Final Report*. London: HMSO.

Lampman, R. (1971) *Ends and Means of Reducing Income Poverty*. New York: Academic Press.

Landry, C (2000) *The Creative City: A Toolkit for Urban Innovators*. London: Earthscan.

Landry, C. and Bianchini, F. (1995) *The Creative City*. London: Demos.

Lansley, S., Goss, S., and Wolmar, C. (1989) *Councils in Conflict. The Rise and Fall of the Municiapal Left*. Basingstoke: Macmillan.

Larner, W. (2003) Neoliberalism? *Environment and Planning D: Society and Space*, 21: 509–12.

Larner, W. and Craig, D. (2005) After neoliberalism? Community activism and local partnerships in Aotearoa New Zealand. *Antipode*, 37, 3: 402–24.

Lawless, P. (1981) *Britain's Inner Cities. Problems and Policies*. London: Harper and Row.

Lawless, P. (1988) *Britain's Inner Cities*. London: Paul Chapman.

Lawless, P. (1996) The inner cities. Towards a new agenda. *Town Planning Review*, 67, 1: 21–43.

Lawless, P. (2004) Locating and explaining area-based urban initiatives: New Deal for Communities in England. *Environment and Planning C: Government and Policy*, 22: 383–99.

Lawless, P. and Ramsden, P. (1990) Sheffield in the 1980s. From radical intervention to partnership. *Cities*, 7, 3: 202–10.

Lea, J. (1997) Postfordism and criminality, in Jewson, N. and MacGregor, S. (eds.), *Transforming Cities. Contested Governance and New Spatial Divisions*. London: Routledge.

Le Corbusier (1929/1987) *The City of Tomorrow*. London: The Architectural Press.

Lees, L. (2003a) The ambivalence of diversity and the politics of urban renaissance: the case of youth in Downtown Portland, Maine. *International Journal of Urban and Regional Research*, 27, 3: 613–34.

Lees, L. (2003b) Visions of "urban renaissance": the Urban Task Force report and the Urban White Paper, in Imrie, R. and Raco, M. (eds.) *Urban Renaissance? New Labour, Community and Urban Policy*. Bristol: Policy Press.

Lees, L. (ed.) (2004) *The Emancipatory City? Paradoxes and Possibilities*. London: Sage.

Lefebvre, H. (1996) *Writings on Cities*, translated and edited by Kofman, E. and Lebas, E. Oxford: Blackwell.

Lehmann, N. (1991) *The Promised Land*. London: Macmillan.

Levitas, R. (2000) Community, utopia and new Labour. *Local Economy*, 15, 3: 188–97.

Lewis, N. (1992) *Inner City Regeneration. The Demise of Regional and Local Government*. Buckingham: Open University Press.

Lewis, O. (1967) *La Vida: A Puerto Rican Family in the Culture of Poverty – San Juan and New York*. London: Secker and Warburg.

LGA, DTLR, HO, CRE (2002) *Draft Guidance on Community Cohesion*. London: Local Government Association, Department of Transport Local Government and the Regions, Home Office, Commission for Racial Equality.

LGMB (1993) *Fitness for Purpose. Shaping New Patterns of Organization and Management*. Luton: Local Government Management Board.

Lipsky, M. (1979) The assault on human services: street level bureaucrats and the fiscal crisis, in Greer, S., Hedlund, R., and Gibson, J. (eds.), *Accountability in Urban Society: Public Agencies under Fire. Urban Affairs Annual Reviews*, Vol. 15. London: Sage.

Liverpool City Council (1997) *Action Plan – Regeneration Agenda for Liverpool: To Develop a Safer City*. Liverpool: Planning and development services, Liverpool City Council.

Lloyd, P. (1979) *Slums of Hope? Shanty Towns of the Third World*. Harmondsworth: Penguin.

Lloyd, R. (2002) Neo-Bohemia: art and neighbourhood redevelopment in Chicago. *Journal of Urban Affairs*, 24, 5: 517–532.

Loftman, P. and Nevin, B. (1996) Going for growth: prestige projects in three British cities. *Urban Studies*, 33, 6, 991–1019.

Loftman, P. and Nevin, B. (2003) Prestige projects, city centre restructuring and social exclusion: taking the long-term view, in Miles, M. and Hall, T. (eds.), *Urban Futures. Critical Commentaries on Shaping the City*. London: Routledge.

Logan, J. and Molotch, H. (1987) *Urban Fortunes. The Political Economy of Place*. Berkeley, CA: University of California Press.

London-Edinburgh Weekend Return Group (1979) *In and Against the State. Discussion notes for Socialists*. London: Publications Distribution Co-Operative.

Loney, M. (1983) *Community against Government: the British Community Development Project, 1968–1978*. London: Heinemann.

Loney, M. (1984) *Poverty and Social Policy, Unit 9 of Social Policy and Social Welfare*. Milton Keynes: Open University.

Low, S. (2003) *Behind the Gates: Life, Security and the Pursuit of Happiness in Fortress America*. London: Routledge.

Lowe, S. (1986) *Urban Social Movements. The City After Castells*. London: Macmillan, 1986.

Lowndes, V. (2001) Rescuing Aunt Sally: taking institutional theory seriously in urban politics. *Urban Studies*, 38, 11: 1953–71.

Lynch, R. (2001) An analysis of the concept of community cohesion, in Cantle, T. *Community Cohesion: A Report of the Independent Review Team*. London: Home Office.

Lynn, L. (1977) A decade of policy developments in the income-maintenance system, in Haveman, R. (ed.), *A Decade of Federal Antipoverty Programs. Achievements, Failures and Lessons*. New York: Academic Press.

Macintyre, S. (1980) *Little Moscows. Communism and Working-Class Militancy in Inter-War Britain*. London: Croom Helm.

McCann, E. (2003) Framing space and time in the city: urban policy and the politics of spatial and temporal scale. *Journal of Urban Affairs*, 25, 2: 159–78.

McCulloch, A. (1997) "You've fucked up the estate and now you're carrying a briefcase!", in Hoggett, P. (ed.), *Contested Communities. Experiences, Struggles, Policies*. Bristol: Policy Press.

McGuigan, J. (1996) *Culture and the Public Sphere*. London: Routledge.

McLaughlin, E. (2002) The crisis of the social and the political materialization of community safety, in Hughes, G., McLaughlin, E. and Muncie, J. (eds.), *Crime Prevention and Community Safety. New Directions*. London: Sage.

McLaughlin, E. and Muncie, J. (1999) Walled cities: surveillance, regulation and segregation, in Pile, S., Brook, C. and Mooney, G. (eds.), *Unruly Cities? Order/Disorder*. London: Routledge.

McLeod, G. and Ward, K. (2002) Spaces of utopia and dystopia: landscaping the contemporary city. *Geografiska Annaler*, 84B, 3–4: 153–70.

McManus, P. (2004) Writing the palimpsest, again; Rozelle Bay and the Sydney 2000 Olympic Games. *Urban Policy and Research*, 22, 2: 157–67.

McNeill, D. (1999) *Urban Change and the European Left. Tales from the New Barcelona*. London: Routledge.

McNeill, D. (2000) McGuggenheimisation? National identity and globalisation in the Basque Country. *Political Geography*, 19: 473–94.

Maginn, P. (2004) *Urban Regeneration, Community Power and the (In)Significance of Race*. Aldershot: Ashgate.

Malanga, S. (2004) The curse of the creative class, *City Journal*, 14, 1. http://www.city-journal.org/html/14_1_the_curse.html

Malpass, P. (2000) *Housing Associations and Housing Policy. A Historical Perspective*. Basingstoke: Palgrave Macmillan.

Manchester City Council (1994) *City Pride. A Focus for the Future. Manchester, Salford and Trafford from the Present into the Twenty-First Century*. Manchester: Manchester City Council.

Marris, P. and Rein, M. (1972) *Dilemmas of Social Reform. Poverty and Community Action in the United States*, 2nd edition. London: Routledge and Kegan Paul.

Marwick, A (1998) *The Sixties. Cultural Revolution in Britain, France, Italy and the United States, c.1958–c.1974*. Oxford: Oxford University Press.

Massey, D. (1999) Imagining globalization. Power-geometries of time-space, in Brah, A., Hickman, M., and Martin, G. (eds.), *Global Futures. Migration, Environment and Globalization*. London: Macmillan.

Massey, D. (2000) Travelling thoughts, in Gilroy, P., Grossberg, L., and McRobbie, A. (eds.), *Without Guarantees: In Honor of Stuart Hall*. London: Verso.

Massey, D. (2004) Geographies of responsibility, *Geografiska Annaler B*, 86, 1: 5–18.

Massey, D., Quintas, P., and Weild, D. (1992) *High-Tech Fantasies: Science Parks in Society, Science and Space*. London: Routledge.

Massey, D., Allen, J., and Pile, S. (eds.) (1999) *City Worlds*. London: Routledge.

Mayer, M. (1992) The shifting local political system in European cities, in Dunford, M. and Kafkalis, G. (eds.), *Cities and Regions in the New Europe*. London: Belhaven.

Mayer, M. (2003) The onward sweep of social capital: causes and consequences for understanding cities, communities and urban movements. *International Journal of Urban and Regional Research*, 27, 1: 110–32.

Mayo, M. (1975) The history and early development of CDP, in Lees, R. and Brake, M. (eds.), *Action Research in Community Development*. London: Routledge and Kegan Paul.

Meegan, R. and Mitchell, A. (2001) "It's not community round here, it's neighbourhood": neighbourhood change and cohesion in urban regeneration policies. *Urban Studies*, 38, 12: 2167–94.

Mellor, R. (1977) *Urban Sociology in an Urban Society*. London: Routledge.

Merrifield, A. (2000) The dialectics of dystopia: disorder and zero tolerance in the city. *International Journal of Urban and Regional Research*, 24, 2: 473–4899.

Middleton, A. (1987) Glasgow and its East End, in Donnison, D. and Middleton, A. (eds.) *Regenerating the Inner City. Glasgow's Experience*. London: Routledge and Kegan Paul.

Miles, M. and Hall, T. (eds.) (2003) *Urban Futures. Critical Commentaries on Shaping the City*. London: Routledge.

Miliband, D. (2006) We want to build communities as well as homes. *The Guardian*, January 10th.

Miller, P. (2002) The economic impact of sports stadium construction: the case of the construction industry in St. Louis, MO. *Journal of Urban Affairs*, 24, 2: 159–174.

Mills, C.W. (1959) *The Sociological Imagination*. Oxford: Oxford University Press.

Milner Holland Report (1965) *Housing in Greater London*. London: Her Majesty's Stationery Office.

Milton Keynes Local Strategic Partnership (2004) *The City that Thinks Differently, Embraces Evolution and Champions Change – Milton Keynes Community Strategy: Our Handbook for Change 2004–2034*. Milton Keynes: Milton Keynes Council.

Mitchell, D. (2003) *The Right to the City. Social Justice and the Fight for Public Space*. New York: Guilford.

Mollenkopf, J. (1983) *The Contested City*. Princeton, NJ: Princeton University Press.

MKELP (2004) *From New Town to International City*. Milton Keynes: Milton Keynes Economy and Learning Partnership.

Molotch, H. (1976) The city as growth machine. *American Journal of Sociology*, 82, 2: 309–30.

Molotch, H. and Vicari, S. (1988) Three ways to build: the development process in the US, Japan, and Italy. *Urban Affairs Quarterly*, 24, 1: 48–69.

Mooney, G. (1998) "Remoralizing" the poor? Gender, class and philanthropy in Victorian Britain, in Lewis, G. (ed.), *Forming Nation, Framing Welfare*. London: Routledge.

Mooney, G. (2004) Cultural policy as urban transformation? Critical reflections on Glasgow, European City of Culture 1990. *Local Economy*, 19, 4: 327–40.

Mossberger, K. and Stoker, G. (1997) Inner-city policy in Britain. *Urban Affairs Review*, 32, 3: 378–402.

Mouffe, C. (1993) *The Return of the Political*. London: Verso.

Moulaert, F., Swyngedouw, E., and Rodriguez, A. (2001) Social polarization in metropolitan areas. The role of new urban policy. *European Urban and Regional Studies*, 8, 2: 99–102.

Moynihan, D. (1969) *Maximum Feasible Misunderstanding*. New York: Free Press.

Moynihan, D. (ed.) (1970) *Toward a National Urban Policy*. New York: Basic Books.

Moynihan, D. (1973) *The Politics of a Guaranteed Income*. New York: Random House.

Mullins, P. (1999) International tourism and the cities of Southeast Asia, in Judd, D. and Fainstein, S. (eds.), *The Tourist City*. New Haven: Yale University Press.

Muncie, J. (2006 forthcoming) Youth governance, neo-liberalism and reconfigurations of the social: configurations and contradictions in contemporary youth justice. *Critical Social Policy*.

Murray, Charles (1984) *Losing Ground: American Social Policy, 1950–1980*. New York: Basic Books.

Murray, Charles (1990) *The Emerging British Underclass*. London: Institute of Economic Affairs.

Murray, Chris (2001) *Making Sense of Place*. Bournes Green: Comedia.

NACRO (2002) *To CCTV or not to CCTV? Current Review of Research into the Effectiveness of CCTV Systems in Reducing Crime*. London: National Association for the Care and Resettlement of Offenders.

Neighbourhood Renewal Unit (2005) *Making it Happen in Neighbourhoods. The National Strategy for Neighbourhood Renewal – Four Years On*. London: Office of the Deputy Prime Minister.

Nellis, M. (2000) Law and order: the electronic monitoring of offenders, in Dolowitz, D., Hulme, R., Nellis, M. and O'Neill, F. *Policy Transfer and British Social Policy. Learning From the USA?* Buckingham: Open University Press.

Newman, J. (2001) *Modernising Governance. New Labour, Policy and Society*. London: Sage.

Newman, O. (1972) *Defensible Space: People and Design in the Violent City*. London: Architectural Press.

Newman, K. and Ashton, P. (2004) Neoliberal urban policy and new paths of neighbourhood change in the American inner city. *Environment and Planning A*, 36, 1151–72.

Newman, P. and Thornley, A. (2005) *Planning World Cities. Globalization and Urban Politics*. Basingstoke: Palgrave Macmillan.

New Urbanism (2005) *New Urbanism. Creating Livable Sustainable Communities*, http://www.newurbanism.org/pages/416429/index.htm

Noble, M., Wright, G., Lloyd, M. et al. (2003) *Scottish Indices of Deprivation 2003: Full Report*. Edinburgh: Scottish Executive.

Noble, M., Wright, G., Dibben, C. et al. (2004) *Indices of Deprivation 2004 (revised)*. Norwich: Her Majesty's Stationery Office.

Norquist, J. (2005) How to avoid the pitfalls of the American way, in *Society Guardian*: 10–11.

Nunn, S. (2001) Cities, space, and the new world of urban law enforcement technologies. *Journal of Urban Affairs*, 23, 3–4: 259–78.

O2C Arc (2003) *The Spirit of Innovation*. Oxford: Cambridge Arc.

Oakley, A. (1998) Public policy experimentation: lessons from America. *Policy Studies*, 19, 2: 93–114.

Oakley, S. (2004) Politics of recollection: examining the rise and fall of DURD and Better Cities through narrative. *Urban Policy and Research*, 22, 3: 299–314.

Oatley, N. (ed.) (1998) *Cities, Economic Competition and Urban Policy*. London: Paul Chapman.

O'Connor, J. (1973) *The Fiscal Crisis of the State*. New York: St. Martins Press.

ODPM (2001) *Urban Policy. Relevant Programmes*. http://www.odpm.gov.uk/stellent/groups/odpm/odpm_control/documents/contentservertemplate/odpm_index.hcst?n=2945&l=2

ODPM (2003a) *Sustainable Communities: Building for the Future*. London: Office of the Deputy Prime Minister, http://www.odpm.gov.uk/stellent/groups/odpm_communities/documents/page/odpm_comm_022184.hcsp

ODPM (2003b) *Sustainable Communities: An Urban Development Corporation for the London Thames Gateway*. A Consultation Paper. London: Office of the Deputy Prime Minister.

ODPM (2004) *Thames Gateway*. London: Office of the Deputy Prime Minister.

OECD (2000) *Urban Renaissance: Belfast's Lessons for Policy and Partnership*. Paris: Organisation for Economic Co-Operation and Development.

OECD (2002) *Urban Renaissance: Canberra. A Sustainable Future*. Paris: Organisation for Co-Operation and Development.

OECD (2003) *Urban Renaissance: Berlin. Towards and Integrated Strategy for Social Cohesion and Economic Development*. Paris: Organisation for Economic Co-Operation and Development.

OECD (2003) *Urban Renaissance: Glasgow. Lessons for Innovation and Implementation*. Paris: Organisation for Economic Co-operation and Development.

Offe, C. (1984) *Contradictions of the Welfare State*. London: Harper Collins.

Olds, K. (2001) *Globalization and Urban Change. Capital, Culture, and Pacific Rim Mega-Projects*. Oxford: Oxford University Press.

Osborn, F. and Whittick, A. (1978) *The New Towns*. London: Leonard Hill.

Osborne, D. and Gaebler, T. (1992) *Reinventing Government. How the Entrepreneurial Sprit is Transforming the Public Sector*. Boston, MA: Addison-Wesley (Page references to 1993 paperback edition, New York: Plume).

Pacione, M. (ed.) (1997) *Britain's Cities. Geographies of Division in Urban Britain*. London: Routledge.

Parkinson, M., Champion, T., Coombes, M. et al. (2005) *State of the Cities: A Progress Report to the Delivering Sustainable Communities Summit*. London: Office of the Deputy Prims Minister.

Pearce, J. (1993) *At the Heart of the Community Economy. Community Enterprise in a Changing World*. London: Calouste Gulbenkian Foundation.

Peck, J. (1996) *Work-Place. The Social Regulation of Labor Markets*. New York: Guilford.

Peck, J. (2001) *Workfare States*. New York: Guilford.

Peck, J. (2002) Political economies of scale: fast policy, interscalar relations, and neoliberal workfare. *Economic Geography*, 78, 331–61.

Peck, J. (2003) Geography and public policy: mapping the penal state. *Progress in Human Geography*, 27, 2: 222–32.

Peck, J. (2005) Struggling with the creative class. *International Journal of Urban and Regional Research*, 29, 4: 740–70.

Peck, J. and Tickell, A. (2002) Neoliberalizing space. *Antipode* 34, 3: 380–404.

Perrons, D. and Skyers, S. (2003) Empowerment through participation? Conceptual explorations and a case study. *International Journal of Urban and Regional Research*, 27, 2: 265–85.

Peterson, P. (ed.) (1985) *The New Urban Reality*. Washington DC: Brookings Institute.

Peterson, P. and Greenstone, D. (1977) Racial change and citizen participation: the mobilization of low-income communities through community action, in Haveman, R. (ed.) *A Decade of Federal Antipoverty Programs. Achievements, Failures and Lessons*. New York: Academic Press.

Pile, S., Brook, C. and Mooney, G. (eds.) (1999) *Unruly Cities? Order/Disorder*. London: Routledge.

Phillips, S.-U. and Yeung, H.W.-C. (2003) A place for R&D? The Singapore Science Park. *Urban Studies*, 40, 4: 707–32.

Piven, F. and Cloward, R. (1972) *Regulating the Poor. The Functions of Public Welfare*. London: Tavistock.

Piven, F. and Cloward, R. (1977) *Poor People's Movements. Why They Succeed , How They Fail*, 2nd edition. New York: Vintage.

Piven, F. and Cloward, R. (1997) *The Breaking of the American Social Compact*. New York: New Press.

Plaza, B. (2000) Evaluating the influence of a large cultural artefact in the attraction of tourism. The Guggenheim Museum Bilbao case. *Urban Affairs Review*, 36, 2: 264–74.

Plowden Report (1967) *Children and their Primary Schools*. London: Her Majesty's Stationery Office.

Pollitt, C. (1993) *Managerialism and the Public Services*, 2nd edition. Oxford, Blackwell.

Popple, K. and Redmond, M. (2000) Community development and the voluntary sector in the new millennium: the implications of the Third Way in the UK. *Community Development Journal*, 35, 4: 391–400.

Porter, M. (1998) *The Competitive Advantage of Nations*. Basingstoke: Palgrave Macmillan.

Poulsen, M., Johnston, R., and Forrest, J. (2004) Is Sydney a divided city ethnically? *Australian Geographical Studies*, 42, 3: 356–77.

Power, A. and Tunstall, R. (1997) *Dangerous Disorder: Riots and Violent Disturbances in Thirteen Areas of Britain 1991–1992*. York: Joseph Rowntree Foundation.

President's Commission (1980a) *Urban America in the Eighties: Perspectives and Prospects*. Washington DC, President's Commission for a National Agenda in the 1980s.

President's Commission (1980b) *A National Agenda for the Eighties*. Washington DC: President's Commission for a National Agenda in the 1980s.

Prime Minister's Strategy Unit (2005) *Improving the Prospects of People Living in Areas of Multiple Deprivation in England*. London: Cabinet Office.

Purdue, D. (2001) Neighbourhood governance: leadership, trust and social capital. *Urban Studies*, 38, 12: 2211–24.

Putnam, R. (1993) *Making Democracy Work: Civic Traditions in Modern Italy*. Princeton, NJ: Princeton University Press.

Putnam, R. (2000) *Bowling Alone: the Collapse and Revival of American Community*. New York: Simon and Schuster.

Raco, M. (2003) Remaking place and securitising space: urban regeneration and the strategies, tactics and practices of policing in the UK. *Urban Studies*, 40, 9: 1869–87.

Raco, M. (2005a) A step change or a step back? The Thames Gateway and the re-birth of the urban development corporations. *Local Economy*, 20, 2: 141–53.

Raco, M. (2005b) Sustainable development, rolled-out neoliberalism and sustainable communities. *Antipode*, 37, 2: 324–47.

Rallings, C., Thrasher, M., Cheal, B., and Borisyuk, G. (2004) *Environment and Planning C: Government and Policy*, 22: 569–82.

Rein, M. (1970) Social planning: the search for legitimacy, in Moynihan, D. (ed.), *Toward a National Urban Policy*. New York: Basic Books.

Reingold, D. and Johnson, C. (2003) The rise and fall of Eastside Community Investments, Inc.: The life of an extraordinary Community Development Corporation. *Journal of Urban Affairs*, 25, 5: 527–49.

Rex, J. (1988) *The Ghetto and the Underclass. Essays on Race and Social Policy*. Aldershot: Avebury.

Richardson, R. (1997) *Towards the Information Society in Southeast Asia? Experiences in Singapore and Malaysia*. A Briefing Report to Northern Informatics. Newcastle: Centre for Urban and Regional Development Studies, University of Newcastle.

Robertson, D. and Judd, D. (1989) *The Development of American Public Policy: the Structure of Policy Restraint*. Glenview, IL: Scott, Foresman.

Robinson, J. (2002) Global and world cities: a view from off the map. *International Journal of Urban and Regional Research*, 26, 3: 531–54.

Robson, B. (1988) *Those Inner Cities. Reconciling the Social and Economic Aims of Urban Policy*. Oxford: Clarendon

Robson, B., Bradford, M., Deas, I. et al. (1994) *Assessing the Impact of Urban Policy*. London: HMSO.

Robson, B., Parkinson, M., Boddy, M., and McLennan, D. (2000) *The State of the English Cities*. London: Department of the Environment, Transport and the Regions.

Rodriguez, A., Swyngedou, E., and Moulaert, F. (2003) Urban restructuring, social-political polarization and new urban policies, in Moulaert, F., Rodriguez, A., and Swyngedouw, E. (eds.), *The Globalized City. Economic Restructuring and Social Polarization in European Cities*. Oxford: Oxford University Press.

Rofe, M. (2004) From "problem city" to "promise city": gentrification and the revitalisation of Newcastle. *Australian Geographical Studies*, 42, 2: 193–206.

Rogers, R. (1997) *Cities for a Small Planet*, edited by P. Gumuchdjian. London: Faber and Faber.

Rogers, R. (1999) *Towards an Urban Renaissance. Final Report of the Urban Task Force*, chaired by Lord Rogers of Riverside. London: E. and F. N. Spon.

Rogers, R. and Power, A. (2000) *Cities for a Small Country*. London: Faber and Faber.

Roger, Tym and Parttners (1998) *Urban Development Corporations: Performance and Good Practice*. London: Department of the Environment, Transport and the Regions.

Rose, N. (1996) The death of the social? Re-figuring the territory of government, *Economy and Society*, 25, 3: 327–56.

Rose, N. (1999) *Powers of Freedom*. Cambridge: Cambridge University Press.

Rossi, P., Berk, R. and Eidson, B. (1974) *The Roots of Urban Discontent. Public Policy, Municipal Instiutions, and the Ghetto*. New York: John Wiley.

Rowntree, S. (1902) *Poverty: A Study of Town Life*. London: Macmillan.

Saito, A. (2003) Global city formulation in a capitalist developmental state: Tokyo and the Waterfront Sub-centre Project. *Urban Studies*, 40, 2: 283–308.

Salcedo, R. and Torres, A. (2004) Gated communities in Santiago: wall or frontier? *International Journal of Urban and Regional Research*, 28, 1: 27–44.

Sandercock, L. (2000) When strangers become neighbours: managing cities of difference. *Planning Theory and Practice*, 1, 1: 13–30.

Sands, G. (2003) Michigan's Renaissance Zones: eliminating taxes to attract investment and jobs in distressed communities. *Environment and Planning C: Government and Policy*, 21: 719–34.

Saunders, P. (1984) Rethinking local politics, in Boddy M. and Fudge, C. (eds.), *Local Socialism? Labour Councils and New Left Alternatives*. London: Macmillan,

Saunders, P. (1986) Reflections on the dual state thesis, in Goldsmith, M. and Villadsen, S. (eds.), *Urban Political Theory and the Management of Fiscal Stress*. Aldershot: Gower.

Savitch, H. and Kantor, P. (2002) *Cities in the International Marketplace. The Political Economy of Urban Development in North America and Western Europe*. Princeton: Princeton University Press.

Lord Scarman (1981) *The Scarman Report: The Brixton Disorders*, April 10–12, 1981. Harmondsworth: Penguin.

Schaffer, F. (1970) *The New Town Story*. London: McGibbon and Kee.

Schneider, G. and Schubert, P. (1997) *Wer baut wo? Die grossen Bauprojekte im Überblick*. Berlin: Jaron Verlag.

Schoon, N. (2001) *The Chosen City*. London: Spon.

Scott, A. (2000) *The Cultural Economy of Cities. Essays on the Geography of Image-Producing Industries*. London: Sage.

Scott, A. (ed.) (2001) *Global City-Regions. Trends, Theory, Policy*. Oxford: Oxford University Press.

Scottish Enterprise (2004) *The Role of Scottish Enterprise in the Economic Regeneration of Scotland*. Prepared for the Ministerial Sub Committee on Regeneration. Glasgow: Scottish Enterprise.

Scottish Executive (2002) *Review of Scotland's Cities – The Analysis*. Edinburgh: The Stationery Office.

Scottish Office (1988) *New Life for Urban Scotland*. Edinburgh: Her Majesty's Stationery Office.

Scottish Office (1990) *Urban Scotland into the 90s. New Life: Two Years On*. London: Her Majesty's Stationery Office.

Seebohm Report (1968) *Report of the Committee on Local Authority and Allied Personal Social Services*. London: Her Majesty's Stationery Office.

Selsdon, A. (ed.) (1985) *The "New Right" Enlightenment*. London: Economic and Literary Books.

Silverman, K. (1996) *The Threshold of the Visible World*. London: Routledge.

Sklair, L. (2005) The transnational capitalist class and contemporary architecture in globalizing cities. *International Journal of Urban and Regional Research*, 29, 3: 485–500.

Smith, M. (1988) *City, State and Market. The Political Economy of Urban Society*. Oxford: Blackwell.

Smith, N. (1996a) *The New Urban Frontier. Gentrification and the Revanchist City*. London: Routledge.

Smith, N. (1996b) Social Justice and the new American urbanism: The revanchist city, in Merrifield, A. and Swyngedouw, E. (eds.), *The Urbanisation of Injustice*. London: Lawrence and Wishart.

Smith, N. (2002) New globalism, new urbanism: gentrification as global urban strategy, *Antipode*, 34, 3: 427–50.

Smithies, B. and Fiddick, P. (1969) *Enoch Powell on Immigration. An Analysis*. London: Sphere Books.

Smyth, P., Reddel, T., and Jones, A. (2004) Social inclusion, new regionalism and associational governance: the Queensland experience. *International Journal of Urban and Regional Research*, 28, 3: 601–15.

Social Exclusion Unit (1998) *Bringing Britain Together. A National Strategy for Neighbourhood Renewal*. London: Her Majesty's Stationery Office.

Social Exclusion Unit (2000) *National Strategy for Neighbourhood Renewal: A Framework for Consultation.* London: Cabinet Office.

Social Exclusion Unit (2001a) *A New Commitment to Neighbourhood Renewal: National Strategy Action Plan.* London: Cabinet Office.

Social Exclusion Unit (2001b) *National Strategy for Neighbourhood Renewal. PAT Audit.* London: Cabinet Office.

Social Exclusion Unit (2004) *Breaking the Cycle. Taking Stock of Progress and Priorities.* London: Office of the Deputy Prime Minister.

Society Guardian (2005) Homes for All. Creating Better Places to Live and Work. Renewing Our Communities. Society Guardian 19.01.05. Produced by the Guardian in association with English Partnerships.

Solesbury, W. (1993) Reframing urban policy. *Policy and Politics*, 21, 1: 31–8.

Solesbury, W. (2002) The ascendancy of evidence. *Planning Theory and Practice*, 3, 1: 90–6.

Sorkin, M. (ed.) (1992) *Variations on a Theme Park: the New American City and the End of Public Space.* New York: Hill and Wang

Southern, A. (2001) What matters is what works? The management of regeneration. *Local Economy*, 16, 4: 264–71.

Staeheli, L. (2003) Women and the work of community. *Environment and Planning A*, 35: 815–31.

Steinbach, C. (2000) *Community Development Corporations in US Civil Society.* USA; Final Report on Case Study, Part 2. Brighton: Civil Society and Governance Programme, Institute of Development Studies, University of Sussex. www.ids.uk/ids/civsoc/final/usa/USA2.doc

Stevenson, D. (2003) *Cities and Urban Cultures.* Maidenhead: Open University Press.

Stewrat, J. (1995) A future for local authorities as community government, in Stewart, J. and Stoker, G. (eds.), *Local Government in the 1990s.* London: Macmillan.

Stewart, M. and Underwood, J. (1982) Inner cities: a multiagency planning and implementation process, in Healey, P., McDougall, G., and Thomas, M. (eds.), *Planning Theory: Prospects for the 1980s.* Oxford: Pergamon.

Stoker, G. (1995) Regime theory and urban politics, in Judge, D., Stoker, G. and Wolman, H. (eds.), *Theories of Urban Politics.* London: Sage.

Stoker, G. (2004) *Transforming Local Governance. From Thatcherism to New Labour.* Basingstoke: Palgrave Macmillan.

Stone, C. (1989) *Regime Politics: The Governing of Atlanta 1946–1988.* Lawrence: University Press of Kansas.

Stone, C. (1993) Urban regimes and the capacity to govern: a political economy approach. *Journal of Urban Affairs*, 15, 1: 1–28.

Sugrue, T. (1996) *The Origins of the Urban Crisis. Race and Inequality in Postwar Detroit.* Princeton, NJ: Princeton University Press.

Swyngedouw, E., Moulaert, F., and Rodriguez, A. (2002) Neoliberal urbanization in Europe: large-scale urban development projects and the new urban policy. *Antipode*, 34, 3: 542–77.

Syms, P. and McIntosh, A. (2004) *Transferable Lessons from the Enterprise Zones.* London: Office of the Deputy Prime Minister.

Taylor, M. (2003) *Public Policy in the Community.* Bristol: Policy Press.

Taylor, M., Craig, G., and Wilkinson, M. (2002) Co-option or empowerment? The changing relationship between the state and the voluntary and community sectors. *Local Governance*, 28, 1: 1–11.

Taylor, P. (2004) *World City Network. A Global Urban Analysis.* London: Routledge.

Teo, P. (2003) The limits of imagineering: a case study of Penang. *International Journal of Urban and Regional Research*, 27, 3: 545–63.

Thake, S. (1995) *Staying the Course. The Role and Structure of Community Regeneration Organisations.* York: Joseph Rowntree Foundation.

Thake, S. and Staubach, R. (1993) *Investing in People. Rescuing Communities from the Margin.* York: Joseph Rowntree Foundation.

Tibbot, R. (2002) Culture club. Can culture lead urban regeneration? *Locum Destination Review, 9,* Autumn: 71–3.

Till, K. (2005) *The New Berlin. Memory, Politics, Place.* Minneapolis, MN: University of Minnesota Press.

Tönnies, F. (1887/1963) *Community and Society (Gemeinschaft und Gesellschaft),* 1963 edition. New York: Harper and Row.

Touraine, A. (1983) *Solidarity. Poland 1980–1981.* Cambridge: Cambridge University Press.

Tranter, P. and Keeffe, T. (2004) Motor racing in Australia's Parliamentary Zone: successful event tourism or the Emperor's new clothes? *Urban Policy and Research,* 22, 2: 169–87.

Troy, P. (2003) Australian cities: politically out of sight and out of mind. *Urban Policy and Research,* 21, 3: 229–31.

Turner, D. and Martin, S. (2004) Managerialism meets community development: contracting for social inclusion? *Policy and Politics,* 32, 1: 21–32.

UN-Habitat (2003) *The Challenge of the Slums: Global Report on Human Settlements.* London: Earthscan.

USHUD (1982) *The President's 1982 National Urban Policy Report.* Washington, DC: US Department of Housing and Urban Development Washington.

US National Advisory Commission on Civil Disorders (1968) *Report of the National Advisory Committee on Civil Disorders* (Kerner Commission). New York: Bantam Books.

Vidal, A. and Keating, D. (2004) Community development: current issues and emerging challenges. *Journal of Urban Affairs,* 26, 2: 126–37.

Wacquant, L (1993a) The return of the repressed. Urban violence, "race", and dualization in three advanced societies, Plenary address to the XVII Encontro Anual da ANPOCS, Caxambu, Brazil, October.

Wacquant, L. (1993b) Urban outcasts: stigma and division in the Black American ghetto and the French urban periphery. *International Journal of Urban and Regional Research,* 17, 3: 366–83.

Wacquant, L. (1999) How penal common sense comes to Europeans: Notes on the transatlantic diffusion of the neoliberal *doxa. European Societies,* 1, 3: 319–52.

Wacquant, L. (2002) From slavery to mass incarceration. Rethinking the "race question" in the US. *New Left Review,* 13: 41–60.

Walker, C. (2002) *Community Development Corporations and Their Changing Support Systems.* Washington, DC: The Urban Institute.

Walklate, S. (1996) Community and crime prevention, in McLaughlin, E. and Muncie, J. (eds.), *Controlling Crime.* London: Sage.

Walklate, S. (2002) Gendering crime prevention. Exploring the tensions between policy and process, in Hughes, G., McLaughlin, E. and Muncie, J. (eds.), *Crime Prevention and Community Safety.* London: Sage.

Wallace, M. (2004) Congressional considerations and urban characteristics in the selection of empowerment zones and enterprise communities. *Journal of Urban Affairs,* 26, 5: 593–609.

Ward, K. and Jonas, A. (2004) Competitive city-regionalism as a politics of space: a critical reinterpretation of the new regionalism. *Environment and Planning A,* 36: 2119–39.

Ward, M. and Watson, S. (1997) *Here to Stay. A Public Policy Framework for Community Based Regeneration.* London: Development Trusts Association.

While, A., Jonas, A., and Gibbs, D. (2004) The environment and the entrepreneurial city: searching for the urban "sustainability fix" in Manchester and Leeds. *International Journal of Urban and Regional Research,* 28, 3: 549–69.

Whitehead, M. (2004) The urban neighbourhood and the moral geographies of British urban policy, in Johnstone, C. and Whitehead, M. (eds.), *New Horizons in British Urban Policy. Perspectives on New Labour's Urban Renaissance.* Aldershot: Ashgate.

Wilks-Heeg, S. and North, P. (2004) Cultural policy and urban regeneration: a special edition of *Local Economy*, *Local Economy*, 19, 4: 305–11.

Williams, R. (1983) *Keywords. A Vocabulary of Culture and Society*. London: Fontana.

Williams, R. (1999) Constructing the European spatial development perspective: consensus without a competence. *Regional Studies*, 33, 8: 793–7.

Wilson, H. (1971) *The Labour Government 1964–1970: A Personal Record*. London: Weidenfeld and Nicolson.

Wilson, J.Q. (1975) *Thinking About Crime*. New York: Basic Books.

Wilson, W. J. (1987) *The Truly Disadvantaged: The Inner City, the Underclass, and Public Policy*. Chicago, IL: University of Chicago Press.

Wilson, W.J. (1992) Another look at "the truly disadvantaged." *Political Science Quarterly*, 106: 639–56.

Winstanley, A., Thorns, D., and Perkins, H. (2003) Nostalgia, community and new housing developments: a critique of new urbanism incorporating a New Zealand perspective. *Urban Policy and Research*, 21, 2: 175–89.

Wiseman, J. (1998) *Global Nation? Australia and the Politics of Globalisation*. Cambridge: Cambridge University Press.

Wolfensohn, J. (2001) The World Bank and global city-regions: reaching the poor, in Scott, A. (ed.), *Global City-Regions. Trends, Theory, Policy*. Oxford: Oxford University.

Wolman, H. (1992) Understanding cross-national policy transfers: the case of Britain and the US. *Governance*, 5, 1: 27–45.

Wood, P. and Taylor, C. (2004) Big ideas for a small town: the Huddersfield Creative Town Initiative. *Local Economy*, 19, 4: 380–95.

World Bank (1991) *Urban Policy and Economic Development. An Agenda for the 1990s*. A World Bank Policy Paper. Washington DC: The World Bank.

World Bank Infrastructure Group Urban Development (2000) *Cities in Transition. World Bank Urban and Local Government Strategy*. Washington DC: The World Bank.

Worpole, K. and Greenhalgh, L. (1999) *The Richness of Cities: Urban Policy in a New Landscape – Final Report*. Stroud: Comedia/Demos.

Wu, F. (2003) The (post-) socialist entrepreneurial city as a state project: Shanghai's reglobalisation in question. *Urban Studies*, 40, 9: 1673–98.

Wu, F. (2004) Urban poverty and marginalization under market transition: the case of Chinese cities. *International Journal of Urban and Regional Research*, 28, 2: 401–23.

Xu, J. and Yeh, A.G. (2005) City repositioning and competitiveness building in regional development: new development strategies in Guangzhou, China. *International Journal of Urban and Regional Research*, 29, 2: 83–308.

Ye, A.G. and Xu, X. (1996) Globalization and the urban system in China, in Lo, F. and Yeung, Y. (eds.), *Emerging World Cities in Pacific Asia*. Tokyo: United Nations University Press.

Young, J. (1999) *The Exclusive Society: Social Exclusion, Crime and Difference in Late Modernity*. London: Sage.

Young, K., Ashby, P., Boaz, A., and Grayson, L. (2002) Social science and the evidence-based policy movement. *Social Policy and Society*, 1, 3: 215–34.

Yusuf, S. and Wu, W. (2002) Pathways to a world city: Shanghai rising in an era of globalisation. *Urban Studies*, 39, 7: 1213–1240.

Zhang, L.-Y. (2003) Economic development in Shanghai and the role of the state. *Urban Studies*, 40, 8: 1549–72.

Zukin, S. (1995) *The Cultures of Cities*. Oxford: Blackwell.

Zukin, S. (2004) *Point of Purchase. How Shopping Changed American Culture*. New York: Routledge.

Index

CPSIA information can be obtained at www.ICGtesting.com
Printed in the USA
LVOW03s1323200814

400085LV00006B/30/P